IMAGE BUYERS' GUIDE

VISUAL RESOURCES SERIES

The Visual Resources Directory: Art Slide and Photograph Collections in the United States and Canada. Ed. by Carla Conrad Freeman; Canadian Editor, Barbara Stevenson

Image Buyers' Guide: An International Directory of Sources for Slides and Digital Images for Art and Architecture. 7th ed. By Sandra C. Walker and Donald W. Beetham

Visual Resources Association_____

Image Buyers' Guide

An International Directory of Sources for Slides and Digital Images for Art and Architecture

Seventh Edition

Sandra C. Walker

The University of Tennessee, Knoxville

Donald W. Beetham

Rutgers, The State University of New Jersey

1999
LIBRARIES UNLIMITED, INC.
Englewood, Colorado

LIBRARIES UNLIMITED, INC.
P.O. Box 6633
Englewood, CO 80155-6633
1-800-237-6124
www.lu.com

Library of Congress Cataloging-in-Publication Data

Image buyers' guide : an international directory of sources for slides
    and digital images for art and architecture / sponsor, Visual
    Resources Association. -- 7th ed. / Sandra C. Walker, Donald W.
    Beetham.
        xxi, 186 p. 22x28 cm. -- (Visual resources series)
        Rev. ed. of : Slide buyers' guide / edited by Norine D. Cashman.
        ISBN 1-56308-658-1 (pbk.)
        1. Art--Slides Catalogs.   2. Art--Slides Directories.   3. Picture
    archiving and communication systems Directories.   4. Art--Computer
    network resources Directories.   I. Walker, Sandra C.   II. Beetham,
    Donald W.   III. Cashman, Norine D., 1949-   Slide buyers' guide.
    IV. Visual Resources Association.   V. Series.
    N4039.I53   1999
    779'.97'0296--dc21   99-16366
                                                                CIP

CONTENTS

PREFACE

The *Image Buyers' Guide* is designed to assist visual resources curators, librarians, teachers, and scholars in identifying sources of images depicting art and architecture. New in this edition is a section of sources for digitized images. The image providers listed are evaluated, whenever possible, on the quality of the images offered, the completeness and accuracy of the identification of the images, and the service rendered in filling orders. The guide is intended to enable purchasers of images to make wise choices in allocating their acquisitions funds.

HISTORY

Six previous editions of the *Guide* appeared in 1970, 1972, 1976, 1980, 1985, and 1990 (titled *Slide Buyers' Guide*). The first four editions were edited by Nancy DeLaurier of the University of Missouri at Kansas City. Norine Duncan (formerly Cashman) of Brown University edited the fifth edition (with Mark Braunstein of Connecticut College) and the sixth edition. The first, second, and fourth editions were published by the Visual Resources Group of the MidAmerica College Art Association (MACAA), and the third edition was published by the College Art Association. During the 29 years that have passed since the first edition, the *Guide* has come to be recognized as a standard reference tool for visual resources curators and librarians. Like most directories, however, it must be updated periodically to retain its usefulness.

Addresses, telephone numbers, and even the names of the image providers change regularly, and this is one reason there is a need for a seventh edition of the *Guide*. Changes have been and will continue to be announced four times a year in the "Slide Market News" column of the *Visual Resources Association Bulletin*. The computer revolution has sparked changes in communication. E-mail addresses and URLs to websites provide easier access to image providers all over the world. Websites provide a medium for image providers to list images without costly mailings. E-mail addresses and URLs also have proven to be fleeting as old computers become obsolete and are replaced. Fortunately, technology has provided a solution to this problem. An Image Providers Directory is available at http://www-rci.rutgers.edu/~beetham/vendor.htm. This URL also is likely to change during the active life of this publication, so the name will stay the same so that it can be located in a web index. The site also will continue to be linked to the Visual Resources Association home page, which is presently located at http://www.oberlin.edu/~art/vra/vra.html. This site can also be located using a web index should the site migrate during the life of this *Guide*.

There has been tremendous change in the nine years since the last edition of the *Guide*. Digitized images have become a reality and are now used in many visual resources collections for students to review images seen in class. The Internet has grown into a popular method of transmitting information, including images, to an international community. E-mail and websites have replaced telex. Museums are forming consortiums such as the Art Museum Image Consortium (AMICO) and the Museum Digital Licensing Collective (MDLC) to license their images to the educational community. The downside has been the loss of many cherished slide providers. There are fewer entries in this edition. Readers will search in vain for Sandak, one of the main sources for images for many years.

METHODOLOGY

A mailing list based on the sixth edition, supplemented by names and addresses from various other sources, was compiled in the summer of 1997. An initial mailing of 494 questionnaires was sent out in September 1997 to presumed slide vendors worldwide. Follow-up mailings (domestic and international) and telephone calls (United States and Canada only) took place from January through June 1998. In all, 140 completed questionnaires were received by July 1, 1998. Other entries were updated by having the vendor mark revisions on a copy of the sixth edition entry. Many U.S. entries, especially for museums, were updated by telephone and E-mail.

When no other sources are stated, the reader may assume that the entry is based on current information from a returned questionnaire, a revised entry, or a telephone conversation. Image vendors from whom no response could be elicited were included in the guide if reasonably current information about them could be obtained from other sources. In such cases, the source of information was noted. If no up-to-date information was available, but the likelihood remained that the vendor still supplies slides, the sixth edition entry was repeated with a note to that effect.

Few entries remain for museums that do not offer slides by mail order. References to these museums are included in the entries for commercial firms that document their collections, and are accessible through the name index.

In all, this edition of the *Image Buyers' Guide* includes slightly more than 300 entries. Most of the data gathered reflect the image market as it existed at the end of 1997. Subsequent changes will be reported in the "Slide Market News" column of the quarterly *Visual Resources Association Bulletin*, which serves as a running update of the *Image Buyers' Guide* between editions. Changes in addresses, telephone numbers, URLs, and the like will be updated in the Image Providers Directory at http://www-rci.rutgers.edu/~beetham/vendor.htm.

The evaluation committee was composed of 15 professional visual resource curators who volunteered to share their experience and judgments with the editors. Some members of the committee were able to meet at the 1998 annual conference of the Visual Resources Association in Philadelphia, where sample slides supplied by the image providers were viewed. All committee members submitted written comments on forms provided by the editors, and each applied the numerical rating system to the vendors from whom they had purchased slides.

The first appendix represents the mailings that did not result in entries. To the best of our knowledge the image providers listed here no longer sell slides or digital images. The second appendix consists of a bibliography of art history textbooks for which slide sets are available, with references to the vendors who offer them.

The subject index was compiled from vendors' catalogs, brochures, and lists when possible. Statements on the questionnaire defining the scope of the vendors' holdings were used as well. The alphabetically arranged subject headings used in the sixth edition were retained, with minor revisions.

ARRANGEMENT

Changes in Order of the Entries in 7th Edition

The way the entries are ordered and numbered has changed from previous editions to facilitate the addition of digital image providers. There are two major sections: Digital Images and Slides. Separate sections will allow the user to browse either for digital images or slides. The organization within both sections is the same as in previous editions. Organizations that sell both digital images and slides appear in both sections. The entries are the same except that the evaluations appear only in the slide section.

Numbering

The primary purpose of the numbers is to locate vendors through the indexes. Thus, each image provider is given one unique number that may appear in either or both sections. The holdings for any image provider will be similar in either medium. Because the entries are identical, it is unimportant if the reader finds the entry in the wrong section. There will be gaps in the numbers due to entries appearing in only one section. Cross-references are inserted into the Slide section. Because there are fewer entries in the Digital Image section, the introduction of cross-references in that section would have overwhelmed the reader.

The arrangement of data within an entry follows the standard of the sixth edition. The following headings are employed as organizational devices:

Price Range: quick range of prices for company's slides

Profile: scope of subject coverage and amount of holdings

Photography: method of creating or acquiring masters for slide production

Production: method of making copies for sale

Documentation: identification supplied in catalogs or with slides or digital images

Purchasing: prices and business practices

Rental: terms on which slides may be borrowed for temporary use

Digital Products: digital images and how they are sold

Other Products: notation of other audiovisual items offered for sale

Other Sources: distributors or independent vendors

Expansion Plans: stated plans for the expansion of the company

Textbooks: slide sets sold to be used with textbooks

Evaluation: ratings on quality, documentation, and service

GENERAL INFORMATION

Conventions and assumptions observed in the entries are as follows:

Original photography is presumed to have been carried out in the presence of the depicted work of art or architecture unless reliance on secondary sources is indicated.

Documentation (catalogs, lists, brochures, slide identifications, labels, texts, and audiocassettes) is in English unless stated otherwise.

All prices stated in entries are subject to change. Payment in the currency of the country in which the vendor is located is preferred or required unless alternatives are stated. State sales tax may apply.

All slides obtainable from sources listed in this guide are presumed to be copyrighted.

In placing international telephone calls, additional prefixes may be required (varying from country to country). Consult directory assistance if necessary.

VALIDITY

The informational content of entries in this guide is derived primarily from statements by the image providers. It was impractical, if not impossible, to verify the accuracy of their responses to the questionnaire. When respondents left blanks on the returned questionnaires, the items in question were omitted from the entry unless the information could be derived from a brochure or catalog.

EVALUATIONS

The "Statement on Slide Quality Standards" (1979), reproduced in the Introduction, represents an attempt by professional slide curators to define the criteria by which slides should be evaluated. The editor and evaluation committee applied these guidelines to the vendors listed in this guide whenever our experience provided substantial evidence. The user should bear in mind, however, that our evaluative ratings are based, by necessity, on samples of the vendor's total production and service.

For the previous two editions, the ratings values of excellent, good, fair, and poor were used in the evaluations. This edition reverts to the earlier values of excellent, good, acceptable, and usable within limitations. These values seem less subjective in rating the usefulness of the image to the teaching of art and art history.

Ratings in this edition are:

4 excellent

3 good

2 acceptable

1 usable within limitations

for each of the following areas:

Quality: photography and production

Documentation: completeness and accuracy of identifications in catalog and/or on labels

Service: promptness and accuracy in filling orders, equity of policies, fairness in dealing with dissatisfied customers, and general helpfulness

In practice, a range was often assigned to reflect either variation in the vendor's quality/documentation/service or a difference of opinion among the evaluators. The ratings are a composite of ratings submitted to the editor by the evaluators, based on their experience as slide buyers. Whenever samples were submitted by image providers, their quality was rated by the evaluation committee at the Visual Resources Association meetings in Philadelphia in March 1998.

Although the system of evaluation in this edition will be helpful to all readers, it is designed particularly to benefit experienced professionals who are discriminating slide buyers. For less experienced buyers, we recognize the need for designating image providers who can be relied on for better than average quality, documentation, and service. Such image providers are marked by an asterisk (*) in the left margin. We understand that small budgets and lack of staff compel some institutional purchasers to build their collections by making a few large purchases, minimizing the time and effort needed for selection. For their benefit, we offer the following list of vendors whose holdings are large and provide general coverage of the history of art and architecture in single slides and small sets.

Hartill Art Associates **(007)**

Davis Art Slides **(047)** [previously Rosenthal Art Slides]

Saskia Cultural Documentation, Ltd. **(086)**

Scala Fine Arts Slides **(287)** (Distributed in the United States by Davis Art Slides **(047)**

University of Michigan **(096)**

We offer these recommendations with the following reservation: Many smaller and more specialized vendors offer excellent slides and should not be overlooked. The subject index of this guide can be used to identify the image providers appropriate to meet specific needs.

CONCLUSION

The *Image Buyers' Guide* is more than a directory of slide or digital image sources, although the listing and evaluation of image providers are its primary functions. The guide has as a secondary mission the education of both vendors and consumers. Since 1979, when the "Statement on Slide Quality Standards" was first disseminated, the quality of slides on the market has improved significantly. The "Slide Quality Standards," which were published in the fourth edition of the *Slide Buyers' Guide*, informed image providers of the criteria by which visual resource professionals judge the quality of their productions. Slide purchasers have used the standards to develop their own critical skills, exerting a real influence on the slide market through discriminating allocation of their acquisitions funds.

ACKNOWLEDGMENTS

We are indebted to the Executive Board of the Visual Resources Association, which has encouraged our work on this edition of the *Image Buyers' Guide*. In particular, Joe Romano, VRA's Past President; Jenni Rodda, VRA President; and William Broom, VRA Secretary, have responded to our requests for information and for funding of the initial questionnaire mailing with promptness. We are especially grateful to Norine Duncan (formerly Cashman), who allowed us to scan and edit the sixth edition of the *Slide Buyers' Guide*, thereby reducing our workload. Nancy DeLaurier acted in an advisory position to our committee, and we acknowledge her insightful comments, particularly in the early stages of our work on this project. This publication could not have been produced without the enthusiastic contributions of the 15 members of the committee who assisted us with verification of addresses and evaluation of slide samples. Bonita Billman has performed an extraordinary job of providing information and evaluations, particularly for image providers in Britain and Norway. Leigh Gates contributed extra efforts in providing and checking contact information in the greater Chicago area. Special acknowledgment should be mentioned for Jeannette Mills and Micheline Nilson, who assisted us with providing an evaluation area for the committee during the 1998 VRA Conference in Philadelphia. We are also grateful to Jennifer Brasher, who assisted with verification of information in Australia, and to Maryly Snow, who provided information on digital image providers. And, certainly, we appreciate the cooperation of the image providers.

At Rutgers, Dr. Sarah McHam, Chair of the Department of Art History, has been unwavering in her support and encouragement. The harmonious work environment she has created has been very conducive to making progress on major projects. In the Visual Resources Collection, Associate Curators Kimberly Byrd, Gabrielle Rose, and Zbynek Smetana have taken responsibility for maintaining the slide collection and have deftly managed most daily crises. Their advice and counsel has been invaluable. Dr. Penny Small has provided valuable technical support for the collection, and her efforts have helped facilitate the completion of this project.

An undertaking like this cannot be completed without having a profound effect on the home life. Donald Beetham's wife, Mary, has forborne boxes of material strewn about the house, and the long hours of compilation, with patience and good humor. Her advice has been wise and timely. John, Michael, Sarah, and Belinda also have patiently endured Beetham's preoccupation with the project and have assisted in numerous ways.

At Tennessee, Dr. Norman Magden, Head, Department of Art, and the Art History professors have encouraged Sandra Walker's participation in this project. William Bishop, Slide Clerk for the Visual Resources Collection, has cheerfully assisted with photocopying materials and with the day-to-day operation of the Visual Resources Collection during this endeavor.

The patience and encouragement of Walker's husband, Martin, and her daughter, Christie, have greatly influenced the outcome of this project. Christie's assistance with folding questionnaires and stuffing envelopes for a mailing list of more than 500 image providers is gratefully acknowledged.

Donald W. Beetham
Rutgers, The State University of New Jersey

Sandra C. Walker
The University of Tennessee, Knoxville

INTRODUCTION

Few of the image providers listed in this guide are companies whose sole or major production consists of 35mm slides or digital images of art and architecture. Some companies supply images of art as well as other subjects. The intended audience for these images may be educational institutions (often at the secondary level) or tourists. Art and architectural subjects may be emphasized or may be merely one of many subjects offered. One image provider is best known for sales of art supplies to practicing artists. Some commercial entities, such as architectural firms, publishers, and commercial photographic studios, issue images as a sideline to their major activity. A number of companies are exclusively or primarily distributors of images produced by others.

All these image providers have in common a profit motive; they are businesses with images as their products. Images also may be purchased from individuals. Artists, scholars, and teachers often make available slides they have taken of their own work or the subjects they study, especially slides shot while traveling abroad. Nonprofit institutions comprise the other large category of image providers. Foremost among them are art museums, which usually sell slides of selected works in their permanent collections as part of their educational mission. Some have their images produced in-house. Others contract with outside firms for photography and/or production. Slides or CD-ROMs are usually sold in the museum shop and by mail order. Exhibitions are sometimes documented, but the necessity of obtaining permissions from lending institutions and/or copyright holders frequently discourages museum personnel from offering this service. Museums will often carry out "special photography," making a new slide of a previously unphotographed work to satisfy a particular request. Prices for this service are usually much higher than for slides kept in stock.

Galleries may offer slides of work by artists they represent. Even if slide sales are not a routine activity, a gallery may be willing to lend slides for duplication.

Some nonprofit institutions without permanent collections of art sell slides documenting exhibitions, architecture, or work in various collections. Staff members of visual collections in educational institutions sometimes carry out photographic documentation projects, making slides available to other institutions without profit. There are even a few nonprofit institutions committed primarily to visual documentation.

The preceding survey of image providers is offered to demonstrate that images on the market come from such diverse sources that variation in quality is only to be expected. The method of obtaining master slides is the point at which image providers first make choices that distinguish their products from those of others. Although certain deficiencies in an original transparency or negative can be corrected in production, in general, high-quality slide copies depend on setting and adhering to high standards in the original photography. The following outline revised from the fourth edition explains the various means by which originals can be obtained to serve as masters for the production of slides.

1. The slide vendor or an employee may photograph directly from the work of art. Extensive travel may be required in this instance, the cost of which is passed on to the consumer. On-site photography is conducted by two types of vendors:

   a. Professional art photographers who arrange in advance to shoot in museums during hours when the museums are closed to the public. These photographers pay fees and/or royalties to the museums. They are allowed to use tripods and professional lighting equipment. Their results are, on the whole, the best that can be obtained.

   b. Traveling scholars or tourists may photograph in museums during regular hours, in available light, while hand-holding their cameras. Some of these slides are excellent, but others may suffer from any of the following deficiencies: glare, deep shadows cast by the frame, inadequate or uneven lighting, color distortion caused by a mismatch of film type and lighting conditions, fuzzy focus, perspective distortion, image size too small or cropped, poor selection of views of architecture and sculpture.

2. Vendors may borrow or rent transparencies (35mm slides or larger format) from the owner of the work of art, paying a flat fee or royalties from sales. This method is standard procedure for some suppliers; others use it only when photography in person is not possible. Even when a substantial fee is paid, this method is usually less costly, and certainly requires less effort, than traveling to photograph on site. The disadvantage of this method, however, is that the vendor is dependent on museums and galleries to supply images of good quality.

3. A vendor may purchase outright or pay royalties for slides shot by a variety of individuals (see 1b above). Slides with flaws can be improved at the professional production facilities of large, established slide dealers. Vendors of this type are usually selective in their acquisition of slides from individuals, which likewise contributes to higher quality overall.

4. A few vendors sell slides shot on a copystand from secondary materials—books, periodicals, printed ephemera, photographic prints, and other slides. In such cases, consumers should be made aware of the source of the slides, or they will probably assume that the original images were photographed on site. Some secondary materials (plates from rare books, for instance) are legitimate sources for slides as long as permission has been obtained from the owner and/or copyright holder of the work photographed.

EVALUATION

Judging the quality of slides and digital images is no easy task. It is an endeavor in which experts may sometimes disagree over particular examples. Some general principles can be agreed on, however. The following document, issued in 1979 by a committee of professional visual resource administrators, defines the criteria by which slides should be evaluated. The statement was subsequently endorsed by the Art Libraries Society of North America and by the Visual Resources Association.

Statement on Slide Quality Standards

COLOR: The color should be as true as possible to the original work of art, neither over nor underexposed, nor off-color due to the lighting or the film type.

FILM: The film should have fine-grained resolution, and color should be stable with a minimum shelf-life of ten years. Duplicate slides should be newly printed as far as possible to maximize their shelf-life. High contrast in duplicate slides should be controlled. The film should be clean with no dirt or scratches on the surface nor duplicated onto the film from the master transparency or negative. The size 24 X 36mm is preferable; the supplier should indicate other sizes if used.

PHOTOGRAPHY: The slides must be in focus and full-frame as far as possible without being cropped. Lighting should be adequate and even throughout and without glare or reflections. In photographing paintings and buildings, distortion should be avoided.

INFORMATION: Accurate and complete information is necessary: artist's full name, nationality and dates, title of the work, medium, date and dimensions if known, and location. Cropped slides should be identified as such, and details should be described. An indication of the orientation is important, especially on details and abstract works of art. It should be clear which is the front of the slide.

It is important to indicate whether the slide will be an original or a duplicate; specific information on the source of the slide, film type, and processing would be appreciated. Return and replacement policies should be spelled out.

PRICE: The price of the slide should fairly reflect the costs of production and distribution.

Carol Terry, Committee Chairman
Stanford University (formerly)
Rhode Island School of Design (presently)

Nancy DeLaurier
University of Missouri at Kansas City (formerly)
Retired

Eleanor Fink
National Museum of American Art, Smithsonian Institution (formerly)
Getty Art History Information Program (presently)

Stanley Hess
Cleveland Museum of Art (formerly)
Nelson-Atkins Museum of Art (presently)

Linda Bien
Concordia University, Montreal

DIGITAL IMAGES

The criteria for producing quality digital images is similar to the requirements for an excellent slide. Color and density should be accurate and true to the original. The image should be in focus. The entire painting or work of art should be included in the image. Lighting should reflect the conditions and the subject; a painting should be evenly lit. There should be no glare or shadows. Resolution is the issue in question because it affects file size. Suffice to say, the greater the resolution, the more accurate the image.

As with slides, the source image is extremely important to the final quality of the resulting digital image. At the time of this writing, unlike slides, the best images are not being produced from the art objects themselves. As a rule, museums are scanning 4" x 5" transparencies and other photographic materials. Failing the availability of a large-format transparency, 35mm slides or negatives scan very well. The equipment to accurately scan original paintings is not a mainstream option at the time of this writing. Presumably this technology will be developed in the near future.

Resolution standards for digital images also have not been determined at this time. The most common use of digital images of artworks is on interior intranets for individual study. For this .JPG or .GIF formats in a file size of about 2040K usually is adequate. The .JPG and .GIF formats were developed to move images quickly across the Internet. These file formats are called "lossy" formats because pixel data is lost in the conversion. The resulting files are relatively small, and a reasonable number of .JPG or .GIF images can be stored on a hard drive or CD-ROM.

To displace slides in the classroom, digital images will require much higher resolution. The .BMP and .TIF file formats are adequate, but the resulting files are very large and require massive amounts of storage. This need for massive storage may be a permanent requirement as the technology develops. New formats being developed, such as flash-pix, will produce very large files that are similar in size to .BMP or .TIF files. The main advantage of the new file formats is that smaller files can easily be extracted from the main file.

Because of the newness of the technology and the lack of standards for the images in various file formats, we reluctantly decided not to provide evaluations of digital image providers in this edition. Most of the digital images being sold, at the time this is being written, are in the more abbreviated formats and are adequate for study purposes. The expertise of the technical staff and the work being performed at image consortiums, such as the Art Museum Image Consortium (AMICO), is impressive, and the methodology is a step toward developing a standard for classroom images of artworks. We urge image producers to take note of the progress of this work.

For users, the best guide to digital image quality of a vendor may be to take note of the slide evaluations if the image provider sells both types of images. If images are being scanned from slides, quality images will rarely be produced from poor slides. Does the vendor make an effort to correct color and density of the digital images? It also should be noted that slide providers are increasingly offering the option of a license so the users can scan the slide themselves.

SLIDE PHOTOGRAPHY AND PRODUCTION

The photographic images purchased from an image provider usually result from two separate events: the original photography of the work or art, and the production of the sale copy. Sometimes the image sold will be an original. In that case the photographer will take a large number of exposures of each work or view for future sale. Needless to say, these original images are the most coveted and the most expensive to produce; the image provider may have to store these images for many years before they are purchased.

A number of factors affect the overall quality and accuracy of color of an original photographic image. These factors include the film, equipment (especially lenses), filters, lighting conditions, compositional skills, and creativity. The production of accurate copies also requires the proper choice of film, specialized equipment, skill, and careful attention to detail. Image providers selling the best images excel in all these areas. Defects caused by deficiencies in most of these areas are readily apparent at the time of sale. Many image providers will allow the purchaser to reject poor reproductions. The overall quality of commercial slides has improved manyfold since Nancy DeLaurier produced the first *Slide Buyers' Guide* in the 1970s.

Unseen at the time of purchase is the permanence of the color in a transparency. Academic teaching slide collections are extremely harsh environments for photographic images. The most important slides are repeatedly projected for long periods of time. In some departments, slides are left in lighted boxes for student study. The cumulative effect of light causes slides to fade. All films eventually will fade under the cumulative exposure to light, but some fade faster than others. The choice of film stock and the processing of these films will determine the stability of color dyes.

Previously, producers and buyers were dependent on conventional wisdom and manufacturers' data for information about film stability. Henry Wilhelm, in his book *Permanence and Care of Color Photographs: Traditional & Digital Color Prints, Color Negatives, Slides & Motion Pictures* (Grinnell, IA: Preservation Publishing, 1993), has produced independent data on the performance of films. Two slide films perform better than others in stability tests. Kodachrome is the film of choice if the image is stored in the dark and projected only rarely or not at all. Fujichrome outperforms all other films in resisting fading under projection conditions. Fujichrome Velvia 50 is a high-resolution film that is comparable to the resolution of Kodachrome 25 (Wilhelm, 678-79).

Slides sold by image providers are generally either duplicated from master slides using a slide duplicating film or "printed" from negatives onto negative stock (making a positive). Kodak Ektachrome #5071 is the most popular slide duplicating film. Kodak produces a K/8071 for duplicates from Kodachrome originals and Ektachrome SO366 for electronic flash duplicators. Fuji duplicating film is a better choice because of its superior stability in light conditions. The reader will note only two slide producers using Fuji duplicating film in this *Guide*: Visual Publications and the Bodleian Library. Both of these producers are in the United Kingdom. Many slide producers and commercial photo labs will likely switch films during the life of this *Guide* as the availability and acceptance of Fuji duplicating film grows. It also should be noted that Ektachrome duplicating film is the second-best choice of all the other methods of producing copies of master photographs.

For large scale production, slides are produced from master negatives, or internegatives are made from the original slides. Eastmancolor print film #5384 is the film most commonly used to produce the new slide from the negative. This film is more stable than Vericolor slide film #5072 but not as stable as Kodachrome in dark storage conditions. Neither film is as stable as Fujichrome or Ektachrome in resisting fading due to light.

MOUNTING AND PACKAGING OF SLIDES

Most slides are mounted in glassless binders of plastic or cardboard. Glass-binding is occasionally offered, usually as an option, at greater cost. Unmounted slides (i.e., a strip of film) are sometimes available at reduced cost. Slides should be stored by the image provider in a manner that protects them from dust and scratches, and they should be packed carefully to prevent damage during shipment. Some vendors insert slides into plastic sleeves or shrink-wrap small sets; although this solution provides excellent protection during shipment, long-term storage in this condition is not advisable unless the plastic is of archival quality.

DOCUMENTATION

Identification of images is necessary to slide buyers, first to select and purchase slides and later to classify, label, and file them within an existing collection. Most slides are keyed to the catalog or to a list sent with the order; some arrive labeled or accompanied by labels to be applied to the slides after binding. The completeness of identification varies among vendors. Desirable elements of a full identification are enumerated in the "Statement on Slide Quality Standards."

The text of booklets supplied with slide sets is of variable quality. A few vendors offer scholarly commentaries that are truly valuable. Most texts are not oriented to a scholarly audience, however, and many are virtually useless. Chatty "lecture notes" are no substitute for full identification of the images.

PURCHASING

Business practices are usually explained in an image provider's catalog. Instructions for placing orders should be followed carefully to avoid delay in filling the order. In some cases, delivery time may be shortened by ordering from a distributor. Purchase of slides from distributors usually results in higher prices for the consumer but eliminates the inconvenience of placing multiple orders, corresponding in foreign languages, paying in foreign currencies, and waiting for overseas shipments to arrive.

Most vendors require prepayment from individuals but will invoice institutions. Unless prepayment is required, image buyers are wise to withhold payment until the images are received and evaluated. If the slides are satisfactory, payment should be processed promptly.

When purchasing from a vendor for the first time, it is wise to consider in advance what can be done if the images prove to be unsatisfactory. Each provider has a policy on accepting returned images if a customer is not pleased. Some vendors send slides "on approval" for a specified period, usually not exceeding 30 days. Within this time, the purchaser may return some or all (depending on the particular vendor's policy) of the slides—provided, of course, that the slides have not been damaged by the customer. An invoice will then be issued for the number of slides actually kept. From the consumer's point of view, approval orders are highly desirable. Not only can materials that do not meet quality standards be rejected, but the views ordered can be compared with those already in a collection to verify that the new slides are truly needed.

Unfortunately, some slide buyers, including institutions, have abused this privilege. Therefore, many vendors are reluctant to trust new customers and will not send orders on approval. A few vendors will accept no returns whatsoever, a policy that should alert slide buyers to order with caution. In such an instance, a small test order is advisable.

Legitimate reasons for returning slides include poor photographic technique, production flaws, fading from film deterioration already evident at the time of receipt, unremovable dirt or scratches, and damage during shipment. Some of these problems can be rectified by the vendor sending another copy of the same slide. In other cases, a refund or credit toward substitute slides is needed. A vendor also should be willing to exchange slides that were sent erroneously; that is, the slides shipped are not those requested.

A few general hints on ordering are offered here for inexperienced slide buyers.

1. Test new vendors with a small initial order, especially if prepayment is required and/or returns are forbidden.

2. When ordering slides from a museum, specify a maximum price you are willing to pay for special photography if you are not sure a "ready-made" is available.

3. Place orders for an economically profitable number of slides. Shipping charges are proportionally higher per slide on small orders, to say nothing of the cost in effort by the buyer and vendor and perhaps the intermediary purchasing department.

4. Proofread orders carefully, especially if slides are designated by numbers. Ask the purchasing department to photocopy your list to avoid errors in retyping. If the purchaser makes a mistake, the vendor has no obligation to rectify it.

5. Designate a specific recipient and address to whom the slides should be sent.

6. Check orders as soon as possible on receipt for accuracy and quality. Generally, returns should be mailed within two weeks of the date of receipt unless a longer period of review has been agreed on.

7. Insure returned merchandise.

COPYRIGHT CONSIDERATIONS

Most contemporary works of art are copyrighted, as are many others produced in the twentieth century. Permission from the copyright owner and, if requested, payment of fees are required by law when copies of the images are made and distributed. Compliance with copyright law is time-consuming and adds to the expense of slide production. Most professional art slide companies obtain permissions as standard procedure.

A slide produced from a work of art may itself be copyrighted by the photographer or producer, and/or by the institution that owns the original work of art. Most slides obtainable today are indeed copyrighted. Commercial slide vendors regard the copying of their productions without permission as an infringement of copyright law. The statement issued in May 1983 by the Slide Producers' Association was updated in March 1998, and the most recent statement is reproduced below. The Visual Resources Association has not endorsed the statement. Slide buyers, however, need to be informed of the position of the vendors on this issue.

Clarification on Copyright from the Slide Producers' Association

March 26, 1998

The vendors of slides in the field of education relating to art and art history wish to publish the following statement in keeping with United States, Canadian, and International Copyright Law:

All slides of art or architecture—whether originals or duplicates—are the original creation of the company producing them, and are thus protected under International Copyright Laws. Such slides are sold under the express condition that they are to be used for teaching and studying purposes only and may be projected via normal slide projector for classroom and lecture use. No purchased slide may be reproduced or transmitted by any other means, electronic or mechanical, including photocopy, slide duplicator, video recording, or any information storage and retrieval system now known or to be invented, without permission in writing from the producer and other rights holders. Permission to digitize slides is contingent upon permission and signing of a site license agreement as well as payment of licensing fees.

As a further clarification, since these slides are produced for the specific purpose of teaching, scholarship and research, the normal "fair use" clause allowing single copies to be made by individuals for these purposes does not apply. Since virtually the only market for these slides is comprised of the very teachers, students, scholars, and visual resource people who would be interested in copies, any copying activity whatsoever is a form of direct damage to the producer of the original image. Therefore, any unauthorized copying of slides must be considered in violation of copyright law and in violation of professional ethics. Any authorized copying must be agreed upon in writing.

The matter of professional ethics is especially important, since the production of high quality slides for teaching and research purposes can occur only if there is close cooperation based on trust between the artist and/or owner of the object being photographed and the photographer on the one hand, and between the photographer and the purchaser of the image on the other. If directors of museums or historic buildings believe that the conditions under which they granted permission to photograph their objects are being violated, they will not grant such permission in the future. If photographers (who incur large up-front expenses) have the already limited potential for sales undermined—or their efforts at achieving maximum quality subverted—through the production of pirated duplicates, the delicate network of trust and cooperation breaks down and continued production of visual material may be in jeopardy. In the interest of scholarship it is therefore crucial that every person involved in the use of visual images exercise ethical responsibility in meticulously honoring and protecting all copyright provisions.

Saskia, Ltd. Cultural Documentation
Davis Art Slides

NOTE TO USERS OF THIS GUIDE

Many of the larger commercial vendors, as well as a few museums, maintain mailing lists to keep regular customers informed of new offerings. Requests to be added to mailing lists are welcomed by such vendors, who routinely send out mailings to promote their products. Most museums, some smaller companies, and individuals, however, often prefer not to mail information unless it is requested by a customer who seriously intends to place an immediate order. If a vendor keeps a mailing list, this fact has been noted at the beginning of the documentation section of the entry. Users of this guide are asked to refrain from soliciting catalogs from vendors indiscriminately, simply to have the catalogs on file. Small vendors are able and willing to correspond with buyers who will actually do business with them but cannot afford to mail ten catalogs for every one that results in a sale. If the correspondence generated by this guide is helpful to their business rather than a nuisance, slide vendors will be more likely to respond to questionnaires for future editions of this guide.

EVALUATION COMMITTEE

Bonita L. Billman
Visual Resources Curator
Department of Art, Music, and Theatre
Georgetown University, Washington, DC

Mark Braunstein
Visual Resources Librarian
Connecticut College, New London

Leigh Gates
Slide Librarian, MacLean Visual Resources Collection
Ryerson Library, Art Institute of Chicago

Miranda Howard Haddock
Western Michigan University, Kalamazoo

Joyce Henderson
University of Arizona, Tucson

Christine Hilker
Visual Resources Director, School of Architecture
University of Arkansas, Fayetteville

Randi Millman-Brown
Slide Curator, Department of Art History
Ithaca College, Ithaca, NY

Kathryn Poole
Visual Collections Librarian, Rotch Library
Massachusetts Institute of Technology, Cambridge

Martha C. Smith
Assistant Librarian, Art History and Humanities Library
State University of New York, Purchase

Diane Upchurch
Arizona State University, Tempe

Leslie J. Walker
Curator, Art History Department
State University of New York-Buffalo, Amherst
    Campus

Michael Williams
Librarian
National Gallery of Canada, Ottawa

Susan Jane Williams
Visual Resources Curator, Art and Architecture Library
Yale University, New Haven, CT

Loy Zimerman
Slide Curator, Art Department
California State University, Long Beach

PART I

DIGITAL IMAGE PROVIDERS

At the time of manuscript preparation during 1998, the provision of digital images for art and architecture is in its early stages. While the group of providers of digital images is much smaller than the group providing traditional slide images, this is an area of rapid growth. Several of the slide providers now provide digital images as well, and many others have expressed interest in providing digital images in the near future. Where this interest was expressed on the questionnaires, that information has been provided in the entries. Those seeking images should contact traditional slide providers to determine whether digital images become available from them following the publication of this directory.

Evaluations are not provided for digital images in this edition. A brief statement on the state of the medium, the need to develop standards, and criteria for evaluation can be found in the Introduction.

The entries for digital image providers who are also traditional slide providers are numbered the same as for the slide provider entry.

Other resources for finding digital images include:

Clearinghouse of Image Databases http://128.196.228.12/images/image_projects.html

Image Databases on the Net

http://sunsite.Berkeley.edu/Imaging/Databases/

The websites mentioned above do not sell images but may point the searcher to image resources.

CONSORTIUMS

001 Art Museum Image Consortium (AMICO)

URL: http://www.amico.net/

Profile: Information obtained from the AMICO website. AMICO is a not-for-profit consortium of institutions with collections of art, who have come together to improve educational access to the documentation of objects in their care. Further information about joining AMICO, and details of its license terms and programs, is available at the Consortium's website. AMICO's Management Consultants are Jennifer Trant and David Bearman, who may be contacted via E-mail links from the website. Twenty-three North American art museums formed AMICO as a project of the Association of Art Museum Directors Educational Foundation Inc. in October 1997. In June 1998, AMICO incorporated as an independent nonprofit organization run by its members and opened membership to institutions worldwide. A summary of obligations and benefits is available at the website. Full museum members agree to provide digital multimedia documentation for a minimum of 500 images per year until the museum collections are completely documented. The 1998/1999 membership dues for museums (in U.S. dollars) range from $2,500 to $5,000 depending on the annual operating budget. A select group of universities will be the first to receive the AMICO Library of multimedia documentation of museum collections in the

1998/1999 academic year. Together the AMICO University Testbed Participants and AMICO members will explore issues related to the licensing and delivery of multimedia museum documentation to higher education. The University Testbed Project plans to provide access to more than 20,000 works of art. Fees for higher education institutions are based on the size of university or college and range from $2,500 to $5,000 per year (U.S. dollars). Testbed universities will receive a 25% reduction in license fees for the academic years 1999/2000 through 2006/2007 (the equivalent of two years of free licenses). The AMICO Library will be available under license to all higher education institutions in the 1999/2000 academic year. Access to the AMICO Library during the University Testbed Project is being provided by the Research Libraries Group (RLG), Mountain View, California, USA. RLG will offer access to universities under subscription beginning in the 1999/2000 academic year. AMICO is in discussions with the California Digital Library initiative and the OhioLINK Consortium to act as distributors to their higher education constituencies beginning with the 1999/2000 academic year. A number of other distributors will serve public libraries and kindergarten through grade 12 educational institutions beginning in 1999/2000.

✦ MUSEUMS PARTICIPATING IN AMICO (AS OF JUNE 1998):

    Albright-Knox Art Gallery, Buffalo, NY

    Art Gallery of Ontario, Toronto, ON

    Art Institute of Chicago, Chicago, IL

    Asia Society Gallery, New York, NY

    Center for Creative Photography, Tucson, AZ

    Cleveland Museum of Art, Cleveland, OH

    Davis Museum and Cultural Center, Wellesley College, Wellesley, MA

    Fine Arts Museum of San Francisco, San Francisco, CA

    International Museum of Photography, George Eastman House, Rochester, NY

    J. Paul Getty Museum, Los Angeles, CA

    Los Angeles County Museum of Art, Los Angeles, CA

    Metropolitan Museum of Art, New York, NY

    Minneapolis Institute of Arts, Minneapolis, MN

    Montreal Museum of Fine Arts, Montréal, PQ

    Musée d'art contemporain de Montréal, Montréal, PQ

    Museum of Contemporary Art, San Diego, CA

    Museum of Fine Arts, Boston, MA

    National Gallery of Canada, Ottawa, ON

    National Museum of American Art, Washington, DC

    Philadelphia Museum of Art, Philadelphia, PA

    San Francisco Museum of Modern Art, San Francisco, CA

    San Jose Museum of Art, San Jose, CA

    Walker Art Center, Minneapolis, MN

✦ UNIVERSITY TESTBED PARTICIPANTS FOR 1998/1999 ACADEMIC YEAR (AS OF JUNE 1998):

    Boston College, Chestnut Hill, MA

    California State Universities, CA

    Carnegie Mellon University, Pittsburgh, PA

    Columbia University, New York, NY

    Harvard University, Cambridge, MA

    Herron School of Art, Indianapolis, IN

    Indiana University-Purdue University, Indianapolis, IN

    Long Beach, Long Beach, CA

    Princeton University, Princeton, NJ

    Rochester Institute of Technology, Rochester, NY

    San Jose State, San Jose, CA

    University of Alberta, Edmonton, AL

    University of Illinois:

        Urbana-Champaign, Urbana, IL

        Chicago, Chicago, IL

    University of Leiden, Leiden, The Netherlands

    University of Texas, Austin, TX

    University of Toronto:

        Toronto, ON

        Mississauga, Mississauga, ON

        Scarborough, Scarborough, ON

    Washington University, St. Louis, MO

Wellesley College, Wellesley, MA

Western Michigan University, Kalamazoo, MI

Production and Documentation: All documentation is to be provided to AMICO in the format set by the AMICO Technical Committee. Members of AMICO share in the technical expertise of AMICO staff, contractors, and other AMICO members.

Purchasing: Licensed use of images is available to all members of AMICO, both museum and university participants, by annual subscription fees ranging from $2,500 to $5,000 (in U.S. dollars) dependent on annual budget for museums and size of institution for universities. Members of AMICO have the opportunity, with staff assistance as needed, to collaborate on solving a range of common information technology- and rights-related problems confronting museums. AMICO members may also choose to launch joint funding applications to benefit their collaborative work. The AMICO Library will be available under license to all higher education institutions in the 1999/2000 academic year.

002   Artweb

France, Germany, United Kingdom
URL: http://www.bridgeman.co.uk

Profile: Information obtained from the Bridgeman Art Library website (Library News section). The Bridgeman Art Library, London, United Kingdom; Reunion des Musées Nationaux, Paris, France; and Bildarchiv Preussischer Kulturbesitz, Germany, are discussing and outlining a venture to produce a joint online service of more than 300,000 images from more than 1,400 museums, photographers, private collections, and individual artists. Artweb is currently in an organizing stage and plans to be a centrally managed database for both commercial and cultural purposes to provide multilingual research, selection, ordering, and downloading of images 24 hours a day. Copyright information on how to clear permission for reproduction will be provided for the images. Technical work is being carried out by ImageFinder Systems of Zurich, Switzerland. A prototype is currently being developed to attract external investment, and grant funding is expected from the European Commission's Info2000 scheme.

003   Image Technology in Museums and Art Galleries (ITEM)

IVAIN
University College Suffolk
Rope Walk, Ipswich, Suffolk IP4 1LT
United Kingdom
Telephone: 44(0)1473 296672
FAX: 44(0)1473 230054
E-mail: ivain@ecna.org
URL: http://item.suffolk.ac.uk

Profile: Information obtained from website. The ITEM Knowledgebase website is hosted by the University College of Suffolk, United Kingdom, and is an endeavor of the not-for-profit International Visual Arts Information Network (IVAIN). This electronic resource is replacing the previously published hardcopy ITEM (published since 1991 in association with CIDOC—the Documentation Committee of the International Council of Museums). The electronic version will be updated monthly as compared to the twice-yearly hardcopy updates. ITEM is an international resource of information about the planned and implemented uses, worldwide, of image databases and interactive multimedia intended to further the accessibility of, knowledge of, and interest in European and world cultural heritage, particularly in relation to the visual arts (including photographs), museums, architecture, and archaeology. ITEM collects and disseminates descriptive text (in English and the language of original production) and technical information (in English only), together with production and publisher contact names and addresses relating to projects under development and completed published or museum-resident image database and interactive multimedia projects. ITEM has subscribers in 22 countries worldwide, who include Museums, Universities, Libraries, Cultural Authorities, information managers, IT Developers and researchers. Web browsers may view demonstrations by selecting from the Sample Titles (artinact 1, Charles Rennie Mackintosh, Musée d'Orsay—An Interactive Tour, National Museum of American Art, Smithsonian, and Paul Klee). Each of the sample titles retrieves content descriptors, technical development information (format, required equipment specifications, etc.), screen shots, and contact information for purchasing the multimedia item. The website has a search capability, but the full abilities of the search are retrievable only by subscription.

004   Museum Digital Licensing Collective, Inc. (MDLC)

URL: http://www.museumlicensing.org/

Profile: Information obtained from the MDLC website. The Museum Digital Licensing Collective, Inc. is a nonprofit, nonstock corporation, incorporated in the state of Delaware, formed to provide financial assistance for the digitization of original materials in museums and collecting institutions; to manage the storage, distribution, and licensing of digitized materials to educational institutions, libraries, museums, commercial companies, and the public; and to develop and distribute related technical and computer services. The MDLC is sponsored by the American Association of Museums, which will always appoint a majority of the MDLC's Board of Directors. According to a diagram located on the MDLC website, the Board of Directors will include appointees from the AAM, individual museums, and educational institutions. Initial contracts for computer services will be with the University of California at Berkeley and Cornell University. Sun Microsystems has donated hardware to Berkeley Library for use by the MDLC. The initial donation-funded digital collection will be materials relating to nineteenth-century North American culture. However, from the start, all MDLC facilities and services will also be available to any museums and original-materials-collecting institutions with any type of collection that has digital materials it would like to distribute and license through the MDLC, providing such materials meet the technical and documentation standards set by MDLC members. Licensing income is expected to build a revenue stream to continue funding digitization projects to build the digital library and to make the MDLC self-supporting. The MDLC will be developed through a collaborative Task Force process over a 9 to 12 month Organizing Phase, which began in June 1998. It is anticipated that the MDLC will be a membership organization, with members including museums, educational, and other institutions with original collections, and the American Association of Museums. Commercial licensing will be handled by an MDLC Commercial Licensing Agency and controlled by the MDLC, with features determined by the Task Force Museums during the Organizing Phase.

✦ POLICY TASK FORCE PARTICIPANTS (as of June 1998) include:

Amon Carter Museum

Arthur M. Sackler Gallery and Freer Gallery of Art

Carnegie Museums of Pittsburgh

Chicago Historical Society

Children's Museum of Indianapolis

Cornell University

Frederick R. Weisman Art Museum

Harvard University Art Museums

Heard Museum

Henry Ford Museum and Greenfield Village

Historic New Orleans Collection

Historical Society of Washington, DC

Library of Congress

Museum of Science and Industry

National Museum of American History

New York Public Library

North Carolina Museum of Art

Peabody Museum of Archaeology and Ethnology

University of California at Berkeley

Worcester Art Museum

These museums and institutions are participating in the Organizing Phase without further obligation to join the MDLC because it is unrealistic to expect an institution to commit to becoming a member of an organization that has not yet been fully established. The participants of the Organizing Phase will explore how the best interests of the institutions can be realized in a licensing collective.

Production and Documentation: Standards for digitization and documentation will be developed through a collaborative process with Organizing Phase members, experts, and research groups, such as the Consortium for the Computerized Interchange of Museum Information (CIMI). Major research libraries' computer departments will serve as storage and distribution centers for digitized materials. The University of California at Berkeley and Cornell University are initial repositories. Searching and display software is to be developed by Berkeley, Cornell, and other educational institutions as well as commercial companies, such as Sun Microsystems.

Purchasing: Initial financing will be through donated funds and project finance loans; $650,000 Organizing Phase budget; estimated $10 million funding requirements over five years (in U.S. dollars).

Nonexclusive licensing of standard images; exclusive licensing of value-added or enhanced images arranged through MDLC financing or MDLC initiated software. Licensing will be available to any educational institution for use in education and research with licensing contracts based on terms and conditions to be developed by MDLC. It is expected that site licensing to educational institutions will begin in Spring 1999. The MDLC will not charge for the use of MDLC materials for the first three years. While a nominal shipping and handling fee may be imposed, the intent is to give colleges, universities, and K-12 school systems every incentive to explore integrating digitized materials in their research and teaching, and by so doing introduce educational institutions to the MDLC and its databases. Universities, colleges, and library associations will participate from the beginning in the planning and development of the MDLC, including the setting of site license fees. The pricing schedule will be jointly designed by the museums and universities. Two prototype demonstrations are currently available at the MDLC website. Cornell University has provided a demonstration of the Fuertes Collection of bird drawings, and the University of California at Berkeley has provided a demonstration on California history.

005   Museums Online

URL: http://www.museums-online.com

Profile: Information obtained from website. The Museums Online website provides links to cultural institutions worldwide as well as a Cultural Image Archive. Features of the Cultural Image Archive include a free search service for selection of images to license for publishing, website design, advertising, and other uses. After searching and retrieval of thumbnail images, selections can be ordered online.

Participants listed on the website include:

✦ PARTNERS:

Laboratorie de Recherché des Musées de France, Le Louvre

Musée des Tissus et des Textiles Anciens, Lyons, France

National Museum of Western Art, Tokyo, Japan

Natural History Museum, Stockholm, Sweden

State Historical Museum, Moscow

University of California at Berkeley (Museum Informatics Project)

✦ COMPANIES:

Art Resource, New York, NY

Grolier Interactive Europe/On Line, Paris, France

Hewlett-Packard, Cupertino, CA

National Centre for Science Information Systems, (NACSIS), Tokyo, Japan

Questor System Inc., Pasadena, CA

SCALA Archivio Fotografico Editoriale, Florence, Italy

✦ PROFESSIONAL BODIES REPRESENTING ARTISTS:

Pyramide Europe, Paris, France

Societies for Protection of Intellectual Property Rights, SOFAM, Brussels, Belgium

Documentation: Searching by artist returns ULAN (Union List of Artist Names from the Getty Information Institute, Santa Monica, CA) listings for artists. Selection from the list of artists then retrieves thumbnails of images by the selected artist with text information including Title, Author [Artist], Period or Date, Location, Type of Work, Copyright Holder, and License Plate [Alphanumeric Identification Code].

CANADA

Digital Image Providers

006   Archivision

6A Brooklyn Ave.
Toronto, Ontario M4M 2X5 Canada
Telephone: (416) 469-3443
FAX: (416) 469-4412
Attn: Scott Gilchrist, Photographer/Owner
E-mail: director@archivision.com
URL: http://www.archivision.com

This vendor also sells slide products and is listed in the slide provider section of the directory.

Price Range: Slides, $2.00 to $3.00; digital products, various plans available. See below.

Profile: Gilchrist left his position as Slide Curator at the School of Architecture, University of Toronto, in 1992 to create a commercial slide distribution company. Archivision was started by a slide curator to specifically meet the needs of slide curators. The goal remains to provide professional and extensive photographic documentation of the built environment, extending coverage to drawings from original sources where available, backed by extensive documentation, and all at the lowest price. In five years the archive has grown from several thousand images to close to 40,000.

The following services are provided:

1. Custom duplicate slides can be made to order in-house.

2. Slides can be ordered in standard plastic mounts, Gepe glass mounts, or unmounted, and in sets or as singles.

3. OVERVIEW SERVICE: An overview from the larger sets can be selected by the company at a number specified by the curator.

4. APPROVAL SERVICE: Duplicate slides can be sent on approval. This service allows the slide curator to pull only the desired slides, returning the rest.

5. Custom in-house digital files may be ordered with the slides or in lieu of the slides.

6. Extensive slide ID's are supplied with all slides/images.

7. SEARCH SERVICE: Extensive menu-driven search engines are available at the website.

8. LANGUAGE SERVICE: Slide ID's can be translated into French, Italian, Spanish, Dutch, or German for a fee.

In October 1996, Archivision launched a website. The site now displays more than 2,000 images for preview by potential clients. The online catalog lists every subject in the archive alphabetically and is searchable via nine menu-driven search engines. Updates are also posted on the website. Furthermore, an Editorial module keeps clients up-to-date on policy changes and future travel plans. With the launch of the website the company also launched Digital Services, fully outlined at the site, including policies on where images may be made available. Thumbnails already on the site can be purchased and downloaded directly from the site upon approval.

Clearly the new web technologies will benefit Archivision's clients in that they can now preview many of the images and keep up-to-date with new acquisitions.

Slide Photography: Onsite photography: Slides (35mm format only) are professionally taken by Scott Gilchrist in front of the original building, garden, sculpture, or art in public. A Nikon F-90 body is used with the following lenses: Nikkor 28mm f3.5 perspective corrective lens, Nikkor 18mm f3.5 rectilinear lens, and Nikkor AF 80-200 f2.8 ED zoom. All slides are made with the use of a tripod, on Fuji Velvia 50 film (exterior conditions) and Kodak EPY-64 (interiors with tungsten light). In addition various corrective filters may be used, especially a Nikon circular polarizer for haze. Studio photography: Slides (usually 35mm, large format for selected works) are taken by a professional studio photographer using appropriate lighting, film (usually Kodak EPY-64), and equipment.

Slide Production: Ordered slides are custom duplicated from the original slide (the original is usually on Fuji Professional Velvia 50 film) on a Beseler Deluxe Slide Duplicator with a 75/4.0 Apo-Rodagon D 1:1 lens. Ektachrome #5071 duplicating film is used for long life and contrast control. E6 processing is by Steichenlab, a local professional photographic lab.

Documentation: Catalog sent to mailing list with update following each documentation trip.

Purchasing Slide Products: Individual, $3.00 each; in sets, $2.00 each (unmounted); add $1.00 for Gepe mounts; minimum order $50 with discounts as follows: 5%, $501-$800; 10%, $801-$1,500; 15%, $1,501-$3,000; 20%, $3,001-$6,000; 25%, more than $6,000. Mail, fax, or E-mail a list of subject titles with corresponding codes and purchase-order number. Unmounted slides, no shipping fee; Quickpoint mounts, add 4% shipping; Gepe mounts, $1.00 per slide and 5% shipping.

Purchasing Digital Products: PhotoCD and web images. Equipment includes Agfa Studioscan llsi; MAC 7200/90. Windows and MAC formats are available, with tech support also available. Original slide scanning at resolutions of 72 dpi only for thumbnails; 82 dpi for larger sizes upon request. Photolook and Photoshop are used as manipulation software for color correction and cropping to provide both entire and detail views. Both individual slides and sets are available in digital format for multi-user, networked usage in .JPG format. Mail, fax, or E-mail list of subject titles with corresponding codes and purchase-order number and type: full-screen only or full-screen w/thumbnails. Digital products are shipped on floppy disk ($2.50 per disk), 100MB Iomega Zip Disk ($25.00 per disk), or SyQuest cartridges (customer supplies), or E-mailed as attachment ($5.00 preparation charge). Images can be purchased as PhotoCDs, $2.95 per images in sets; $3.25 selected by Archivision; $4.00 selected by customer.

Expansion Plans: The company plans to document architecture, gardens, and sculpture in Egypt, Israel, Jordan, Scotland, and England in 1999.

Museums

012   Canadian Museum of Civilization

100 Laurier Ave., P.O. Box 3100
Hull, Quebec J8X 4H2 Canada
Telephone: (819) 776-7000
FAX: (819) 776-8300
Attn: Louis Campeau, Photo Archives Research Officer
URL: http://www.civilization.ca

This museum also offers slide products and is listed in the slide provider section of the directory.

Profile: The Canadian Museum of Civilization is a Crown Corporation comprising Canada's National Museum of History and Anthropology and the Canadian War Museum. This entry refers to the CMC only. The collection has more than 300,000 images of museum collections, exhibitions, and events, plus historical photograph collections dating from the late nineteenth century (primarily ethnographic subjects). 200,000 images have been digitized in Kodak PhotoCD, and a large website has been established. These and other initiatives make the collection more accessible.

Photography: Original slides are photographed by a professional staff photographer on site at the museum. Photography is primarily in color. Film size and stock varies. For further information, photographer must be consulted.

Production: For actual image duplication, slides or negatives are sent out to professional photo labs. Digital images are produced under contract by Danka Imaging (formerly Kodak Imaging Systems). CMC does not provide copies of images other than from its own collection.

Documentation: Printout from computerized artifact or image database can be provided if requested. Image is labeled with museum catalog number.

Purchasing: Individual slides are priced at $2.50 each. Slide discounts may be negotiated; contact museum for details. Client is invoiced when order is filled. No prepayment required. VISA and MasterCard accepted. Turnaround time dependent on complexity of order. Orders usually shipped by Canada Post. Postage added. No minimum order. Payment for digital product is similar to slides. Contact museum for digital product prices.

Digital Products: CD-ROMs and PhotoCDs are offered in Windows format. Scanned originals include 35mm, 2¼ or 4" x 5", 35mm negatives, and black-and-white negatives in all sizes. The scanning is done with a Kodak Professional PhotoCD Scanner to the resolutions provided in the PhotoCD Image Pack. Manipulation of scanned images is carried out with Kodak Proprietary Imaging PIW 4220 v7.6. Images are color-corrected and can be cropped to detail if ordered by purchaser. The format is .PCD, but can be converted. Viewing software can be Corel, Adobe, L-View, and so forth. Payment arrangements similar to slides. One-time and multiuser formats are offered, but images cannot be networked.

Expansion Plans: Brochures, mailing list, access to electronic catalog, website development.

017   Provincial Museum of Alberta

12845 – 102 Ave.
Edmonton, Alberta T5N 0M6 Canada
Telephone: (403) 453-9100
FAX: (403) 454-6629
URL: http://www.pma.edmonton.ab.ca/

This museum also offers slide products and is listed in the slide provider section of the directory.

Profile: The museum's emphasis is on the natural history of Alberta but includes ethnology, folk life, Western Canadian history, government history, and archaeology.

Photography: Photography of an artifact or specimen in the museum's collections can be arranged. In this case, the client pays all the photography fees as well as any borrowing fees.

Rental: 35mm slides: A loan agreement is signed by the borrower; loan return dates are open to renewal; the loan states terms regarding use, copyright, fees, credit-line requirements, etc.

Digital Products: Kodak PhotoCDs are produced from slides and photographs. The scanning of originals is done by a commercial business in 5 resolutions at 300 dpi. Formats include .PCD, .JPG, .GIF, .BMP, and .TIF. Kodak PhotoCD Access Plus software or other viewing software is required to view the images.

UNITED STATES

Digital Image Providers

026   Art Images for College Teaching (AICT)

Minneapolis College of Art & Design
2501 Stevens Ave. South
Minneapolis, MN 55404
Telephone: (612) 874-3781
Attn: Allan T. Kohl
E-mail: allan_kohl@mn.mcad.edu
URL: http://www.mcad.edu/AICT/index.html

This image provider also offers slide products and is listed in the slide provider section of the directory.

Price Range: Provides slide duplicates of AICT images for $1.25.

Profile: AICT has 500 images on the website and 2,000 to 3,000 images on PhotoCDs that can be loaned to institutions for copying.

Purchasing: $1.25 per duplicate slide. Website images are free.

Digital Products: CD-ROMs and web images.

*028   Art on File

1837 E. Shelby
Seattle, WA 98112
Telephone: (206) 322-2638
FAX: (206) 329-1928
Attn: Rob Wilkinson
E-mail: artofile@wln.com
URL: http://www.artonfile.com

This vendor also sells slide products and is listed in the slide provider section of the directory.

Profile: Art on File was founded in 1982 by photographers Rob Wilkinson and Colleen Chartier to document recent developments in public art, architecture, and design. The company concentrated initially on public art and then evolved into the documentation of a full range of public-space design including architecture, landscape architecture, and urban design. Most of the slide documentation concentrates on contemporary projects; however, some historic topics are covered with a strong connection to contemporary developments in art and architecture. A grant from the National Endowment of the Arts, sponsored by the VRA, helped to expand the company's geographical coverage. Today, the images document projects from North America, Europe, and Asia.

By January 1, 1998, the company will have 62 slide and digital collections with more than 8,000 images. Beginning in early 1998, Art on File will announce all new offerings through its website. A comprehensive printed catalog will no longer be produced, although postcard reminders of new offerings and the website address will be distributed several times per year. The website is actually a fully functional database with keyword access to the entire library, a simple ordering procedure, and thumbnail images of 98 percent of the image library. The company has continued the tradition of producing extensive annotations for each project documented. Because of the contemporary nature of many of the projects photographed, the annotations often include original research and interviews with the artists and designers. Art on File intends to continue this tradition. Ninety-eight percent of the 35mm slide library has been scanned and is available to clients. Images are delivered on CD-ROM in whatever format is desired for either PCs or Macintosh computers. Clients may order entire collections or individual projects. More than 7,000 images will be available for viewing. Art on File is also collecting a series of QTVR scenes to be offered in late 1998. These digital panoramas will supplement the still digital images and slides offered by the company.

Photography: Art on File produces its own photography with a few exceptions noted in the online catalog and annotations. All photographs are produced on location by photographers Rob Wilkinson and Colleen Chartier.

Slide Production: The company uses principally Kodak film products (at 100 ASA), selected based upon the type of conditions found. The slides are duplicated by a local professional lab that uses

Kodak #5071 slide duplication film. Although most of the original photography is 35mm format, a medium-format camera with perspective correction is used for architecture.

Documentation: A catalog is available and an update is sent to the mailing list each spring.

Purchasing: Slides are available individually or in sets priced as follow: $.50 per slide in sets/$4.00 per slide individually; digital images $4.00. Discounts not available at present, but policy is being reviewed. Purchase orders are accepted by fax, E-mail, or letter. Orders are usually shipped within two weeks of receiving them. If additional time is required at the duplicating lab, clients are notified to this effect at the time the order is received. A shipping fee of $6.00 is charged for each order. Approval plans are available.

Digital Products: PhotoCDs are available in either Windows or MAC format with tech support available. A recent-model MAC or PC with a CD-ROM drive is required for viewing. Original transparencies (not duplicates) are scanned using a Kodak PhotoCD Workstation at three resolutions: 300K, 1MB, and 4.5MB. Photoshop and Debabilizer software is used for color correction and cropping. Both entire and detail views are available. Both individual images and sets are available for multiuse. Numerous software can be used for viewing, including Adobe Photoshop.

Art on File's digital images are site-licensed for campus use, which restricts access to current students, faculty, and staff. Digital images may not be transferred to another institution, copied, or reproduced in any form without permission from Art on File, Inc. Digital images are licensed through a signed site license agreement. A standard form is used for this purpose. Orders are filled within one week if the images have been previously scanned and corrected. A shipping and handling charge of $6.00 is added to each order. Rush development of image orders is possible depending on inventory of contemporary public slides.

Other Products: A CD-ROM product called Public Art: Seattle is being marketed that contains several hundred Art on File images sponsored and funded by the Seattle Arts Commission and the National Endowment of the Arts.

Expansion Plans: 1998 plans include the documentation of a number of new projects in Spain, Germany, and England and other locations in North America. Suggestions for projects to document are always encouraged. Art on File has been steadily developing a library of QTVR panoramas that document important historical and contemporary projects around the world. This library is currently not available, but

the first version will be released soon. This product will enable educators and students to explore, in 360-degree space, noteworthy buildings, site-specific artworks, urban spaces, and landscapes. QTVR is the most effective new media available for the exploration of natural or built space. As always Art on File encourages comments and criticisms about the company's work and makes every effort to incorporate appropriate changes as indicated. The company is currently investing in a higher production level for new photography, a streamlined ordering process through the World Wide Web and the creation of new media resources such as QTVR.

029a   Arts of the United States

Lamar Dodd School of Art
University of Georgia
Athens, GA 30602

Profile: The Carnegie Study of the Arts of the United States was begun in 1955 to "illustrate the nature and quality of American Art and American civilization." The project was funded by the Carnegie Corporation of New York and directed by Lamar Dodd. Victor and Harold Sandak supervised the production of the photographic materials. The set contained 4,155 images of all facets of American art from the sixteenth century to the mid-twentieth century. Following the cessation of the Sandak business in 1997, the negatives for the Arts of the United States project were returned to the University of Georgia in July 1998. Plans are being formulated as to how to make the images accessible. Thomas Polk, of the University of Georgia, expects the negatives to be digitized. Announcement as to the availability of these images will be disseminated through the *VRA Bulletin* "Slide Market News" column and through the Image Providers Directory at http://www.rci.rutgers.edu/~beetham/vendor.htm.

This site also will continue to be linked to the Visual Resources Association home page, located at http://www.oberlin.edu/~art/vra/vra.html.

035   Calderca Inc.

10709 Cleary Blvd., #202
Plantation, FL 33324
Telephone: (954) 452-2699
Attn: Jose Luis Colmenares
E-mail: CALDERCA@aol.com

This vendor also sells slide products and is listed in the slide provider section of the directory.

Profile: Collection of around 30,000 slides of architecture, developed over 20 years by Professor Jose Luis Colmenares. A graduate of the University of Texas at Austin, with several architectural degrees, Professor Colmenares has taught for 17 years and lectured widely in Europe, the USA, and Latin America. He offers 188 sets, ranging from 10 to 150 slides per set of architecture in situ, with a brief essay on the subject of each set. Sets include a wide range of thematic subjects, such as gothic architecture, neoclassical architecture in France, and high-tech architecture, and sets on individual architects. Sets include European, North American, and Latin American architects. Contact Professor Colmenares for a list of sets.

Photography: All the slides were photographed by Professor Jose Colmenares, in situ, over a period of 20 years. Because the collection consists of 30,000 slides, several types of film have been used, but mainly Kodachrome 64, Ektachrome 64, and Fujichrome 50.

Production: Slide sets are duplicated on Ektachrome 64 film and mounted in plastic.

Documentation: Each slide is numbered and individually identified, including: name of building, architect, date, location, and point of view. Accompanying texts are explanations and critical reviews that could be used as lecture notes.

Purchasing: Slides are sold in sets, ranging from set of 10 priced at $30 to set of 150 priced at $450. Set prices do not include shipping. Place order by listing set numbers. If the order is for less than $180 (U.S.), the order can be placed by E-mail or telephone and the purchaser will be billed later. For orders totaling more than $180 (U.S.), send a check payable to CALDERCA Inc. Allow 3 to 4 weeks for delivery. Special requests are available if groups of slides are needed for a particular academic course.

Digital Products: Slides can be ordered in CD-ROM format. Contact Professor Colmenares for details.

038   Chronicle Books/Eden Interactive

Customer Service
275 Fifth St.
San Francisco, CA 94301

Telephone: (800) 722-6657
Eden Interactive Technical Support:
(415) 241-1450
FAX: (800) 858-7787
URL: http://www.chronbooks.com

Profile: Primarily a book publisher, this company produced a CD-ROM titled American Visions: Art from the Roy Neuberger Collection through its Eden Interactive associate, founded in 1992. The CD-ROM is available in either MAC or Windows format and includes the artists Jackson Pollock, Milton Avery, Alexander Calder, Stuart Davis, Mark Rothko, Georgia O'Keeffe, Jacob Lawrence, and others. The interactive CD-ROM includes more than 200 works of art by 140 different artists and commentaries by art authorities, as well as QuickTime video clips of selected artists, and is a winner of the 1994 Invision Award and a Four Mice winner, one of the Top 50 CD-ROMs, from *MAC User Magazine*. The suggested retail price is $49.95. ISBN 0-8118-1142-5.

Other Sources: CD-ROM is also available from Crystal Productions.

*039   Cirrus

542 S. Alameda St.
Los Angeles, CA 90013
Telephone: (213) 680-3473
FAX: (213) 680-0930
Attn: Cameron Whiteman or Jean Milant
E-mail: CCirrus@aol.com
URL: http://www.LACN.org

This vendor also sells slide products and is listed in the slide provider section of the directory.

Price Range: $.50/slide to $25.00 for Cirrus CD-ROM; digital images to be downloaded from website: LACN.org (Faces of LA) as of January 2, 1998.

Profile: Jean R. Milant founded Cirrus Editions, originally located in Hollywood, in 1970. From the beginning, it was a publisher of original graphics and multiples by Southern California artists. The fully equipped workshop produces fine prints (using lithography, silkscreen, and etching) by such contemporary artists as Peter Alexander, John Baldessari, Vija Celmins, Ed Moses, Bruce Nauman, Joan Nelson, Lari Pittman, and Ed Ruscha. Cirrus Gallery was established in 1971 and from that time, it became a major contemporary art gallery exhibiting new and exciting Southern California artists.

Cirrus is a participant in "Faces of LA," which is a project of the Getty Museum's LA Culture Net. This promotes access to cultural resources through online networks. A consortium of Los Angeles museums and libraries and Cirrus has created a virtual database composed of digital materials from their collections that illustrate the places, monuments, events, culture, and history of the peoples of Southern California, and that represent themselves as local cultural institutions. Cirrus has included 1,000 images that will be accessible through this website. In addition to the digital images, Cirrus offers slides photographed professionally from the original works of art.

Photography: Original works photographed by a professional photographer.

Production: Generally, the slides are duplicated by an outside vendor from 35mm originals to high-quality 35mm duplicates.

Documentation: The Los Angeles County Museum of Art published a catalogue raisonné of the Cirrus Editions archive. This includes 60 color and 400 duotone reproductions. It is available from Cirrus for $65. Key text fields will be available with digital images on website.

Purchasing: Slides are priced at $.50 each, individually or in sets. Discounts for volume purchases and for educational institutions. Cirrus requires payment or large institution purchase order with the order, and orders are filled each week. Shipping charges are additional.

Digital Products: The Getty Information Institute contracted with Luna Imaging, Inc., a well-regarded service bureau in Venice, CA, to scan Cirrus master slides and provide digital image files. These are now available in most formats and in a range of resolutions. Luna has corrected the original images for color distortions. Complete views of the Cirrus work of art is available with zoom detail.

040 Clearvue/eav

6465 N. Avondale Ave.
Chicago, IL 60631-1996
Telephone: (800) CLEARVU ([800] 253-2788)
(8 A.M. to 4:30 P.M. CST, M-F)
FAX: (800) 444-9855
URL: http://www.clearvue.com/home.html

Profile: Information from catalog and website. Company sells CD-ROMs, videotapes, and filmstrips suitable for use in elementary schools through colleges. Catalog is available on request and indicates grade level. Curriculum materials including artist biographies and links to other websites are available at website. CD-ROMs are available in both MAC and Windows formats and singly or in lab packs. Topics include art history and culture, art appreciation, individual artists, design, art processes and techniques, photography, electronic art, and careers in art. CD-ROM prices begin at $75 (U.S. funds) for individual CD-ROMs. Purchase orders, checks, and credit cards are accepted. Orders from outside the USA must be prepaid. Shipping charges are additional. A 45-day preview period is available and must be requested on institutional letterhead or purchase order or be prepaid. Prepaid orders may be returned within 45 days for credit, exchange, or refund. Purchases from Clearvue/eav include limited performance rights and may be used only in face-to-face education in a single location. Network usage requires payment of additional licensing fees where permission can be granted for such usage.

045 Crystal Productions

1812 Johns Dr., P.O. Box 2159
Glenview, IL 60025
Telephone: (800) 255-8629 (Outside U.S. & Canada [708] 657-8144)
FAX: (800) 657-8149 (Outside U.S. & Canada [708] 657-8149)
E-mail: custserv@crystalproductions.com
URL: http://www.crystalproductions.com

This vendor also sells slide products and is listed in the slide provider section of the directory.

Profile: Information from catalog and website. Company sells CD-ROMs, videodiscs, videotapes, posters, art prints (Shorewood Prints and New York Graphic Society Prints), books, games, filmstrips, and slide sets including sets from the American Craft Council. Selected CD-ROM titles include *History Through Art, The Hermitage, Exploring Modern Art* (Tate Gallery), *Microsoft Art Gallery* (The National Gallery, London), *Renaissance, Impressionism, The Ultimate Frank Lloyd Wright, American Visions: 20th Century Art from the Roy R. Neuberger Collection, Survey of Western Art,* and *The Electronic Library of Art: European and American Art.* The company also sells timelines and color wheels. Topics include art, art history, architecture, and multicultural series.

Products are suitable for elementary to college-age audiences with intended audience noted in catalog.

Documentation: Catalog available on request and sent to mailing list annually. Format and hardware requirements are noted in catalog. Most CD-ROMs listed in recent catalog are available in both Windows and MAC formats.

Purchasing: Purchase orders, credit cards, and checks are accepted. All payments must be in U.S. funds. Material can be returned within 30 days if not satisfactory. Preview period of 30 days on all products except books and CD-ROMs. Preview requests should be made on institutional letterhead or purchase order. Shipping charges additional (7% of total or minimum of $3.50). Order shipped within 7 to 10 days of receipt of order. Rush shipping available for additional charge.

050　Dick Blick Co.

P.O. Box 1267
Galesburg, IL 61501
Telephone: (800) 447-8192 (orders only)
or (800) 723-2787 (customer service)
FAX: (800) 621-8293
E-mail: info@dickblick.com
URL: http://www.dickblick.com

This vendor also sells slide products and is listed in the slide provider section of the directory.

Profile: Company sells CD-ROMs, videotapes, and art and educational supplies and offers more than 200 slide sets. Art and architecture covered from prehistory to the present. Several sets offered are coordinated with textbooks. Very large survey set also available, 800 slides for $1,049.90. Selected CD-ROM titles include *Van Gogh, Michelangelo, Leonardo* and *History Through Art Series* (9 CD-ROMs).

Production: Most sets produced by Universal Color Slides (90%, according to Universal).

Documentation: Slide sets listed in general catalog ($3.00). New catalog issued annually. Identification of individual slides not provided in catalog, but slides themselves labeled.

Purchasing: Order form included in catalog. Slides sold in sets only, ranging in size from 10 slides to 800 slides. Quantity discounts figured into price structure, with per-slide cost about $2.00 in small sets. Postage added (10% on prepaid orders). Special prices quoted for very large orders. Minimum

charge card order $10.00. Prepayment required except from institutions or companies with Dun & Bradstreet rating. Credit card charges accepted. Slides kept in stock and shipped within two to three weeks, usually via UPS. Rush orders filled within one week; no surcharge. Returns accepted for refund within ten days. "All sales guaranteed."

Digital Products: CD-ROMs on individual artists (Van Gogh, Michelangelo, Leonardo) and History Through Art series (9 CD-ROMs). The individual artist CD-ROMs are priced at $49.95 each, and the price of each CD-ROM in the History Through Art series is $75.00 or the entire set can be purchased for $600.00. All prices are in U.S. dollars.

Other Sources: Mail orders should be sent to the nearest office. Besides the central office listed above, orders may be addressed to one of the following:

Dick Blick East	Dick Blick West
P.O. Box 26	P.O. Box 521
Allentown, PA 18105	Henderson, NV 89015
Telephone:	Telephone:
(215) 965-6051	(702) 451-7662
FAX: (215) 965-4026	FAX: (702) 451-8196

Also, retail stores located in 10 U.S. cities.

Other Products: Videotapes.

Evaluation: See Universal Color slides **(095)**.

051　Digital Arts & Sciences

1301 Marina Village Pkwy.
Alameda, CA 94501
Telephone: (800) 449-6220 (orders) or
(510) 814-7200, x632
FAX: (510) 814-6100
Attn: Theresa Cronis
E-mail: theresac@dascorp.com
URL: http://www.dascorp.com

Profile: Information from 1998 flyer and from Theresa Cronis, Marketing Manager. Company sells art CD-ROMs, ImageAXS, and ImageAXS Pro image management software, and EmbARK collections management and cataloging software. Digital Arts & Sciences also markets the Museum System for Windows, a Gallery Systems product. Fine art collections on CD-ROM include: *Masterworks of Japanese Painting (Etsuko and Joe Price Collection), Great Paintings— Renaissance to Impressionism (Frick Collection), Ancient Egyptian Art (Brooklyn Museum), 1000 Years of Russian Art (State Russian Museum, St. Petersburg),*

Masterpieces of World Art (Harvard University Art Museums), Robert Mapplethorpe—An Overview, Robert Mapplethorpe—The Controversy, and *Robert Mapplethorpe—The Catalogue Raisonné.* CD-ROMs are available in either Windows or MAC formats or in a Windows/MAC Hybrid format.

Purchasing: Prices range from $59.95 to $349.95, depending on title. Purchase orders, checks, and credit cards (VISA and MasterCard) are accepted. Shipping charges and sales tax for California residents will be added to orders. Prices are in U.S. dollars. Information packets on the software products are available without charge.

055   European Access

U.S. and European Offices
U.S. Office: Mark Carrow
1647 Grove St.
San Francisco, CA 94117
Telephone: 1 (415) 749-1660
FAX: 1 (415) 776-1525
E-mail: mark@euroaccess.net

European Office: Thomas Gaida
Maternplatz 8
50996 Köln (Cologne), Germany
Telephone: 49 (221) 935 9054
FAX: 49 (221) 9359055
E-mail: thomas@euroaccess.net
URL: http://www.euroaccess.net/

Profile: Company markets CD-ROMs produced by Digital Arts & Sciences. CD-ROM titles available from Euroaccess include *The Frick Collection, The Brooklyn Museum, The State Russian Museum, Masterworks of Japanese Painting,* and *Robert Mapplethorpe.*

056   Films for the Humanities & Sciences

P.O. Box 2053
Princeton, NJ 08543-2053
Telephone: (800) 257-5126 or (609) 275-1400
(8:30 A.M. to 5:00 P.M. EST)
FAX: (609) 275-3767
E-mail: custserv@films.com
URL: http://www.films.com

Profile: Information from catalog and website. Company has been in business for more than 25 years, providing educational media. Company offers more than 5,000 videotape, CD-ROM, and videodisc programs in subject areas appropriate for schools, colleges, and public libraries. Programs are available with public performance rights. Company is U.S. and Canadian distributor for World Microfilms (221). Website has searchable categories including BBC Collection, architecture and urban studies, arts, multicultural studies, philosophy, ethics and religion, and women's studies among others. Selected CD-ROM titles include *Ancient Civilization of the Mediterranean, Cyber Rome, English Architecture on CD-ROM, Japan 2000, Leonardo da Vinci on CD-ROM,* and *Renaissance of Florence on CD-ROM.*

Documentation: Catalog available on request and updates regularly sent to mailing list. Website is searchable by subject or category. Format (Windows or MAC) is noted, but hardware requirements are not listed in catalog. Not all titles are available in both formats.

Purchasing: Purchase orders, credit cards, and checks are accepted. Prices are in U.S. dollars. Online ordering and payment by credit card is available. Shipping charge additional (6% of total or minimum of $5.95).

058   G. K. Hall

An Imprint of Macmillan Publishing USA, a Simon and Schuster Co.
866 Third Ave., 17th Floor
New York, NY 10022
Telephone: (800) 261-8763 (orders) or (212) 702-6789
FAX: (800) 562-1272 or (212) 605-9350

Profile: The company has been known for many years as a publisher of library reference books and is now offering *Athena: Classical Mythology on CD-ROM, Avery Index,* and *National Portrait Gallery-Smithsonian Institution Permanent Collection of Notable Americans on CD-ROM. Athena* is an interactive database with summaries and source citations for more than 1,200 myths culled from 44 works of major significance. Approximately 500 classical images and illustrations of the gods, goddesses, and other mythological characters are included.

Documentation: Brochure available from G. K. Hall on request or information is available at website. Format and hardware requirements are noted in brochure and on website. *Athena* is available in both MAC and Windows formats and is available in both single-user and multiuser versions. A free demonstration package is available on request.

Purchasing: Purchase orders, credit cards, and checks accepted. Online ordering is available at website. Prices are listed in U.S. dollars and do not apply to international shipments. Contact nearest representative for international orders (links to representatives at website). Shipping and handling fees are free on all prepaid and standing orders.

061 Hedrich-Blessing Photography

11 W. Illinois St.
Chicago, IL 60607
Telephone: (312) 321-1151
FAX: (312) 321-1165
Attn: Michael Houlahan or Bob Shimer
E-mail: hedrich@hedrich-blessing.com
URL: http://www.hedrich-blessing.com/

This vendor also sells slide products and is listed in the slide provider section of the directory.

Profile: Hedrich-Blessing specializes in architectural and interior design photography, so the images are limited to that area. All the material that is sold is created from assignments that were completed for clients. Images are sold individually.

062 Image Directory

Academic Press, A Division of Harcourt Brace & Company
525 B St., Suite 1900
San Diego, CA 92101-4495
Attn: Project—John Elliott, Marketing Manager
Online Products, Academic Press
Telephone: (619) 699-6233
E-mail: jelliott@acad.com
Attn: Technical—Kaaran Webb, Project Manager
Image Directory, Academic Press
Telephone: (619) 699-6379
E-mail: kwebb@acad.com
Attn: Copyrights & Permissions—Dr. J. Scott Bentley
Senior Editor, Academic Press
Telephone: (619) 699-6387
FAX: (619) 699-6715
E-mail: jsbentley@acad.com
URL: http://imagedir.com

Profile: Information from website and from Clearinghouse on Image Information (http://www.library.arizona.edu/images/image_projects.html). The Image Directory is an online database of information on art images from museums and collections around the world and includes painting, sculpture, architecture, textiles, photography, ethnographic pieces, decorative objects, maps, and more. Subscribers can retrieve detailed data on each artwork, contact numbers for rights and reproduction information and licensing fees, and a link to the image provider's website. Many entries are accompanied by low-resolution images, provided by the Image Directory's network of participating museums, libraries, societies, and other institutions. A demonstration is available free of charge at the Image Directory website.

✦ PARTICIPATING INSTITUTIONS (AS OF JUNE 1998):

Abby Aldrich Rockefeller Folk Art Center, Williamsburg, VA

Academy of Natural Sciences

American Craft Museum

American Textile History Museum

Anacostia Museum—Smithsonian Institution, Washington DC

Ancient World Slides

Archivision

Art Gallery of Western Australia, Perth

Art on File, Inc.

The Asia Society, New York

Avery Architectural and Fine Arts Library, Columbia University

Berkeley Art Museum/Pacific Film Archives

Berkshire Museum

Blackader-Lauterman Library of Architecture and Art, McGill University

Braithwaite Fine Arts Gallery—Southern Utah University

The Brooklyn Museum of Art, NY

Canadian Museum of Civilization, Hull

Chicago Architecture Foundation

The Colonial Williamsburg Foundation

Columbus Museum of Art, Columbus, OH

Crawford Municipal Art Gallery

Crocker Art Museum

Dallas Museum of Art, TX

Davis Publications—Rosenthal Art Slides

Delaware Art Museum

Derek Fell's Horticultural Picture Library

The Design Library

Elizabeth Ney Museum

Florida State University Museum

Foundation for Latin American Anthropological Research

Fort Wayne Museum of Art, IN

George Eastman House—International Museum of Photography

Gilcrease Museum

Goucher College

Guiseppe Mazza

Harold Stump Architectural Foundation

Harper Horticultural Slide Library

Hartill Art Associates

Historic New Orleans Collection

Hunter Museum of Art

Huntington Library, Art Collections, and Botanical Gardens

Icarus, U.K.

The Jewish Museum

Leanin' Tree Museum of Western Art

Magnolia Plantation and Gardens, Charleston, SC

Media for the Arts

Mediaflex

Michigan State University Museum

Montreal Museum of Fine Arts

Munson-Williams-Proctor Institute

Museum Boijmans Van Beuningen

Museum of Antiquities, University of Newcastle-upon-Tyne, U.K.

Museum of Fine Arts, St. Petersburg, FL

The Museum of Modern Art, NY

Museum of Northern Arizona

Museum of the City of New York

National Museum of African Art—Smithsonian Institution, Washington DC

National Museum of American Art—Smithsonian Institution, Washington DC

National Museum of American History—Smithsonian Institution, Washington DC

National Postal Museum—Smithsonian Institution, Washington DC

The Natural History Museum, London

Newberry Library

North Carolina Museum of Art

Noyes Museum

Oliver Radford Architecture Slides

Philbrook Museum of Art—Chapman Library

Pilgrim Society & Museum

Portland Art Museum

Preservation Society of Newport County

Princeton University Department of Art and Archaeology

Richmond Art Museum, VA

Rijksmuseum, Amsterdam, The Netherlands

Rockwell Museum

Royal British Columbia Museum of Art, Victoria

San Diego Museum of Art, CA

Saskia Ltd.

Seth C. Jayson

Shelburne Museum, VT

South Dakota Art Museum

Southeastern Architectural Archive

Southwest Museum

Sterling and Francine Clark Art Institute

The Stuart Collection—University of California, San Diego

Studio-Museum of Elizabeth O'Neill Verner

Suffolk County Vanderbilt Museum

Superstock

Tacoma Art Museum, WA

Textile Museum

Timken Museum of Art

Toronto Historical Board, ON

Tweed Museum of Art—University of Minnesota, Duluth

UC Berkeley Architecture Slide & Photograph Library, CA

UCLA—Armand Hammer Museum of Art, Los Angeles, CA

Utah Museum of Fine Arts

Vancouver Art Gallery, BC

Widener University Art Collection & Gallery

Williams College Museum of Art

Wright Museum of Art, Beloit College

Agreements with other institutions are being negotiated. See website for updated list of participating institutions.

Purchasing: Access to the Image Directory is sold by subscription. There are three types of subscription available. Annual Site License Subscription allows unlimited users at an institution (e.g., library) with access controlled through the use of IP addressing. Cost is $1,500 per year, per institution (U.S. dollars). Customer signs a physical site license and pays through conventional means (non-Web). Members of Academic Press's IDEAL program are eligible for a 15% discount on this subscription. Annual Commercial/Organization Subscription allows up to 60 users with access controlled through use of secure passwords. Cost is $300 per year for the first 10 users and $200 (U.S. dollars) for each additional 10 up to a total of 60. The customer signs up and pays via a secure Web order form. Purchase orders and/or credit cards are accepted. One-month subscription allows one user unlimited use for one month with access controlled through the use of a secure password. Cost is $40 per month (U.S. dollars). Individual subscriptions are also available in three-month, six-month, and one-year increments. The customer signs up and pays with a credit card via a secure Web order form. Typical individual subscribers include graphic designers, art students, and professors.

Documentation: Stuart Glogoff, Manager of the Clearinghouse on Image Information, reports that the Image Directory includes 105,000 records with thumbnail .GIF images (2,000) as of June 1998. He describes the Image Directory as an online union catalog of information on art images, including such information as the title, artist, date, medium, materials, and dimensions. Full contact information is listed so that users can obtain rights and reproduction information from the image provider. Links to the Getty Information Institute's Union List of Artist Names (ULAN) and the Art & Architecture Thesaurus (AAT) provide comprehensive, standardized information on artists' names and art and architecture terms. Another feature is the Times and Places Page, which includes maps and timelines taken from *Gardner's Art Through the Ages* and allows a user to explore the geographic, historical, and political context in which a given artwork was created. Another feature allows records and images selected during one session to be saved for retrieval in a subsequent session.

063 Insight Media

2162 Broadway
New York, NY 10024-6620
Telephone: (800) 233-9910 (9:30 A.M. to 6:00 P.M. EST) or (212) 721-6316
FAX: (212) 799-5309

Profile: Information from brochure. Company sells videotapes and CD-ROMs on art and architecture topics. Selected CD-ROM titles from a recent brochure include *Leonardo the Inventor, Introduction to Archaeology, Exploring Ancient Architecture,* and several CD-ROMs for creating floor plans.

Documentation: Brochures sent periodically to mailing list. Format (Windows or MAC) noted in brochure, but no information noted on hardware requirements.

Purchasing: Individual CD-ROMs in recent brochure priced from $99.00 to $119.00 (U.S. dollars). Purchase orders, credit cards, and checks accepted. Shipping charge additional (5% of total with minimum charge of $5.00). Shipping is free if check is sent with order.

064 Instructional Resources Corporation

1819 Bay Ridge Ave.
Annapolis, MD 21403
Telephone: (800) 922-1711
FAX: (410) 268-8320
E-mail: ircemail@aol.com

Profile: The several large slide sets "American History," "Western Civilization," and "World History" have been converted to CD-ROM and videodisc. The brochure notes that these discs are interactive for student use as well as being suitable for the classroom. The "American History" disc includes 200 paintings and 115 historical maps among the 2,512 images. There are "hundreds of paintings" included in the 3,936 images on the "Western Civilization" disc. The "World History" disc (non-European History) contains 2,400 images; 320 of these are works of art.

Purchasing: Each set is shipped on 30-day approval. 5% is added to invoice for shipping and handling. One year guarantee for defective parts. The disks are $95 each for a single copy, $375 for 5 copies, $496 for 10 copies, and $995 for 25 copies. The three titles are sold together for $245.

073   Media for the Arts (formerly Budek)

360 Thames St., Suite 2N
P.O. Box 1011
Newport, RI 02840-6631
Telephone: (800) 554-6008 or
(401) 845-9600
FAX: (401) 846-6580
Attn: Elizabeth Allen, Director
E-mail: artmfa@art-history.com
URL: http://www.art-history.com

This vendor also sells slide products and is listed in the slide provider section of the directory.

Profile: Media for the Arts has been in business since 1948 serving the art and music enthusiast and educator with visual materials designed to enhance, enliven and educate. Company has 30,000 color slides on architecture, sculpture, painting, and archaeology. Slides are sold in sets only.

Documentation: Annual catalog sent to mailing list.

Purchasing: The price for each slide set depends upon the mount selected and the size of the slide set. The number of slides is indicated in parentheses. Standard sets average 10 slides. Super sets, designated by catalog number ending in -4, average 40 slides. Standard sets are priced at $15.00 (cardboard mounts) and $19.00 (Gepe glass mounts), and Super Sets (-4) are priced at $59.00 (cardboard

mounts) and $76.00 (Gepe glass mounts). Any other special pricing is denoted in catalog. All prices are subject to change without notice. Quantity discounts are offered. Contact vendor for details. All prices are FOB Newport, RI, 30 days NET. Please add 7% to the total of your order to cover postage/handling insurance for U.S. and Canadian shipments. There is a $6.00 minimum shipping charge. On overseas orders, please state shipping preference. Shipping and Receiving claims must be made within 10 days of receipt of order. There is a 10% surcharge for any orders needed prior to our normal 14-day ARO. Please allow enough delivery time when ordering. Videos may take 3 weeks for delivery. Only firm orders are accepted for videos and CD-ROMs. They are not available for preview. There are no returns except for manufacturer's guarantee. Slide sets are available for 30-day approval privileges. Institutional purchase orders are accepted. Orders from individuals must be prepaid either by check or credit card (MasterCard and VISA accepted).

Digital Products: CD-ROMs in both Windows and MAC formats. Laserdiscs. Selected titles include: The Art Historian (Ancient to Medieval $49.95 and Renaissance to Modern $49.95); History Through Art—Series of nine titles $675.00 (individual titles $75.00 or lab packs of five CDs $225.00); Early American History Through Art ($75.00 or Lab packs of five CDs $225.00); Art of the Western World (Laserdisc) 10 titles 1-9: $100.00 each.

Other Products: VHS videotapes.

084   Reindeer Company

P.O. Box 7429
Boulder, CO 80306
Telephone: (800) 952-6844 or
(303) 938-6844
FAX: (303) 938-6847
Attn: Rebecca Cook
E-mail: becky@reindeer.com

Profile: Company focused on producing multimedia for art and art history. Their first product was *The Art Historian, Volume I* and *Volume II*. Volume I covers Ancient to Medieval, and volume II covers Renaissance to Modern and Asian, African, and Oceanic. The interactive CD-ROMs contain more than 1,200 images gathered from more than 300 museums and text and test questions written by current scholars from academic institutions across the

United States. *The Art Historian* is available in both MAC and Windows formats.

Documentation: Brochure available on request that includes hardware requirements, contributing scholars, and a partial listing of schools using the program as well as a content description and screen shots.

Purchasing: Available for single use or site license for multiuse. Payment in U.S. funds is requested. Contact company for pricing.

Other Products: *Absolute Music* CD-ROM to be available August 1998.

Other Sources: *The Art Historian* is also available from Media for the Arts **(073)**.

*086   Saskia, Ltd. Cultural Documentation

5 Horizon Ln.
Freeport, ME 04032
Telephone: (877) SASKIA2 or
(877) 727-5422
Attn: Renate Wiedenhoeft
E-mail: info@saskia.com
URL: http://www.saskia.com

This vendor also sells slide products and is listed in the slide provider section of the directory.

Profile: Approximately 20,000 color slide titles offered of art and architecture of Western Europe, dating from Ancient Greece through the early twentieth century, with emphasis on the Italian Renaissance, Italian and northern Baroque painting, and nineteenth-century French and German painting. This company has more than 30 years of experience documenting museum objects. Color slides offered as originals and some as duplicates. New slides continually added. For more than 30 years, Saskia has documented the history of Western art in Europe—working in the major repositories of France, Italy, Germany, Austria, Greece, Turkey, and Scandinavia from Ancient Greece to the beginning of the twentieth century. Saskia has already incorporated the most advanced technologies: digital images, interactive website browsing, online ordering and searching, and credit card purchases. Museum collections documented selectively as follows:

AUSTRIA

Gemäldegalerie der Akademie der Bildenden Künste, Vienna

Historisches Museum (Museum der Stadt Wien), Vienna

Kunsthistorisches Museum, Vienna

Österreichische Galerie im Belvedere, Vienna

Schatzkammer, Vienna

BELGIUM

Musées Royaux des Beaux-Arts de Belgique, Brussels

DENMARK

Thorvaldsen Museum, Copenhagen

FINLAND

Finnish Architecture Museum, Helsinki

FRANCE

Musée du Louvre, Paris

GREECE

Acropolis Museum, Athens

Archaeological Museum, Delphi

Archaeological Museum, Olympia

National Archaeological Museum, Athens

GERMANY

Alte Pinakothek, Munich

Germanisches Nationalmuseum, Nuremberg

Glyptothek, Munich

Schloss Charlottenburg, Berlin

Staatliche Museum zu Berlin, East Berlin

Staatsgalerie, Stuttgart

Städelsches Kunstinstitut, Frankfurt-am-Main

Stiftung Preussischer Kulturbesitz, Berlin (Gemäldegalerie, Kupferstichkabinett, Nationalgalerie, and Schloss Grünewald)

Suermondt-Ludwig Museum, Aachen

Wallraf-Richartz Museum and Museum Ludwig, Cologne

HUNGARY

Museum of Fine Arts, Budapest

ITALY

Galleria Borghese, Villa Borghese, Rome

Galleria degli Uffizi, Florence

Galleria dell'Accademia, Florence

Galleria dell'Accademia, Venice

Galleria Doria Pamphili, Rome

Galleria Nazionale d'Arte Antica, Rome (Palazzo Barberini & Palazzo Corsini)

Galleria Palatina, Palazzo Pitti, Florence

Galleria Spada, Rome

Museo Archaeologico Nazionale, Naples

Museo Campano, Capua

Museo Capitolino, Rome

Museo del Duomo, Florence

Museo del Duomo, Siena

Museo di Palazzo Venezia, Rome

Museo e Gallerie Nazionale di Capodimonte, Naples

Museo Nazionale del Bargello, Florence

Palazzo Rosso, Genoa

Pinacoteca di Brera, Milan

Pinacoteca Nazionale, Bologna

Pinacoteca Nazionale, Siena

NETHERLANDS

Centraal Museum, Utrecht

NORWAY

Bergen Billedgalleri Permanenten, Bergen

Historisk Museum, University of Bergen, Bergen

Nasjonalgalleriet, Oslo

Rasmus Meyers Samlinger, Bergen

SPAIN

Madrid, Prado

SWEDEN

Goteborgs Konstmuseum, Gothenburg

Nationalmuseum, Stockholm

Uppsala Universitets Konstsamling, Uppsala

SWITZERLAND

Offentliche Kunstsammlung-Kunstmuseum, Basel

UNITED STATES

California Palace of the Legion of Honor, San Francisco, CA

Cleveland Museum of Art, Cleveland, OH

Denver Art Museum, Denver, CO

M. H. DeYoung Memorial Museum, San Francisco, CA

Metropolitan Museum of Art, New York, NY

Nelson-Atkins Museum of Art, Kansas City, MO

North Carolina Museum of Art, Raleigh, NC

Photography: Museum photography conducted at times when collections are closed to the public. Kodak color scale often photographed with work of art. Background cloth usually hung in galleries when photographing freestanding objects. Professional studio equipment used. Artworks are photographed by a professional art historian/photographer using Kodak and Fuji film under controlled conditions using constantly upgraded professional equipment.

Original 35mm slides (4" x 5" in some cases) are photographed directly in front of the work of art on Kodak EPT5037 and Fuji film.

Production: Duplicates printed on standard Kodak duplicating film #5071. Originals inserted in window of 3" x 5" index cards or (formerly) mounted in thin paper masks. Duplicates color corrected and mounted in cardboard or plastic. Frames not masked prior to duplication.

Documentation: Mailing list kept. Free catalog available and updated catalogs regularly sent to mailing list. Slides accompanied by full identifications imprinted on mounts or index cards. Documentation is obtained from museums and does not always reflect scholarly disagreements about attributions. Orientation not marked.

Purchasing: See website and/or catalog. Slides are priced at $3.25 each for duplicates, $6.75 each for originals, and $7.50 each for limited-edition originals. Discounts: 5% for 20 slides or more; 10% for 50 slides or more; 15% for 100 slides or more. University purchase orders accepted; prepayment required (including credit cards) for individuals. Orders filled in 3 to 10 days.

Digital Products: PhotoCDs and web images are available. PhotoCDs are available in both Windows and MAC formats, and tech support is provided. For viewing, 24-bit color monitors are recommended; 16-bit color will suffice. Original 35mm slides and some 4" x 5" transparencies are scanned. All images are offered in three resolutions: 1024 x 1536, 512 x 768, and 128 x 192 pixels. Adobe Photoshop is used for manipulation including color correction and cropping. Both entire and detail views are offered. Kodak Pro PhotoCD Scanning with manual correction is used for production of digital images. Image Formats: Saskia offers three separate resolutions on the same CD-ROM: high-resolution, 1024 x 1536 pixels, ca. 1MB filesize; screen-size, 512 x 768 pixels, ca. 200KB filesize; and thumbnail-size, 128 x 192 pixels, ca. 20KB filesize. All are .JPG compressed files in 24-bit color.

For viewing, any software capable of viewing the above formats is usable. Saskia suggests integrating images into an image database, either a commercially available product (e.g., EmbARK) or developing an intranet-type solution. Digital images are licensed for network use, allowing for multiple access from different locations. Payment terms are same as slides. Currently network licenses run five years with a 25% renewal fee for an additional five-year term. License fees are between $3.50 and $4.00 per image depending on quantity. Additional fees apply for small orders.

Other Products: Black-and-white 8" x 10" photographic prints of items in St. Peter's Basilica, Rome.

Expansion Plans: Saskia is on a continuous and systematic program to digitize their archive of original color slides (overall views as well as details). Close to 3,000 images were available at the end of 1997, including most of the works offered in Italian Renaissance and Ancient Art. Documentation of new collections will depend upon the interest and sale of existing slides. Saskia has already assembled a rich and diverse archive with which to teach art history and plans to make wider use of it through modern technology.

Textbooks: Lists available for images to accompany textbooks including *Gardner's Art Through the Ages,* Stokstad's *Art History,* Hartt's *Italian Renaissance Art,* and Gilbert's *Living with Art.*

Evaluation: (6th ed.) Quality, 3 to 4; documentation, 3 to 4; service, 3 to 4. Photography of paintings, including well-selected details, especially fine. Valuable coverage of collections in Europe.

*095 Universal Color Slide Co.

8450 S. Tamiami Trail
Sarasota, FL 34238-2936
Telephone: (800) 326-1367
FAX: (800) 487-0250
Attn: Marjorie Crawford
E-mail: ucslide@aol.com
URL: http://www.universalcolorslide.com

This vendor also sells slide products and is listed in the slide provider section of the directory.

Price Range: $2.25 to $2.90 per individual slide, depending on quantity. Slide sets also available.

Profile: The company has been in business for more than 50 years. The current owners have continually upgraded and added to the slide collection since 1984. Personal customer service representatives are available to answer questions about the collection.

More than 8,000 different slide images offered. Periods covered are from prehistoric through 20th century. More than 50 different slides sets available. Some sets are correlated to books, including the major art history/appreciation texts. Company may make images available on PhotoCD if customers are interested.

Photography: Originals are photographed by professional photographers on staff using Ektachrome ASA 64 professional film (tungsten). Original slides also supplied by artists or galleries. Transparencies supplied by museums.

Production: Originals are duplicated in-house on Ektachrome #5071 and mounted in cardboard mounts. Professional inkjet printing is used for slide information.

Documentation: A catalog is sent to mailing list once or twice each year. Slide number, artist name or period, artist birth and death date, title of work, date of work, medium, dimensions, location, and asterisk for orientation in projector is printed on slides with high-quality inkjet printer.

Purchasing: Individual slides are priced at $2.25 to $2.90 each, depending on quantity ordered. Slide sets start at $29.55. Call for details; volume discounts available. No minimum order. Schools and universities need to supply purchase orders. A 2% prepayment discount is offered.

Shipping charges prepaid and added to invoice. Call for quote. Special shipping and handling available. International orders must prepay in U.S. dollars. Turnaround time 3 to 21 days depending on quantity.

Digital Products: PhotoCDs available in both Windows and MAC formats.

Other Products: Books, videotapes, reproductions, CD-ROMs, slide cabinets, sorters, projectors, resource sets.

Expansion Plans: Expanding into areas of contemporary art. Slide curriculum guides are becoming available with slide sets at no extra charge.

Textbooks: *History of Art* by Janson; *History of Art for Young People* by Janson; *A Basic History of Art* by Janson; *Gardner's Art Through the Ages* by Tansey and Kleiner; *Art History* by Stokstad; *American Art of the 20th Century* by Hunter and Jacobus; *A History of Western Art* by Schneider Adams; *History of Modern Art* by Arnason; *Discovering Art History* by Brommer; *Art: A History of Painting, Sculpture and Architecture* by Hartt; *Modern Art* by Hunter and Jacobus; *Art Past/Art Present* by Wilken, Schultz, and Linduff; *Art & Civilization* by Lucie-Smith; *The Visual Experience* by Hobbs and Salome; *Art: The Way It Is* by Adkins Richardson; *Varieties of Visual Experience* by Burke Feldman; *The Story of Art* by Gombrich; *Art Forms* by Preble; *Women Artists: An Illustrated History* by Heller. Others available by request.

099 Yale University Press

U.S. and British Offices
P.O. Box 209040
New Haven, CT 06520-9040
Telephone: (203) 432-0960
FAX: (203) 432-0948
E-mail: custserv.press@yale.edu

British Office:
23 Pond St., Hampstead
London NW3 2PN England
Telephone: (171) 431-4422
FAX: (171) 431-3755
E-mail: tom.buhler@yaleup.co.uk
URL: http://www.yale.edu/yup/

Profile: Yale University Press was founded 90 years and 7,000 titles ago by a young graduate and his wife, George Parmly Day and Wilhelmina, in 1908. Currently, Yale University Press is a separately endowed department of the University with its own Board of Governors. During this century, the Press has won many notable literary awards, including several Pulitzer Awards. Yale University Press was

one of the first university presses to publish electronic multimedia with its debut CD-ROM, *Perseus,* and others including Albers's *Interaction of Color* and the *Complete Illustrated Catalog of the National Gallery, London. Perseus* is an interactive CD-ROM on Ancient Greece that includes complete and selected works of 31 authors in Greek with classic English translations from the Loeb Classical Library; a collection of 25,000 images of architecture, sculpture, coins, and vases with detailed catalog entries; an extensive atlas of Ancient and present-day Greece; an online version of the Liddell-Scott Intermediate Greek-English Lexicon; an encyclopedia of major historical and mythological figures, places, and terms; and a chronological summary of the major historical and cultural events from the archaic period to Alexander the Great, with links to the rest of the Perseus database. *The Complete Illustrated Catalog of the National Gallery, London* includes color images; it is searchable by artist or category and provides biographical information on the artist as well as catalog entries for the images.

Documentation: Format and hardware requirements, as well as content descriptions, are available at the website. Information is also provided via telephone service.

Purchasing: Online ordering is available at the website, or orders may be placed through conventional means. Purchase orders accepted.

Museums

106 Art Institute of Chicago

Michigan Ave. at Adams St.
Chicago, IL 60603
Telephone: (312) 443-3655
Attn: Image Rights Department

This museum also offers slide products and is listed in the slide provider section of the directory.

Profile: Color slides available of masterpieces in the permanent collection. New slide titles continually added.

Photography: Slides and large-format transparencies shot by staff photographer in a studio using Ektachrome ASA 100.

Production: Duplicated on Ektachrome #5071. Color-corrected and contrast-controlled. Mounted in cardboard.

Documentation: Comprehensive list available. Slides imprinted on mounts or keyed to list. Orientation marked by asterisk or slide number.

Purchasing: Slides sold singly or in sets. Single slides made to order, $5.00 each from existing transparencies. If new photography required, $25.00 per item charged. Postage charge of $2.50 added to all orders. Prepayment required.

Other Products: CD-ROM available.

Other Sources: Davis Art Slides (Rosenthal Art Slides) **(047)** offers 1,600 duplicate color slides of works in this museum, available singly. Some 280 slides of drawings and prints are available from the University of Michigan Slide Distribution **(096)**.

Evaluation: (6th ed.) Quality, 3 to 4; documentation, 3; service, 2 to 3. Recent productions show a marked improvement in quality. "The set we bought (twelve Seurat painting slides purchased May 1985) had excellent color images and wonderful details" (Christine Bunting). Sample set of 12 slides of textiles sent in 1984: very good slides, ample information.

132 Freer Gallery of Art

(Smithsonian Institution)
1050 Independence Ave.
Washington, DC 20560
Telephone: (202) 357-4880, x237
FAX: (202) 633-9770
Attn: Scott A. Thompson
E-mail: thompsc@asia.sivm.edu

This museum also offers slide products and is listed in the slide provider section of the directory.

Profile: The Freer Gallery of Art and the Arthur M. Sackler Gallery together comprise the Smithsonian National Museums of Asian Art. The Freer Gallery was established with a bequest from Charles Long Freer and includes Chinese art, Japanese art, Korean art, Indian art, Islamic art, Egyptian art, early Christian and Byzantine art, art of the ancient Near East, and nineteenth-century American painting (especially Whistler). The Freer Gallery provides photographs, slides, and transparencies of objects in the collection, and grants permission to publish images in scholarly and commercial publications.

Photography: Objects are photographed by professional photographers in studios. Large-format

4" x 5" Ektachrome transparencies and 4" x 5" black-and-white negatives are produced in-house.

Production: Duplicate 4" x 5" transparencies and 35mm slides are made from the originals.

Documentation: A mailing list is maintained. Any basic object information available upon request. Slide labels contain title, artist, date, and medium.

Purchasing: Individual slides are priced at $5.00 each. Prepayment is generally required, but university purchase orders are accepted. Stock slides shipped immediately after payment. Special-order slides require 2 to 3 weeks minimum. Minimum U.S. surface shipping $4.50, or rush shipping via Federal Express for $15.00. Fee structure not yet determined for digital images. Contact museum for information. Prepayment is required for digital products, but university purchase orders are welcomed. Orders are usually filled within 2 to 3 weeks.

Digital Products: CD-ROMs in both Windows and MAC formats are available and are produced using a Leaf 4" x 5" film scanner or a Umax flatbed scanner. Original 4" x 5" transparencies, slides, or 4" x 5" black-and-white negatives can be scanned at any resolution, but normally 400 dpi or less is used. Photoshop 4.0 is used for manipulation, including color correction and cropping. Entire views and details can be provided. Any detail, format, resolution, and size can be special ordered. Film can be custom scanned when needed. Any format and any image viewing software can be used. CD-ROMs are provided for one-time or multiuser applications, but not for networked use.

Rental: No rental or borrowing of slides. Rental of 4" x 5" transparencies for publication.

Other Products: Black-and-white 8" x 10" prints sold and 4" x 5" color transparencies rented for publication.

133 Frick Collection

1 E. 70th St.
New York, NY 10021
Telephone: (212) 288-0700
FAX: (212) 628-4417
Attn: Sales and Information Department
URL: http://www.frick.org

This museum also offers slide products and is listed in the slide provider section of the directory.

Price Range: $1.00 to $5.00 for slides and $49.99 for PhotoCD.

Profile: Approximately 100 color slides offered of works in the museum's permanent collection: primarily paintings, with details; also room views, sculpture, and porcelain. New titles occasionally added.

Photography: Original slides shot by staff photographer on Ektachrome ASA 160 using Nikon camera in studio.

Production: Duplicated by a local laboratory on Ektachrome #5071. Color-corrected and contrast-controlled. Mounted in plastic.

Documentation: Free list. Slides labeled. Identifications include name of artist, title of work, and collection.

Purchasing: Individual slides are priced at $1.00 and $5.00. Purchase orders accepted; premade slides sent within the week, custom orders approximately one month.

Digital Products: PhotoCD available in both Windows and MAC formats.

Other Sources: No vendor is authorized by the museum to sell slides of its holdings.

Evaluation: Reprinted from 6th ed. Quality, 3; documentation, 2; service, 3.

152   Minneapolis Institute of Arts

2400 Third Ave. South
Minneapolis, MN 55404
Telephone: (612) 870-3196
FAX: (612) 870-3004
E-mail: hraatz@artsmia.org
URL: http://www.artsmia.org

This museum also offers slide products and is listed in the slide provider section of the directory.

Profile: Slides available of works in the permanent collection, which features paintings, sculpture, drawings, prints, decorative arts, textiles, photography, antiquities, and the arts of Oceania, Africa, the Americas, and Asia. Items not available through Rosenthal Art Slides (now a division of Davis Publications) can be requested; a duplicate will be supplied provided an original master slide is available.

Photography: Originals are photographed by professional staff photographers, who use Kodak E100S film with electronic flash in the studio;

Ektachrome T64 film in galleries with existing tungsten lighting.

Production: Slides from slide library duplicated on Ektachrome #5071 by ProColor, Minneapolis, Minnesota. Color-corrected and contrast-controlled if necessary. Mounted in plastic.

Documentation: All slides produced by Slide Library labeled with full identifications. No catalog or brochure from Slide Library. Brochure available from Davis Art Slides (formerly Rosenthal Art Slides) of 265 slides produced by them. Full identifications sent with permission/licensing information for digital images.

Purchasing: Individual slides are priced at $5.00 each; additional charges may apply if new photography is required. Invoice sent with slides (small orders). Larger orders and orders from institutions should include a purchase order. Orders usually filled within two weeks (longer time frame if new photography is required). Slides sent via U.S. mail; sleeved and packed in padded mailers. Postage and handling charges added. Slides not sent on approval.

Rental: Rental sets, slides with accompanying curriculum materials, available primarily within the upper Midwest region (USA). Contact the Curriculum Materials Department, (612) 870-3134 for information and brochures.

Digital Products: CD-ROMs in both Windows and MAC formats are produced using PhotoCD and a flatbed scanner. Transparencies, minimum size 2¼", are scanned at resolutions ranging from 150 dpi to 1000 dpi and manipulated with Photoshop for color correction and cropping. Entire views are offered in .JPG format for viewing with Photoshop. CD-ROMs are licensed for one-at-a-time use but not for networked use. Please contact Permissions & Licensing Department, (612) 870-3191, for more information.

Other Products: Please contact Curriculum Materials Department. Two CD-ROMs are available from the Museum Shop: *A Prairie School Gem: The Purcell-Cutts House* and *Prints and Processes*.

*158   Museum of Fine Arts, Boston

465 Huntington Ave.
Boston, MA 02115
Telephone: (617) 369-3724
FAX: (617) 267-9773
Attn: Photographic Sales/Slides MFA Enterprise

E-mail: nluongo@mfa.org (for Photographic Sales)
nfujiwara@mfa.org (for MFA Enterprise)
URL: http://www.mfa.org

This museum also offers slide products and is listed in the slide provider section of the directory.

Profile: Slides had been sold in the Slide Library until August 1996. Slide sales were transferred to the retail division, MFA Enterprise, at that time. Catalog has been discontinued, but slides are available by mail/fax/ E-mail. There are 8,000 images of MFA objects currently in stock for purchase. Special orders are accommodated for other items for which no master slides exist. The 8,000 images, currently part of the sales inventory, are intended to be online in the early part of 1998. These will be for reference and ordering use.

Photography: Images are photographed in-house by MFA photographers from original object. Items are shot in the Photo Studio with appropriate lighting. Images are shot in large format and slides are reduced.

Production: Duplicates of Ektachrome reductions are what customers receive.

Documentation: Slides are accompanied by printed information sheets.

Purchasing: Both individual slides and sets are available. Individual slides are priced at $3.00/slide. No discounts except 10% for MFA members. Sets are priced at approximately $2.00/slide (preselected); sets include from 5 to 250 slides. Prepayment is required: check, VISA, MasterCard, American Express, purchase orders. Orders are filled upon receipt when in stock. Special orders take up to 2 weeks. Rush orders are twice the total cost and guaranteed within a week. Postage and handling varies for U.S./Canada/Europe and on slide quantities.

Rental: Slide rental is allowed for local educators only. Public hours: Monday 10 A.M.-1 P.M., Wednesday 1 P.M.-7 P.M. Call for an appointment.

Digital Products: Contact MFA Enterprises, Rights and Licensing to negotiate use of digital images.

Other Products: Black-and-white photos and transparency rentals for reproduction are available through MFA Enterprises, Rights and Licensing.

171   North Carolina Museum of Art

2110 Blue Ridge Rd.
Raleigh, NC 27607-6494

Telephone: (919) 839-6262
FAX: (919) 733-8034
Attn: Museum Shop
URL: http://www2.ncsu.edu/ncma

This museum also offers slide products and is listed in the slide provider section of directory.

Profile: Art Museum owned by State of North Carolina. Collections include: Ancient Classical, Pre-Columbian, African, Judaica, European, American, 20th Century. Sells slides and one CD-ROM.

Documentation: Captions on each slide.

Purchasing: Individual slides are priced at $2.25 each. Purchase orders and charge cards are accepted.

Other Products: Posters, prints, notecards, postcards.

190   Uncommon Objects

(Museum Store for Allen Memorial Art Museum)
Oberlin College
39 S. Main St.
Oberlin, OH 44074
Telephone: (216) 775-2086
Attn: Shirley Hull
E-mail: jenny_wilker@qmgate.cc.oberlin.edu
URL: http://www.oberlin.edu/allenart/

This vendor also sells slide products and is listed in the slide section of the directory.

Price Range: Slides sold singly, $5.00 each plus shipping.

Profile: Offers 300 color slide titles of works in the permanent collection: paintings, sculpture, works on paper, and decorative arts. Slides of the Frank Lloyd Wright House also are available. A few new titles occasionally added.

Photography: Slides shot on Kodak film by an independent professional photographer using Nikon equipment. Objects lit by quartz lamps.

Production: Duplicated on Ektachrome by an independent professional laboratory. Color-corrected and contrast-controlled. Mounted in cardboard.

Documentation: Free list, revised more or less annually. Artist, title, medium, and dimensions given. Slides labeled on mounts. Orientation marked by label placement.

Purchasing: Single slides priced $2.00 each. No discounts. No minimum order. Postage added. Duplicates kept in stock, and orders usually shipped within five days after receipt of payment. Rush orders filled same day if items are in stock, with no surcharge. Slides shot to order within one to three weeks of works not previously photographed; fee of $15.00 per slide charged. Prepayment required on all orders. Returns accepted for exchange or refund if slides are of unacceptable quality.

Digital: The Museum CD-ROM, Masterworks for Learning: A College Collection Catalogue, does include full-screen images of 171 important works in the collection.

These copyrighted images are not downloadable and cannot be used for other purposes. The CD-ROM includes scholarly entries about these 171 works and a complete collection database. It sells for $29.95, plus $5.00 shipping.

Evaluation: Reprinted from 6th ed. Quality, 3; documentation, 3 to 4; service, 3 to 4.

199 Frank Lloyd Wright House & Studio Foundation

951 Chicago Ave.
Oak Park, IL 60302
Telephone: (708) 848-1606 (bookshop)
(708) 848-9518 (catalogue order department)
URL: http://www.wrightplus.org/

This image provider also sells slide products and is listed in the slide section of the directory.

Profile: The Home and Studio served as the private residence and architectural office of Wright during the first 20 years of his professional career, 1889–1909. There are seven $5.50 slide sets (five slides each) of Unity Temple exteriors and Unity Temple interiors, three sets of houses in Oak Park, Wright House (one exterior, four interiors) and Wright Studio (one exterior, four interiors). A boxed set of 20 slides of Falling Water is $15.00.

Digital Products: The following CD-ROMs are sold in the bookshop: the Luna CD-ROM of the *Houses of Frank Lloyd Wright* ($199), an interactive disc of *Falling Water* ($50), and the *Frank Lloyd Wright Companion* ($60).

BRITAIN

211 AVP (Audio-Visual Productions)

School Hill Centre, Chepstow
Monmouthshire NP6 5PH
United Kingdom
Telephone: 01291 625439
FAX: 01291 629671
Attn: Valerie Drewett
E-mail: avp@compuserve.com
URL: http://www.avp.co.uk

This vendor only offers digital products.

Price Range: £39.00 to £89.00 for each CD-ROM (site licenses in addition).

Profile: Originally publishers of slide sets for schools. Now publishers of CD-ROMs and supplier to schools.

Digital Production: PhotoCDs in MAC format, image sets only, for multiuse.

Documentation: Catalog sent to mailing list three times a year. All images are accompanied by descriptive text and sound on CD-ROM.

Purchasing: Catalog prices pro-forma for non-U.K. institutions. Postage and packing in addition.

213 Bodleian Library

Broad St.
Oxford OXI 3BG United Kingdom
Telephone: 01865 277214
FAX: 01865 277187
Attn: Mrs. Rigmor Batsvik/Dr. Bruce Barker-Benfield
E-mail: western.manuscripts@bodley
URL: http://www.bodley.ox.ac.uk/welcome.html

This library also offers slide products and is listed in the slide provider section of the directory.

Price Range: £1.00 to £36.00 (and VAT where applicable).

Profile: Built up since the late 1950s to provide immediate sales from stock of color images from medieval manuscripts, in conjunction with an iconographic card index and other in-house search tools. Medieval manuscripts of the Bodleian Library, Oxford, with others from Oxford College Libraries, and minor coverage of other holdings of the Bodleian Library (printed books and ephemera).

See the Internet site for current free-access imaging projects. The library hopes to develop a color digitizing service on demand, when funding allows.

Photography: Originals shot by staff photographers. Manuscript and other materials photographed flat or on cradle under vertical Nikon camera, lit previously by photo Pearl lights and now by Bowens flash.

Production: The older stock of master negatives (filmstrips and individual slides) was mostly filmed from the originals in the library's own photographic studio on Eastmancolor negative film #5247, from which copies for sale are now printed on Fuji 3518 film. New slides are now both filmed from the originals in the studio and copied from the resulting masters on Kodak Ektachrome professional film ASA 100.

Documentation: Filmstrips and slide sets accompanied by identification lists.

Purchasing: Individual slides are available for £1.00 plus postage and packing (and VAT where applicable). Sets as unmounted filmstrips: six levels £6.00–£36.00 + P&P (and VAT). Prepayment required. Stock slides and filmstrips supplied within one week of receipt of payment (pro forma invoice sent if required). Overseas orders sent by airmail post at standard charge of £6.00 [P&P]. Less for internal U.K. orders.

Other Products: The library's photographic studio supplies nonstandard 35mm images and other types of photographs (large-format color transparencies, black-and-white bromide prints, microfilms) to order, with a waiting period of two to three months.

214   Bridgeman Art Library (London and New York)

London Office:
17-19 Garway Rd.
London W2 4PH United Kingdom
Telephone: 0171 727 4065
FAX: 0171 792 8509

New York Office:
65 E. 93rd St.
New York, NY 10128 USA
Telephone: (212) 828-1238

FAX: (212) 828-1255
Attn: Robin M. Eichel
E-mail: info@bridgeman.co.uk (London)
URL: http://www.bridgeman.co.uk

This image provider offers only digital products.

Profile: Founded in London in 1972 by Harriet Bridgeman. For more than 25 years, Bridgeman Art Library has provided reproduction rights to more than 100,000 works of art in more than 800 collections worldwide. The New York Branch Office opened in June 1997, and states, "We provide an expert research service, we are fully digitized and also provide copyright database information."

Browsers can view 4,000 of the 100,000 images on the CD-ROM catalog, visit the website, or make use of the library's free-text-keyword research service. Bridgeman's website states they have received European funding to test the most efficient means of delivering images on the Internet.

Digital Products: CD-ROMs with .JPG images at 100-150 dpi resolution, manipulated with Photoshop software.

Documentation: A catalog is sent to mailing list. Bridgeman Art Library offers a newsletter four times a year.

Purchasing: Bridgeman Art Library does not sell slides. Contact office or visit website for details on services provided.

Rental: Bridgeman Art Library rents 4" x 5" transparencies.

216   British Library Reproductions

British Library
96 Evston Rd., St. Pancras
London NW1 2DB United Kingdom
Telephone: 44 (0) 171 412 7614
FAX: 44 (0) 171 412 7771
Attn: Reproduction Enquiries
E-mail: bl-repro@bl.uk
URL: http://www.bl.uk

This library also offers slide products and is listed in the slide provider section of the directory.

Profile: The British Library has operated a photographic service for many years. Text copies (photocopies), microfilm, and photographs are offered for commercial reproduction. The world-renowned collections include 17 million books and 250,000 unique historical manuscripts. This is a unique source of visual inspiration to scholars, publishers, and advertisers. The library hopes to announce a CD-ROM catalog to permit remote browsing.

Photography: Slides, negatives, and large-format transparencies shot by staff photographers. Nikon equipment and Ektachrome ASA 64 are used for 35mm slides, with lighting by electronic flash.

Production: Duplicates are made in-house on Ektachrome #5071 film.

Purchasing: Prices vary. Individual slides are available. At the time of writing (November 1997) the price for the first slide is £10.21, and thereafter slides are priced at £8.17 each. Prices are reviewed in April each year. The pictures themselves are prepaid. Reproduction rights fees are paid on publication of the picture.

Rental: Large transparencies are hired for three months, and 35mm slides as well.

Digital Products: CD-ROMs are being prepared using MAC equipment with large-format transparencies scanned and then manipulated with Adobe Photoshop software.

Other Products: Large-format transparencies, black-and-white prints, microfilm, paper copies.

226 Oxford University Press (London, USA, and Canada)

Worldwide Offices can be located at website.
James Arnold-Baker, Secretary to the Delegates and Chief Executive
Great Clarendon St.
Oxford OX2 6DP United Kingdom
Telephone: 01865 56767
FAX: 01865 56646

U.S. Office: Edward W. Barry, President
Oxford University Press, Inc., USA
198 Madison Ave.
New York, NY 10016
Telephone: (212) 726-6000
FAX: (212) 726-6440

Canadian Office: Oxford University Press, Canada
70 Wynford Dr.
Don Mills, Ontario M3C 1J9 Canada
FAX: (800) 665-1771 or (416) 441-0345
E-mail: custserv@oupcan.com
URL: http://www.oupcan.com/index.shtml

Profile: Legally owned by the University of Oxford (England), but a large publishing house of educational books, Oxford University Press is probably best known as the publisher of the *Oxford English Dictionary* (OED), available in CD-ROM since 1992. Not a company in the normal sense, having no shareholders, but owned by the "Chancellor, Master and Scholars of the University of Oxford," which is the official term for the body corporate as defined in an act of parliament in 1571. Apparently the only CD-ROM offered for art or architecture is *Frank Lloyd Wright: Presentation and Conceptual Drawings*. This four CD-ROM set was produced by Luna Imaging in California and includes nearly 5,000 drawings by Wright. More than 860 projects are included, ranging from private homes, banks, and office buildings to skyscrapers, apartment buildings, museums, and schools. The drawings span Wright's career, from student drawings of 1887 to his last rendering in 1959. *The Frank Lloyd Wright Quarterly*, in its Winter 1996 issue, stated that this CD-ROM package "is a scholarly work, professionally packaged and masterfully presented. The image quality and color reproduction are state-of-the-art."

Documentation: Information is available at the website on content, but little information was found on format and hardware requirements. Information from a 1995 brochure indicates that the CD-ROM package is available only in Windows format for an SVGA monitor, with 60MB of free hard disk space preferred.

Purchasing: Price quoted on the website from OUP USA is $2,250. Online ordering is available. Telephone ordering is available for Canadian residents paying with credit card from the following telephone numbers: in Toronto (416) 441-2941 (request Customer Service); outside Toronto (800) 387-8020. Oxford University Press recommends ordering from nearest OUP office for best service.

230 World Microfilms Publications, Ltd.

23 N. Wharf Rd.
London W2 1LA United Kingdom
Telephone: 0171 262 2178
FAX: 0171 262 1708
Attn: S. C. Albert
E-mail: microworld@ndirect.co.uk
URL: http://www.microworld.ndirect.co.uk/wmcats.htm

This vendor also offers slide products and is listed in the slide provider section of the directory.

Profile: Slide sets available in addition to more numerous microform titles. Thousands of duplicate color slide titles offered in sets in the following series: Pidgeon Audio Visual Library of Tape/Slide Talks, RIBA Exhibitions, Masters of Architecture, Historic Houses, The Indian World, and Artists Talking. Exhibitions documented at the Royal College of Art's Henry Moore Gallery and at the Heinz Gallery of the Royal Institute of British Architects. Slides available of manuscripts in the Lambeth Palace Library, London, and of the Winchester Bible. New sets continually added. World Microfilms is gradually entering CD-ROM market, mainly with illuminated manuscripts.

Photography: Originals shot in various formats on various films by various photographers, including staff and independent professionals. In recent correspondence with a slide curator in the United States, Mr. Albert stated that the company could not afford to hire professional photographers to shoot originals of architectural monuments, and therefore often relied upon the work of the architects themselves or architectural historians and lecturers. In quite a lot of cases, photographs (even if they are quite old) of buildings at the time of completion have been used to depict the work as the architect intended. Film used in approximately 50% of original work is Kodak #5247.

Production: Slides produced on Fuji positive film or Kodak's Eastmancolor #5384 print film by Filmstrip Services, Ltd., London. Some slides of historic houses produced by Trans-Globe, a separate company that formerly used unstable film; presumably these are now printed on the low-fade Eastmancolor. Color-corrected and contrast-controlled. Mounted in "Geimuplast" mounts and shipped in boxes.

Documentation: Mailing list kept. Free brochures sent monthly announcing new sets. Contents lists available on request. Imprinted on mounts, keyed to contents list accompanying each set. Orientation marked only when necessary. Audiotapes included in the tape/slide talks.

Purchasing: The North American distributor for slides and CD-ROMs is Films for the Humanities (see that entry for address). Slides sold in sets only. Minimum order one set. Prices listed in brochures. Discount given on prepaid orders. Prepayment required from individuals, purchase orders from institutions. Shipping and insurance costs added. Payment accepted in pounds sterling or U.S. dollars. Sets kept in stock and usually shipped within 7 to 10 days.

Rush orders sent by return post if goods in stock; no surcharge. Slides not sent on approval, but defective slides will be replaced.

Digital Products: CD-ROMs, Windows format with Tech Support. Minimal equipment needed for viewing: 8MB RAM/486/SVGA. Images are scanned from color microfilm in 256 colors and color corrected with Alchemy software used for manipulation. Alchemy offers the purchaser the opportunity to enlarge the image *ad infinitum*, thus allowing the finest detail to be seen as clearly as possible. CD-ROMs are sold for multiuse, networked applications with Alchemy viewing software included in CD-ROM. As for slides, the North American Distributor for CD-ROMs is Films for the Humanities.

Other Products: Microforms, CD-ROMs, videotapes, computer programs, audiotapes.

Expansion Plans: Continuing publication of slides, tape/slides, microforms, videotapes, and audiotapes.

246   National Gallery Picture Library

Trafalgar Square
London WC2N 5DN United Kingdom
Telephone: 44 (0) 171 747 2814/2515
FAX: 44 (0) 171 753 8178
Attn: Belinda Ross
E-mail: picture.library@ng-london.org.uk
URL: http://www.nationalgallery.org.uk

This image provider also offers a slide product and is listed in the slide provider section of the directory.

Profile: Entry reprinted from the 6th edition with some new information. Approximately 1,130 color slides offered of works in the permanent collection and a few items on loan: European paintings of the thirteenth to twentieth centuries. Most slides are duplicates, but a few originals remain, mostly of less-popular subjects. A few new titles added occasionally.

Photography: Currently, originals are 8" x 10" transparencies shot by staff photographers with a Sinar system on Ektachrome ASA 100 professional film #6122. Daylight flash used. Original slides were mostly shot on Agfachrome 5OL; a few may be on Ektachrome EPD ASA 200 daylight film.

Production: Printed from internegatives by Walter Scott Laboratories, Ltd., Bradford, on Fuji #8816.

Color-corrected and contrast-controlled. Most mounted in plastic, some (originals) in cardboard.

Documentation: Free catalog. Artist surname and title of work given. Supplements issued approximately twice yearly. Most slides are labeled. Additional information available in published catalogs of the collection. Orientation marked on most slides.

Purchasing: Slides sold singly, 50 pence each. No minimum order. Postage added. Order form provided. Prepayment in pounds sterling required from pro forma invoice. International postal money orders accepted, as well as credit cards. Slides kept in stock and shipped within two to three weeks after receipt of payment. Rush orders sent within four days at no extra charge. Slides not sent on approval, and returns not accepted.

Digital Products: CD-ROM, The Complete Illustrated Catalogue, covers the entire collection and is offered for sale or loan.

Evaluation: Quality, 3 to 4; documentation, 2 to 4; service, 3 to 4.

ECUADOR

257 Group for the Promotion of Art & Design

Roca 549, DPTO. 602
Quito, Ecuador, South America
Telephone: (593-2) 506175
FAX: (593-2) 566714
E-mail: JBREILH@ CEAS.MED.EC
Attn: Dr. Jaime Breilh

Profile: The recently formed nonprofit group, Group for the Promotion of Art & Design, has just released its first multimedia endeavor, a CD-ROM on the Ecuadorian sculptress Germania Breilh. Information from the group indicates that the interactive CD-ROM provides information on this Latin American expressionist artist of the 1930s and 1940s and images of her works, some of which can be rotated on the viewing screen. Animations and video clips about the expressionist movement in South America, its historical context, and its relation to artistic movements in North America, Mexico, and Europe are also included. The format is bilingual (English and Spanish). Dr. Breilh reports that the Group for the Promotion of Art & Design is at work on a second CD-ROM, about the basics and history of graphic design, planned to be available soon.

Documentation: Information is available from Dr. Breilh via E-mail, and a printed brochure about the CD-ROM is available on request.

Purchasing: The CD-ROM on Germania Breilh is available for $55.00 plus $5.00 shipping (U.S. dollars). Purchase orders are accepted. Wire transfer of funds and orders via mail are also accepted. The purchase price of the CD-ROM entitles the purchaser to use it for academic presentations and on university networks. Windows and MAC formats are available.

FRANCE

264 L'agence photographique de la Reunion des Musées Nationaux

(formerly Services Techniques et Commerciaux de la Reunion des Musées Nationaux)
10, rue de l'Abbaye
75006 Paris, France
Telephone: 33 1 40 13 46 00
FAX: 33 1 40 13 46 01
Attn: Monsieur le directeur
E-mail: photo@rmn.fr
URL: http://www.rmn.fr/

This vendor also offers slide products and is listed in the slide provider section of the directory.

Profile: Did not respond to questionnaire. Entry from 6th edition updated where possible from website. Slides and CD-ROM of works in the Louvre and 33 other French national museums offered. Works from the following collections are represented:

Paris:

Galerie Nationales du Grand Palais

Musée des Arts d'Afrique et d'Océanie

Musées des Arts Asiatiques - Guimet

Musée des Arts et Traditions Populaires

Musée Eugéne Delacroix

Musée d'Ennery

Musée Hebert

Musée Jean - Jacques Henner

Musée du Louvre

Musée Gustave Moreau

Musée du Moyen Age - Thermes de Cluny

Musée de l'Orangerie des Tuileries

Musée d'Orsay

Musée Picasso

Musée Auguste Rodin

Ille-de-France (provincia parisina):

Musée des Antiquités Nationales

Musée de Céramique

Musée Fontainebleau

Musée des Granges de Port - Royal

Musées de Malmaison et de Bois - Préau

Musée de la Renaissance

Musées de Versailles et de Trianon

Acquitaine:

Musée du Chateau de Pau

Musée de la Préhistorie

Bourgogne:

Musée Magnin

Corse:

Musée de la Maison Bonaparte

Limousin:

Musée Adrien Dubouché

Pays-de-la-Loire:

Musée des Deux Victoires

Picardie:

Musée de Compiégne

Musée de la Coopération Franco - Américaine

Poitou-Charentes:

Musée de L'ille d'Aix

PACA:

Musée Fernand Léger

Musée Message Biblique - Marc Chagall

Musée Picasso "La Guerre et la Paix"

Photography: Original transparencies shot on Ektachrome by photographers employed by the Réunion des Musées Nationaux. (Ed. Note: Ceased production.)

Production: Printed from internegatives on low-fade Eastmancolor film. Mounted in cardboard. Versailles and Fontainebleau sets produced elsewhere.

Documentation: Mailing list kept of customers interested in exhibition coverage. Free catalog and supplements. Artist and title listed. Slides labeled. Since January 1983, label information consists of artist, artist's dates "if necessary," title, date if known, location, dimensions, and materials. "Diafiche" sets of 10 slides accompanied by text in French, English, German, and Spanish.

Purchasing: Slides sold singly or in sets. Some slides available only in sets. Single slides offered only of objects in the Louvre, the Musée d'Orsay, and the Orangerie des Tuileries. Large sets (18, 30, and 42 slides) also offered. Minimum order 54 francs. Airmail postage added. Order form provided. Prepayment required by traveler's check, money order, or check.

Other Products: Videocassettes, Super 8 films, microfiche. Large-format transparencies rented for reproduction.

Evaluation: Quality, 3; documentation, 3; service, 2. Good color and sharpness, but some problems noted with dust, scratches, and cropping. Documentation improved on recent sets, but merely adequate on older ones.

GERMANY

268   K. G. Saur

Verlag Ortlerstrasse 8
D-81373
München (Munich), Germany
Telephone: 49 (0) 89 76902-0
FAX: 49 (0) 89 76902-150
E-mail: 100730.1341@compuserve.com
URL: http://www.saur.de/cdhome2.htm

Profile: K. G. Saur has been a publisher of library reference books for many years. In 1993, Saur began publishing a series of CD-ROMs titled Digital Information System for Art and Social History (DISKUS). This series has been edited by Bildarchiv Foto Marburg, German Documentation Centre for Art History, Phillips-Universität Marburg, and Computer & Letteren, Rijksuniversiteit Utrecht.

Documentation: The DISKUS CD series gives access to the collections of major museums participating in the program "Computer Aided Cataloguing in Major Museums," supported by the Volkswagen Foundation. All pictures are included as top-quality images on the individual CD-ROMs. Each image is accompanied by full background information (e.g., information on artist, exhibition and bibliography). The first five CD-ROMs produced are available in German only, with later ones in German or English for user menus and help functions. The CD-ROMs are available in Windows format. Current titles in the DISKUS series are: *The Russian Avant-Garde, Ludwig Collection, Printed Portraits: 1500–1618; from the Prints Collection, Germanisches Nationalmuseum, The Political Poster in the GDR 1945–1970, Photographic Perspectives from the Twenties, Italian Drawings of the 14th to 18th Century in the Kupferstichkabinett, The Paintings of the Nationalgalerie* (Nationalgalerie der Staatlichen Museen zu Berlin), *Wallraf-Richartz-Museum Cologne, Collection of Paintings and Sculptures, Posters from World War One 1914–1918* (compiled by Deutsches Historisches Museum, Berlin), *Political Allegories and Satires from the Prints Collection of the Germanisches Nationalmuseum, Political Badges from the Imperial Age and the Weimar Republic, Films Posters of the Austrian National Library,* and *1848-Politics, Propaganda, Information and Entertainment from the Printing Press* (edited by Deutsches Historisches Museum, Berlin). Titles scheduled for future release include: *Picture Gallery Berlin, Plakate in der DDR* (edited by Deutsches Historisches Museum-Berlin), *Gemälde-und Skulpturenkatalog* (edited by Nationalgalerie, Berlin), *Plakate der 30er Jahre* (edited by Kunstbibliothek, Berlin), and *Altdeutsche und niederländische Zeichnungen* (edited by Universitätsmuseum, Göttingen).

Purchasing: Prices for the currently available CD-ROMs are listed on the website at 88.00 deutsche marks each. Online ordering is available.

ITALY

*287 Scala Fine Arts Slides

SCALA Istituto Fotografico Editoriale S.p.A.
Via Chiantigiana 62 - I
50011 Antella, Florence, Italy
Telephone: (055) 641-541
FAX: (055) 644-478
URL: http://scala.firenze.it

This vendor also offers slide products and is listed in the slide provider section of the directory.

Profile: Entry reprinted from 6th edition with updated address and distributor information. Some information from website. Nearly 10,000 duplicate color slide titles offered of art and architecture history of all periods, with emphasis on works in Italian collections. New sets occasionally produced from an archive of more than 80,000 transparencies. European churches documented in 55 eight-slide sets (TAC series). Italian painting surveyed in 122 twelve-slide sets (SAD series). Scala is the official photographer for most Italian museums and for several other European museums. Major exhibitions documented. Museum collections represented in Scala sets include the following:

Castello Sforzesco, Milan

Galleria Borghese, Rome

Galleria degli Uffizi, Florence

Galleria dell'Accademia, Venice

Monumenti, Musei e Gallerie Pontificie, Vatican City Museo Archaeologico, Florence

Museo Archaeologico Nazionale, Paestum

Museo di San Marco, Florence

Museo Intemazionale delle Ceramiche, Faenza

Museo Nazionale di Villa Giulia, Rome

Museo Poldi Pezzoli, Milan

Palazzo Pitti, Florence

Pinacoteca di Brera, Milan

Victoria and Albert Museum, London

Photography: Original large-format transparencies shot by professional staff photographers on Kodak film using Sinar view cameras.

Production: Printed from internegatives on Eastmancolor #5384 at Scala Istituto Fotografico Editoriale, Florence. Color-corrected and contrast-controlled. Mounted in cardboard. Packaged in plastic sleeves.

Documentation: Free list, in English, of set titles available from Davis Art Slides, Worcester, MA (Scala distributor in the United States and Canada) **(047)**. Slides labeled in Italian and keyed to accompanying identification list or booklet. Texts often multilingual (English, Italian, French, and German) or sometimes available in one of various languages by request. Images thoroughly identified in most cases; dates of works sometimes lacking. Orientation marked.

Purchasing: U.S. and Canadian orders must be addressed to Davis Art Slides **(047)**. Slides sold in sets only, with price list available. The Scala website (English or Italian) includes an online catalog of 30,000 low-resolution, watermarked images. The website also offers the Scala Archives on CD-ROM and image licensing. Customers can receive, on request, a CD-ROM catalog with images.

Other Sources: Scala sets occasionally sold by Miniature Gallery (225) at discount prices; when Scala slides are in stock, an issue of *Art-Slide News* will announce their availability.

SWITZERLAND

306 Schweizerisches Landesmuseum

(Swiss National Museum)
Museumstr.2
8006 Zurich, Switzerland
Telephone: (01) 218 65 39
FAX: (01) 211 29 49
Attn: Mrs. Jeanette Frey
E-mail: jeanette.frey@slmnet.ch
URL: http://www.slmnet.ch

This museum also offers slide products and is listed in the slide provider section of the directory.

Price Range: 20 Swiss francs to 400 Swiss francs.

Profile: The photo archive of the Swiss National Museum contains pictures of the objects in the museum since its foundation in 1898. The collections cover archaeological objects through to the twentieth century and arts and crafts, including nineteenth- and twentieth-century photography. Existing collection of pictures includes 350,000 black-and-white prints, 30,000 slides, and 10,000 color transparencies. In two to three years, part of the photo archive will be shown on the Internet for researchers. 20,000 slides already are digitized; digital photography is planned before 2000. Download through Internet or satellite network planned after 2005.

Photography: Original photography is carried out by Staff Professional Photographers, Otto Knel and Donat Stuppan. Equipment used includes: Camera: Sinar (4" x 5" up to 20 x 25cm), for reportage: smaller formats (6 x 6cm, 24 x 36mm). Two photo studios in-house. Different kinds of film are used, but normally Kodak Ektachrome and Ilford for black-and-white.

Production: Slides are duplicated.

Documentation: Catalog is sent to mailing list and updated when museum prices change, usually every three to four years. List with short text in German is included with slide orders.

Purchasing: 20 Swiss francs for 24 x 36mm; 100 Swiss francs for 4" x 5" or larger. Orders by fax or letter. Prepayment or invoice sent with material. Slides not sent on approval. Rush orders filled immediately and sent by Federal Express or DHL where required, at cost of the client. Normal delay: two weeks.

Rental: Rental of 4" x 5" Ektachromes or 24 x 36mm slides is available. Contact museum for details.

Digital Products: Kodak PhotoCD; Scan with Agfa DuoScan from 24 x 36mm original. Manipulated with Photoshop and color-corrected. .PCT and .JPG formats are available; others may be supplied if required. Digital products available for one-time, nonnetworked use. .JPG format requires Photoshop to view. Digital product delivered on floppy disk or CD-ROM within three weeks; protected by watermark. Federal Express/DHL etc. when required at cost to client.

Other Products: Listings from the object database and the picture database (almost all kinds of objects concerning Swiss history).

Expansion Plans: Choice of posters and slides, digital products for the Museum Shop and Internet.

CANADA

006   Archivision

6A Brooklyn Ave.
Toronto, Ontario M4M 2X5 Canada
Telephone: (416) 469-3443
FAX: (416) 469-4412
Attn: Scott Gilchrist, Photographer/Owner
E-mail: director@archivision.com
URL: http://www.archivision.com

This vendor also offers digital products and is listed in the digital section of directory.

Price Range: Slides, $2.00 to $3.00; digital products, various plans available. See below.

Profile: Scott Gilchrist left his position as Slide Curator at the School of Architecture, University of Toronto, in 1992 to create a commercial slide distribution company to specifically meet the needs of slide curators. The goal remains to provide professional and extensive photographic documentation of the built environment, extending coverage to drawings from original sources where available, backed by extensive documentation, and all at the lowest price. In five years the archive has grown from several thousand images to close to 40,000.

Services:

1.   Custom duplicate slides can be made to order in-house.

2.   Slides may be ordered in standard plastic mounts, Gepe glass mounts, or unmounted, in sets or as singles.

3.   OVERVIEW SERVICE: Archivision can select an overview from the larger sets at a number specified by the curator.

4.   APPROVAL SERVICE: Duplicate slides may be sent on approval. This service allows the slide curator to pull only the desired slides, returning the rest.

5.   Custom in-house digital files may be ordered with the slides or in lieu of the slides.

6.   Extensive slide ID's are supplied with all slides/images.

7.   SEARCH SERVICE: Extensive menu-driven search engines are available at the website.

8.   LANGUAGE SERVICE: Slide ID's can be translated into French, Italian, Spanish, Dutch, or German for a fee.

A website now displays more than 2,000 images for preview by potential clients. The online catalog lists every subject in the archive alphabetically, and is searchable with nine menu driven search engines. Updates are also posted on the website. Furthermore, an editorial module keeps clients up-to-date with policy changes and future travel plans. Along with the website, Archivision also launched Digital Services, fully outlined at the site, including policies on where images may be made available. Thumbnails already on the site may be purchased and downloaded directly from the site upon approval.

Slide Photography: On-site photography: Slides (35mm format only) are professionally taken by the owner, photographer Scott Gilchrist, in front of the original building, garden, sculpture, or art in public. A Nikon F-90 body is used with the following lenses: Nikkor 28mm f3.5 perspective corrective lens, Nikkor 18mm f3.5 rectilinear lens, and Nikkor AF 80-200 f2.8 ED zoom. All slides are made with the use of a tripod, on Fuji Velvia 50 film (exterior conditions) and Kodak EPY-64 (interiors with tungsten light). In addition, various corrective filters may be used, especially a Nikon circular polarizer for haze. Studio photography: Slides (usually 35mm, large format for selected works) are taken by a professional studio photographer using appropriate lighting, film (usually Kodak EPY-64), and equipment.

Production: Ordered slides are custom duplicated from the original slide (the original is usually on Fuji Professional Velvia 50 film) on a Beseler Deluxe Slide Duplicator with a 75/4.0 Apo-Rodagon D 1:1 lens. Ektachrome #5071 duplicating films used for long life and contrast control. E6 processing is by Steichenlab, a local professional photographic lab.

Documentation: Catalog sent to mailing list with update following each documentation trip.

Purchasing Slide Products: Individual, $3.00 each; in sets, $2.15 each (unmounted); $2.35 per slide for overview/custom set selected by Archivision; add $1.00 for Gepe mounts; minimum order $50 with discounts as follows: 5%, $501-$999; 10%, $1,000-$2,999; 15%, $3,000-$5,999; 20%, $6,000+. Mail, fax, or E-mail list of subject titles with corresponding codes and purchase order number. Unmounted slides, no shipping fee; Quickpoint mounts, add 4% shipping; Gepe mounts, $1.00 per slide and 5% shipping.

Purchasing Digital Products: PhotoCD and web images. Equipment includes Agfa Studioscan IIsi; MAC 7200/90. Windows and MAC formats are available with Tech Support also available. Original slide scanning at resolutions of 72 dpi only for thumbnails; 82 dpi for larger sizes upon request. Photolook and Photoshop are used as manipulation software for color correction and cropping to provide both entire and detail views. Both individual slides and sets are available in digital format for multiuser, networked usage in .JPG format. Mail, fax, or E-mail list of subject titles with corresponding codes and purchase order number and type: full-screen only or full-screen w/thumbnails. Digital products are shipped on floppy disk ($2.50 per disk), 100MB Iomega Zip Disk ($25.00 per disk), or SyQuest cartridges (customer supplies), or E-mailed as attach-

ment ($5.00 preparation charge). Images can be purchased as PhotoCDs, $2.95 per images in sets; $3.25 selected by us; $4.00 selected by customer.

Expansion Plans: Company plans to document architecture, garden, and sculpture in Egypt, Israel, Jordan, Scotland, and England in 1999.

Evaluation: Quality, 3 to 4; documentation, 4; service, 3 to 4.

*007   Hartill Art Associates

Prospect Place, R.R. #6
St. Marys, Ontario N4X 1C8 Canada
Telephone: (519) 229-8752
FAX: (519) 229-8596
Attn: Alec and Marlene Hartill
E-mail: hartills.art@sympatico.ca
URL: http://www3.sympatico.ca/
hartills.art

Profile: Hartill Art Associates have been a registered partnership since 1977 and are specialists in medieval and contemporary architecture. Photography covers 19 countries, from the prehistoric to the twentieth century, in architecture and decorative arts. Company has an archive of approximately 25,000 slides.

Photography: Photography is carried out by the Hartills, who are professionals, using Nikon equipment, tripod and various lenses as appropriate, including telephoto and perspective-correcting. Kodak Kodachrome and Ektachrome films are used.

Production: Duplicate slides are produced on Pro Kodachrome 25 with a Beseler Dual-Mode Duplicator. Slides are produced in-house to custom order only.

Documentation: A catalog is available. Slides are labeled with catalog number. Individual lists are provided with special sets.

Purchasing: Both individual slides and slide sets are available. Individual slides are priced at $3.00 for duplicates and $5.00 for originals with discounts as follows: 1-100, 10%; 250-499, 15%; 500-999, 20%; 1,000+, 25%. Sets are priced at approximately $2.75 per slide for special sets. For orders in North America add 4% shipping. Overseas orders will have actual airmail costs added. Shipments are registered and insured. Purchase orders preferred but will accept fax and E-mail orders. Orders usually completed within three weeks of receipt. Billing in U.S. currency outside Canada on all orders.

Evaluation: Quality, 3 to 4; documentation, 3 to 4; service, 3 to 4.

008 National Archives of Canada

395 Wellington St.
Ottawa, Ontario K1A 0N3 Canada
Telephone: (613) 992-3884
FAX: (613) 995-6274
Attn: Director, Researcher Services Division
E-mail: reference@archives.ca
URL: http://www.archives.ca

Profile: The National Archive's collection of 15 million photographs and 300,000 works of art represents a vital visual resource documenting many facets of Canadian history and culture from the 1840s to the present day. The collections encompass a large variety of subjects relating to Canadian history and social development, including portraits, landscape, cityscape, and architectural views, historical events; and costume and commercial designs. A broad definition of "documentary" has been essential in order to respond to the requirements of changing historical trends; its application to places, people, and events has resulted in a program that encompasses work done in Canada by Canadians and others, as well as done by Canadians at home and abroad. Images will be available through planned NA website.

Photography: Original photography is carried out by in-house photographers and laboratories using 35mm Kodak Ektachrome slide film.

Production: Duplicates made in-house on Ektachrome #5071 or Eastman Fine Grain Release Positive film #5032 (for black-and-white slides). Color-corrected. Contrast controlled in black-and-white slides. Mounted in plastic or cardboard.

Documentation: Free brochure available describing sets. Information provided in booklets in English and French. Orientation marked.

Purchasing: Both individual slides and sets are available. Originals priced at $6.00 each (Canadian funds); duplicates $4.00 each (Canadian funds). Prices same for black-and-white or color. No minimum order. Prepayment required. Duplicates made to order and shipped within three months. No rush orders accepted. Slides not sent on approval, and no returns accepted.

Rental: Transparencies may be borrowed in order to have slides reproduced from them.

009 Ontario Crafts Council

170 Bedford Rd.
Toronto, Ontario M5R 2K9 Canada
Telephone: (416) 925-4222
FAX: (416) 925-4223
Attn: Kathleen Morris, Information Officer

Price Range: $2.50 per slide (Canadian funds).

Profile: The Craft Resource Centre of the Ontario Crafts Council maintains a slide library dating from the creation of the OCC in 1976. Presently there are 362 slide packages in the system documenting the evolution of contemporary Canadian Craft. Slide packages are available for loan or purchase. A slide catalog is available providing descriptions for each. Packages contain slides, sheet of slide descriptions and, at times, additional support material. An Ontario Crafts Council website is planned.

Photography: Originals are photographed by a photographer or supplied by the artist.

Production: Kodak film duplicated by TPS or BGM, Toronto.

Documentation: A catalog is sent to mailing list biannually.

Purchasing: Individual slides are priced at $2.50 per slide (Canadian funds). Purchase orders or prepayment accepted. Slides shipped within one month. Postage or courier charges and applicable taxes apply.

Rental: Two-week loan exclusive of shipping time $10/OCC members; $15 nonmembers plus shipping costs (Canadian funds).

Other Products: Publications pertaining to operating a crafts business, quarterly magazine, portfolios of Ontario craftspeople.

010 Scholastic Slide Services

605 Blair Rd.
Ottawa, Ontario KIJ 7M3 Canada
Telephone: (613) 749-0862
FAX: (613) 749-0862
Attn: Hellmut W. Schade

Profile: Business established in 1976, by professor (now retired) at Carleton University, as a result of extensive photography while participating on excavation teams in Italy and Greece.

Subsequent photography has concentrated on architecture of Canada and USA. Some 45,000 titles available as duplicate slides, featuring Canadian architecture from all provinces except Yukon and Northwest Territories (28,000 items). In addition, slides available of architecture in West Germany, including Berlin (6,000 items); Greece (4,000); France (2,000); the United States (2,000); Italy, including Sicily (1,000); and 500 items each from Switzerland, Spain, Mexico, Peru, and the West Indies. Sculpture and paintings that are part of a building's decoration are included, accounting for approximately 8 percent of total holdings. Less than 2 percent of the slides are black-and-white, these usually being ground plans. New titles continually added.

Photography: All originals (slides and large-format transparencies) shot by Professor Schade using Nikon equipment, tripod, and various lenses including perspective-correcting lens when appropriate. Films used are Kodachrome and Fujichrome (occasionally 4" x 5" Ektachrome).

Production: Duplicated on Ektachrome #5071, color-corrected and processed to exacting standards by a professional lab. Mounted in plastic and shipped in plastic sleeves. Duplicate slides are unconditionally guaranteed against color fading for 10 years.

Documentation: Catalogs and lists are available, and information is sent to a mailing list biannually. All research for catalogs performed by Professor Schade, who until his retirement in 1989 was on the faculty of the School of Architecture, Carleton University. Slides keyed to catalog or list and accompanied by a photocopy of the label on the original slide. Full identifications given, including orientations of buildings. Orientation of slide marked by number placement in upper right corner. Lists of slides that match textbook illustrations (Janson, Gardner, Hartt, and others) are available.

Purchasing: Slides sold singly, $4.00 each (Canadian dollars). Shipping and insurance costs invoiced to customer on orders valued $100.00 or less, free on larger orders (Canadian dollars). Discount of 25% allowed when all slides of a particular building or architect are purchased.

Duplicated upon receipt of order and shipped within two to three weeks except when owner is absent on a photographic excursion.

Other Products: Slide/tape productions with music and narration, including "Paestum: The Greek Temples in Italy" and "Canon: The Development of the Three Classical Orders in Architecture." Each includes 80 slides.

Other Sources: A selection of slides of Canadian architecture (185 items) and Greek architecture (250 items) is available from Davis Art Slides (formerly Rosenthal Art Slides) **(047)**.

Expansion Plans: Transfer of slide images to CD-ROM as prices for this product make it more affordable.

Evaluation: Quality, 3; documentation, 3 to 4; service, 4.

Museums

011 **Art Gallery of Ontario**
317 Dundas St. W.
Toronto, Ontario M5T IG4 Canada
Telephone: (416) 979-6660, x499
FAX: (416) 979-6674 or (416) 204-2697
Attn: Photographic Resources
URL: http://www.ago.net

Price Range: $2.50 for selected titles readily available; $5.00 for duplicate slides; $10.00 for new slides. No catalog.

Profile: Color slide titles offered by Photographic Services. Western art primarily represented: Canadian (historical and contemporary), United States (twentieth century), and European (nineteenth and twentieth centuries). Large group of slides of Henry Moore's work available. Slides of Inuit culture featured: artifacts, sculpture, prints, and drawings. Most slides in inventory are original 35mm Ektachrome film; some are dupes (Ektachrome slide duplicating film). All are fully labeled. Quantities are limited; first come, first served. Slide sets from major exhibitions assembled at the Art Gallery of Ontario have been made available for educational sales only. Effort is made to include titles from private collections, which are not otherwise accessible. In each case a limited number of sets have been produced, and as sets are sold out individual slides may become available. See website for information on sets.

Photography: Slides shot on Ektachrome by staff photographer in studio.

Production: Duplicated in-house on Ektachrome #5071. Color-corrected and contrast-controlled. Slides mounted in cardboard or plastic.

Documentation: Full information provided in catalog and on labels. Slides for public sale are fully labeled (English or French). Other slides keyed to information provided. Orientation marked when necessary.

Purchasing: Orders may be placed in person or by mail (please send as complete a description of your requirements as possible). Generally, a minimum of three weeks is required, but delivery time varies depending upon the complexity of the assignment and the size of the order. Advance payment in Canadian funds is required on all orders. Approved accounts may submit a purchase order. All Ontario orders are subject to Ontario sales tax. All Canadian orders are subject to GST. Service charges for postage and handling will be applied.

Digital Images: Available through AMICO **(001)**.

Other Products: Black-and-white photographs also sold by Photographic Services, and 4" x 5" color transparencies rented for reproduction.

Evaluation: Quality, 3 to 4; documentation, 4; service, 3.

012   Canadian Museum of Civilization

100 Laurier Ave., P.O. Box 3100
Hull, Quebec J8X 4H2 Canada
Telephone: (819) 776-7000
FAX: (819) 776-8300
Attn: Louis Campeau, Photo Archives
Research Officer
URL: http://www.civilization.ca

This museum also offers digital products and is listed in the digital section of the directory.

Profile: The Canadian Museum of Civilization is a Crown Corporation comprising Canada's National Museum of History and Anthropology, plus the Canadian War Museum. This entry refers to the CMC only. The collection has more than 300,000 images of museum collections, exhibitions, and events plus historical photograph collections dating from the late nineteenth century (primarily ethnographic subjects). 200,000 images have been digitized in Kodak PhotoCD, and a large website has been established. These and other initiatives make the collection more accessible.

Photography: Original slides are photographed by a professional staff photographer on site at Museum. Photography is primarily in color. Film size and stock vary. For further information, photographer must be consulted.

Production: For actual image duplication, slides or negatives are sent out to professional photo labs. Digital images are produced under contract by Danka Imaging (formally Kodak Imaging Systems). CMC does not provide copies of images other than from its own collection.

Documentation: Printout from computerized artifact or image database can be provided if requested. Image is labeled with museum catalog number.

Purchasing: Individual slides are priced at $2.50 each. Slide discounts may be negotiated. Contact museum for details. Client is invoiced when order is filled. No prepayment required. VISA and Master-Card accepted. Turnaround time dependent upon complexity of order. Orders usually shipped by Canada Post. Postage added. No minimum order. Payment for digital product is similar to slides. Contact museum for digital product prices.

Digital Products: CD-ROMs and PhotoCDs are offered in Windows format. Scanned originals include 35mm, 2¼ or 4" x 5", 35mm negatives, and black-and-white negatives in all sizes. The scanning is done with a Kodak Professional PhotoCD Scanner to the resolutions provided in the PhotoCD Image Pack. Manipulation of scanned images is carried out with Kodak Proprietary Imaging PIW 4220 v7.6. Images are color-corrected and can be cropped to detail if ordered by purchaser. The format is .PCD but can be converted. Viewing software can be Corel, Adobe, L-View, etc. Payment arrangements similar to slides. One-time and multiuser formats are offered, but images cannot be networked.

Expansion Plans: Brochures, mailing list, access to electronic catalog, website development.

013   McMichael Canadian Art Collection

10365 Islington Ave.
Kleinburg, Ontario L0J 1C0 Canada
Telephone: (905) 893-0344, x255
FAX: (905) 893-2588
Attn: Linda Morita, Archives
E-mail: linda-morita@mcmichael.on.ca
URL: http://www.mcmichael.on.ca

Profile: Slides of works of art in the holdings of the McMichael Canadian Art Collection are reproduced upon request. The permanent collection features works of the Group of Seven and their contemporaries, as well as native and Inuit art of Canada. Please contact the museum for further details.

Photography: Originals are photographed by a professional art photographer using Kodak film.

Documentation: No catalog is available. Contact the museum for available slides. Slides are identified with the following information: artist, title, date of work, medium, size, McMichael Accession number, and name of institution.

Purchasing: Slides are priced at $4.00 each (Canadian dollars). Prepayment required. On receipt of payment, order will take two to three weeks to fill. Shipping charges (by mail or courier) are extra.

Rental: Weekly loans available at $10.00 (Canadian dollars) per week. Deposit or credit card number required. Additional charges for shipping and preparation fee.

Evaluation: Quality, 4; documentation, 4; service, 3 to 4. (Evaluation by a single committee member.)

014   Musée des Beaux-Arts de Montreal

3400, avenue du Musée
Montreal, PQ H3G IK3 Canada
Telephone: (514) 285-1600, xl56
Attn: Slide Librarian

Profile: Entry reprinted from 6th ed. Color slides (originals when available, otherwise duplicates) offered of works in the permanent collection, which features Canadian art; Latin American art; ancient art of the Near East, Greece, Etruria, and the Roman Empire; medieval art; Renaissance through nineteenth-century European art; African art; Oceanic art; Pre-Columbian art; Islamic art; Oriental art; and Mediterranean glass. Museum Boutique sometimes sells five-slide sets derived from temporary exhibitions.

Photography: Original slides shot by staff photographer in studio on Ektachrome (EPY) ASA 50 or Kodak EPP ASA 100.

Production: Duplicated on Ektachrome #5071 by a local laboratory. Color-corrected and contrast-controlled. Mounted in plastic or cardboard. Shipped in boxes in bubble envelopes (large orders) or between two cardboards in paper envelopes (small orders).

Documentation: Free list of Canadian paintings (260 titles). Identifications provided in English and French. Full information given, including museum accession number. Orientation marked.

Purchasing: Slides sold singly by Slide Library, $2.50 each. No minimum order. Duplicates made to order and shipped within three to five weeks. Limited edition sets of five slides sold by Boutique for $10.00 (Canadian funds). Postage added. No rush orders accepted. Payment accepted in Canadian or United States dollars. No returns accepted.

Rental: Slides may be borrowed, in person only, from the Slide Library collection (holdings approximately 35,000 items) for one week, for a fee.

Other Products: Boutique currently offers one videocassette.

Evaluation: Quality, 4; documentation, 4; service, 4. (Evaluation by a single committee member.)

015   Museum of Anthropology

University of British Columbia
6393 N.W. Maine Dr.
Vancouver, BC V6T 1Z2 Canada
Telephone: (604) 822-5087
FAX: (604) 822-2974
Attn: Deb Tibbel
E-mail: tibbel@unixg.ubc.ca
URL: http://www.moa.ubc.ca/

Profile: The museum, designed by Canadian architect Arthur Erickson, is noted for Pacific Northwest art and artifacts. MOA's Great Hall displays huge totem poles, feast dishes, and canoes of the Kwakwaka'wakw, Nisga'a, Gitksan, Haida, and Coast Salish peoples, while the Masterpiece Gallery exhibits carved works in silver, gold, stone, and wood. The outdoor sculpture complex includes two Haida Houses and ten poles and features the work of some of the finest contemporary First Nations artists of the Northwest Coast. The Museum has the world's largest collection of works by Haida artist Bill Reid.

The Koerner Ceramics Gallery features a 600-piece collection of fifteenth- to nineteenth-century European ceramics, as well as specially commissioned ceramics and textiles by contemporary Vancouver artists. The Museum's extensive Visible Storage Galleries make more than 15,000 objects from the collections accessible to the public. Arranged according to culture and use, the Visible Storage Galleries invite individual exploration, comparison, and contrast of materials from cultures from all over the world. Slides of works in the collections are available.

016   National Gallery of Canada

380 Sussex Dr.
P.O. Box 427, Station A
Ottawa, Ontario KIN 9N4 Canada
Telephone: (613) 990-0545
Attn: Slide Sales, Reproduction Rights
and Sales

Profile: Entry reprinted from 6th ed. More than 2,500 color slide titles offered of works in the permanent collection and special exhibitions. Canadian art emphasized (76% of the museum's paintings are Canadian). Slides also available of Chinese, Tibetan, and Indian art; Amerindian and Eskimo art from Canada; Canadian silver; and European painting. The collection of contemporary art, including video and film, is growing. The photography collection, begun in 1967, is outstanding. Exhibition sets offered as limited issues.

Photography: For the most part, slides shot on Ektachrome by staff photographers in studio.

Production: Duplicated on Ektachrome #5071 by the National Film Board of Canada. Color-corrected and contrast-controlled. Mounted in cardboard or plastic. Some sets available unmounted.

Documentation: Mailing list kept. Catalog in French and English distributed free to "best customers." Catalog issued in 1984, priced $12.00 (Canadian funds, as are all amounts in this entry), postpaid. Identifications complete. Slides keyed to catalog. Orientation marked by number placement.

Purchasing: Slides sold only to educational institutions, singly or in sets. Slides in stock $1.95 each. Slides duplicated to order, $10.00 each. Per-slide cost discounted in sets. Otherwise, no discounts given. Minimum order 10 slides unless order is prepaid. Orders filled from stock within a few days. Duplicates made to order shipped within two weeks. On request, slides sent by courier service at customer's expense. Slides usually not sent on approval, and no returns accepted. "We have seldom ever had slides returned."

Evaluation: Quality, 4; documentation, 4; service, 4. (Reprinted from 6th edition; exhibitions sets especially valuable. " 'Three Hundred Years of Canadian Art' set [303 slides] is a standard tool for Canadian courses" [Brenda MacEachern].)

017   Provincial Museum of Alberta

12845 – 102 Ave.
Edmonton, Alberta T5N 0M6 Canada
Telephone: (403) 453-9100
FAX: (403) 454-6629
URL: http://www.pma.edmonton.ab.ca/

This museum also offers digital products and is listed in the digital section of the directory.

Profile: The museum's emphasis is on the natural history of Alberta, but it also includes ethnology, folk life, Western Canadian history, government history, and archaeology.

Photography: Photography of an artifact or specimen in the museum's collections can be arranged. In this case, the client pays all the photography fees as well as any borrowing fees.

Rental: 35mm slides: A loan agreement is signed by the borrower. Loan return dates are open to renewal. The loan states terms regarding use, copyright, fees, credit-line requirements, etc.

Digital Products: Kodak PhotoCDs are produced from slides and photographs. The scanning of originals is done by a commercial business in five resolutions at 300 dpi. Formats include .PCD, .JPG, .GIF, .BMP, and .TIF. Kodak PhotoCD Access Plus software or other viewing software is required to view the images.

018   Royal Ontario Museum

100 Queen's Park
Toronto, Ontario M5S 2C6 Canada
Telephone: (416) 586-5549

Profile: Entry reprinted from 6th ed. No slides of art collection sold by museum shop. Inquiries should be directed to the curator of the appropriate department: Canadiana, European Art, Greek and Roman Art, Egyptian Art, Far Eastern Art, or New World Archaeology. As of 1989, there is no person on the museum's staff who has responsibility for disseminating audiovisual materials.

UNITED STATES

019 Academic Challenge

P.O. Box 4603
Rock Hill, SC 29731
Telephone: (803) 328-8554
E-mail: academic@infoave.net
URL: http://www.quizq.com/

Profile: Entry reprinted from 6th edition with some new information from website. Slide sets sold with or without questions intended for use in quiz bowls. Four hundred slides in all are available, most of works from the Metropolitan Museum of Art, New York, and the National Gallery of Art, Washington, DC. New titles continually added. Slides offered include 22 sets from Dutch masters to Post Impressionists, and each set contains 12 slides.

Photography: Original slides shot by company president, John Alan Presto, in galleries with existing light, using Kodak film or Fujichrome ASA 200.

Production: Duplicated from originals by Photo Pros, Charlotte, North Carolina, on Ektachrome #5071. Color-corrected and contrast-controlled. Mounted in plastic and packaged in Vu-All pouches.

Documentation: Mailing list kept. Free brochure and list of slides (artist, nationality, and title). Call or send E-mail message to request brochure. Slides labeled with artist and title of work; for architecture, architect if known, building name, and location. Category A sets (six slides) accompanied by eighteen questions. Orientation marked.

Purchasing: Order form on reverse of brochure. Sets with questions composed of six slides; without questions, 12 slides. Slides are priced at $1.35 each with a minimum order of $15.00. Postage added. Prepayment or purchase order required. Slides kept in stock and shipped within two weeks. Rush orders shipped on day of receipt; express mailing charges added. Satisfaction guaranteed; returns accepted for refund or exchange.

Evaluation: Reprinted from 6th ed. Quality, based on two samples sent, 2 to 3. Paintings photographed with frames so that actual painted surface does not fill film frame. Documentation 2. No information available on service.

020 American Classical League (ACL)

Miami University
Oxford, OH 45056
Telephone: (513) 529-4116

Profile: Entry reprinted from 6th ed. One hundred duplicate color slide titles offered in four sets: "Ancient Rome," "Roman Forum," "Pompeii," and "Ancient Athens."

Photography: Original slides shot by William M. Seaman, in whose possession they remain.

Production: Duplicates supplied to the American Classical League by Mr. Seaman. According to the 4th edition of this guide, duplicates made by World in Color on Ektachrome #5071.

Documentation: Free catalog listing set titles. Slides labeled.

Purchasing: Each set of 25 slides priced $14.90, plus shipping via UPS ($3.00). Prices discounted 10% for ACL members if order is prepaid. Sets shipped on day of receipt of order. Returns accepted for refund if slides are damaged.

*021 American Committee for South Asian Art (ACSAA)

Color Slide Project
Department of History of Art
Tappan Hall
University of Michigan
Ann Arbor, MI 48109-1357
Telephone: (734) 936-2539
FAX: (734) 647-4121
Attn: Wendy Holden
E-mail: acsaa.slide.project@umich.edu
URL: http://www.umich.edu/~hartspc/acsaa/acsaa.html

Profile: Entry reprinted from 6th ed. More than 8,000 color slides offered. Project established in 1974 to document art and architecture of India, Nepal, Tibet, Sri Lanka, Burma, Thailand, Afghanistan, and Indonesia. Production and distribution supported by grants from the Association for Asian Studies,

Asian Cultural Council, Southeast Asia Art Foundation, and individuals. Five to 10 new sets issued annually (eight in 1989). Southeast Asian collections of the following museums have been extensively photographed:

Bharat Kala Ghavan, Benares (Varanasi), India

Cleveland Museum of Art, Cleveland, OH

Los Angeles County Museum of Art, Los Angeles, CA

Photography: Originals shot by various photographers. Some original slides available for purchase at no additional cost.

Production: Duplicated on Ektachrome from master originals after inventory of originals is depleted.

Documentation: Free catalog, revised annually. List of contents of a particular set sent on request, prior to purchase. Some sets accompanied by books or booklets at no additional cost. Label information imprinted on mounts (since 1982) or provided on self-adhesive labels. Identification extensively detailed.

Purchasing: Sets of 100 slides priced $130 (United States) or $135 (foreign), postpaid. U.S. and Canadian orders sent UPS or parcel post. Foreign orders sent by airmail. Discounts given to advance subscribers. Any five sets (or more) from prior years discounted 10%. Order form included in catalog. Prepayment or purchase order required. Orders of back issues shipped within two weeks. "Any subscriber dissatisfied with the slides may receive a refund upon return of the slides within 60 days."

Evaluation: Quality, 3 to 4; documentation, 2 to 4; service, 1 to 4.

*022 American Library Color Slide Co.

P.O. Box 4414, Grand Central Station
New York, NY 10163-4414
Telephone: (800) 633-3307 or
(212) 255-5356
FAX: (212) 691-8592
Attn: Leonard S. Barton, Director
E-mail: info@artslides.com
URL: http://www.artslides.com

Price Range: $2.50 to $4.00 per slide.

Profile: The American Library Color Slide Co., Inc. was conceived as an encyclopedic source of color slide visual aids for the study of art, architecture, and the humanities in 1939. Since then, it has grown to one of the world's largest archives available

for acquisition, with more than 250,000 color slide images and more than 5,000 didactic sets that cover the entire scope of world cultural history. The first major project in the 1930s was an inclusive photographic survey of then-contemporary American art. It was created with the cooperation of individual artists, art galleries, and museums. By 1940, these efforts were complemented by exhaustive research and extensive travel that allowed the Library on-site access to photograph major paintings, sculpture, and architectural monuments throughout the world. The American Archives of World Art was established as the Library's art history affiliate in the late 1950s. The initial project was to classify, annotate, and index the archives within a detailed historical framework, creating an important scholarly source for the study of visual arts, world history, anthropology, and religion. Next, the Basic Libraries of World Art were compiled; these are expandable slide libraries designed expressly for educational institutions. A decade later, as the Library continued to grow, didactic Survey Sets were introduced and Units of Ten were created to present refined breakdowns of many of the larger Survey Sets. All of these initiatives provided the basis for today's archives.

Documentation: Catalog available. "The American Library Compendium and Index of World Art—Book 1" is a catalog of the holdings. Free detailed literature offering an overview of the book is now available on request. In brief: 550 pages, two indices (one by artist, the other by subject), includes more than 25,000 individual titles with emphasis on world painting and related mediums. Paperbound, $25.00; hardbound, $40.00, plus $5.00 (domestic) shipping.

Expansion Plans: CD-ROMs in the works.

Evaluation: Quality, 1 to 3; documentation, 1 to 3; service, 2 to 3. The samples were rated higher, quality, 2 to 4; documentation, 3 to 4.

023 Canyon Lights World Art Slides (formerly Ancient World Slides)

1127 Eagle Way
Lyons, CO 80540
Telephone: (303) 823-5913
E-mail: SPeirce@prodigy.net

Profile: Company markets slides photographed by art history professor of sites important in Ancient Greece, Ancient Rome, megalithic sites in England, sites in Malta, Sardinia, and Southwestern USA (Native American) prehistoric art.

Photography: Slides are photographed by an art history professor on Fuji professional slide film. All slides are color images. Images have been photographed to achieve an authentic mood. No artificial lighting is used. For example, if the interior of a Roman building has light streaming through an oculus or window into an otherwise dark room, the slide will have extremes of light and dark.

Production: Original slides are duplicated onto Kodak Archival Long Lasting duplicating film.

Documentation: Slide lists are available on request. Slide labels indicate site, location, and name of monument.

Purchasing: Slides are priced at $3.00 per slide in sets or at $3.25 per individual slide. Any slide in a set may be purchased individually. Contact company for information on permission to digitize purchased slides for educational use. University purchase orders and personal checks are accepted. Payment must be in U.S. funds. Shipping charges are extra, and order is filled within three weeks of receipt of order. A 5% discount is offered for prepayment on order.

024   Architectural Color Slides

187 Grant St.
Lexington, MA 02173
Telephone: (781) 862-9431
Attn: Franziska Porges

Profile: Current owner is looking for buyer for collection. Twenty-five thousand duplicate color slide titles offered of architecture and related arts; scope is international. Works in Greek museums and the Museum of Fine Arts, Boston, represented. New titles continually added. Sets available on topics such as the following: "The Functions of Cities," "The Living City," "The City at Night," "City Spaces for People Around the World," and "Katmando Valley Towns."

Photography: Original slides shot with Leica and Nikon equipment by Ms. Porges, an architect, on Kodachrome and Ektachrome.

Production: Duplicated by Kodak.

Documentation: Free single-page information sheet gives titles of lists available. Catalog (16 lists) $3.00, deductible from first order. Slides identified by location, building name, architect, and view; few dates given. Slides keyed to catalog. Sets accompanied by lecture notes or text.

Purchasing: Slides sold singly or in sets. Single slides priced $1.80 each. Discounted 10% on orders

of more than 100 slides. Duplicated to order. Rush orders filled within one week. Sets priced at $88.00 to $170.00.

Evaluation: Reprinted from 6th ed. Quality, 2; documentation, 2; service, 2. No recent samples available for evaluation.

025   Architecture of the World

37 E. 19th St., Second Floor
New York, NY 10003
Telephone: (212) 529-1630
FAX: (212) 749-6399
Attn: Ernest Burden

Profile: Entry reprinted from 6th edition at request of owner. More than 5,000 duplicate color slide titles offered of architecture, emphasizing ancient and modern (especially in the United States, Canada, and South America). Approximately 2,000 slide titles available now beside those listed in the catalog, and 1,000 more to be added by the end of 1989.

Photography: Original slides shot by E. Burden, architect (50%), or by traveling scholars (50%) on Ektachrome ASA 160 using Nikon equipment, including wide-angle, zoom, and perspective-correcting lenses. Tripod used for some shots. "Each site was photographed from an overall view, followed by closer general views and terminated by several close-ups and detail shots."

Production: Duplicated in-house from originals onto Ektachrome ASA 64. (Catalog states that duplicates are on Kodachrome.) Color-corrected and contrast-controlled. Mounted in cardboard.

Documentation: Mailing list kept. Free catalog, indexed. Slides keyed to catalog. Identifications consist of architect, building name, location, and description of view. Dates of construction not given. Orientation not marked (not necessary).

Purchasing: Slides sold singly or in sets. Minimum order 30 slides. Some slides available only in sets, as noted in catalog. Single slides priced $2.15 each. Quantity discounts given. Please address orders to the attention of Ernest Burden. Postage included in price except for foreign orders or orders sent by priority mail. Duplicated to order and usually shipped within two weeks. No rush orders accepted. Prepayment required from individuals and private companies. Purchase order required from educational institutions. Slides not sent on approval, and no refunds or exchanges allowed. However, "each slide is fully guaranteed as to photographic quality and if found defective will be replaced. Claims must be made within two weeks after receipt of merchandise. Returns will not be accepted without prior written permission."

Evaluation: Reprinted from 6th ed. Quality, 2; documentation, 2; service, 2.

026 Art Images for College Teaching (AICT)

Minneapolis College of Art & Design
2501 Stevens Ave. S.
Minneapolis, MN 55404
Telephone: (612) 874-3781
Attn: Allan T. Kohl
E-mail: allan_kohl@mn.mcad.edu
URL: http://www.mcad.edu/AICT/index.html

This image provider also offers digital products. See entry in the digital section of the directory.

Price Range: Provide slide duplicates of AICT images for $1.25.

Profile: AICT has 500 images on the website and 2,000 to 3,000 images on PhotoCDs that can be loaned to institutions for copying.

Purchasing: $1.25 per duplicate slide. Website images are free.

Digital Products: CD-ROMs and web images.

027 Art in America Magazine

817 W. End Ave., Suite 12AA
New York, NY 10025
Telephone: (212) 749-6361
FAX: (212) 749-6399
Attn: Michele Senecal (c/o Power & Senecal Group)
E-mail: powsengrup@aol.com

Profile: Art in America suspended production of the slide sets this past spring (1997). Sets are available for years 1990–1995. Resumption of new editions of the annual offerings is currently awaiting a final decision from the publisher. Before suspension of new sets, limited-issue set of 200 duplicate color slides were released annually, selected by the editors of *Art in America* magazine from the previous year's publications. Contemporary painting, sculpture, drawing, and photography featured. Most major galleries and museums in the United States and abroad represented. Earlier sets not restricted to contemporary art.

Photography: Large-format transparencies shot by professional art photographers on Ektachrome #5271. Images are supplied to the magazine by the artist's gallery or representative for publication in the magazine. They usually are photographed by a professional photographer. Accurate reproduction in the magazine is of paramount importance.

Production: Slides produced by ChroMakers, Stamford, Connecticut. Color-corrected and contrast-controlled. Mounted in cardboard.

Documentation: Mailing list kept. Free brochure issued annually. List of contents available on request. Slides labeled with full identifications, except artist's birth date. Artist's nationality not included prior to 1989 set. References to issue and page number included. Orientation marked.

Purchasing: Orders solicited prior to production. Annual mailings await publisher's decision. List of contents available upon request. Slides labeled with full identifications, except artist's birthdate. Artist's nationality not included prior to 1989 set. References to issue and page number included. Orientation marked. Sets stocked until depleted. Sets are available for years 1990–1995 for $350-$375 per set with shipping included except on international orders. Price of 1995 set $375, postpaid. Editions 1990–1993 are now offered at a discounted price of $350. Shipped via UPS. If in stock, orders filled within two weeks. Rush orders accepted. Prepayment required on noninstitutional orders. Institutions may send prepayment, purchase order, or letter of agreement to purchase. Sets sent on approval; returns accepted for exchange.

Evaluation: Quality, 3; documentation, 3; service, 3.

*028 Art on File

1837 E. Shelby
Seattle, WA 98112
Telephone: (206) 322-2638
FAX: (206) 329-1928
Attn: Rob Wilkinson
E-mail: artofile@wln.com
URL: http://www.artonfile.com

This vendor also offers digital products and is listed in the digital section of the directory.

Profile: Art on File was founded in 1982 by photographers Rob Wilkinson and Colleen Chartier to document recent developments in public art, architecture, and design. The company concentrated initially on public art and then evolved into the documentation of a full range of public-space design including architecture, landscape architecture, and urban design. Most of the slide documentation concentrates on contemporary projects; however, some historic topics are covered with a strong connection to contemporary developments in art and architecture. A grant from the National Endowment of the Arts, sponsored by the VRA, helped to expand the geographical coverage. Today, images document projects from North America, Europe, and Asia.

By January 1, 1998, there were 62 slide and digital collections with more than 8,000 images. Beginning in early 1998, Art on File will announce all new offerings through its website. This image provider will no longer produce a comprehensive printed catalog, although postcard reminders of new offerings and website address will be distributed several times per year. The website is a fully functional database with keyword access to the entire library, a simple ordering procedure, and thumbnail images of 98% of the image library.

Because of the contemporary nature of many of the projects, annotations often includes original research and interviews with the artists and designers. 98% of the 35mm slide library has been scanned and is available to clients. Images are delivered on CD-ROM in whatever format is desired for either PCs or Macintosh computers. Clients may order entire collections or individual projects. More than 7,000 images will be available for viewing. Art on File is also collecting a series of QTVR scenes to be offered in late 1998. These digital panoramas will supplement our still digital images and slides.

Photography: All photographs are produced on location by photographers Rob Wilkinson and Colleen Chartier, founders and owners of Art on File, Inc., with a few exceptions noted in online catalog and annotations.

Slide Production: Kodak film products at (100 ASA) are selected based upon type of conditions. Slides are duplicated by a local professional lab that uses Kodak #5071 slide duplication film. Although most of the original photography is 35mm format, a medium-format camera with perspective correction is used for architecture.

Documentation: A catalog is available, and update is sent to mailing list each spring.

Purchasing: Slides available individually or in sets priced as follow: $.50 per slide in sets/$4.00 per slide individually; digital images $4.00. Discounts not available at present, but policy is being reviewed. Purchase orders are accepted by fax, E-mail, or letter. Orders are usually shipped within two weeks of receiving them. If additional time is required at the duplicating lab, clients are notified at the time their order is received. A shipping fee of $6.00 is charged for each order. Approval plans are available.

Digital Products: PhotoCDs are available in either Windows or MAC format with tech support available. A recent model MAC or PC with CD-ROM is required for viewing. Original transparencies (not duplicates) are scanned using a Kodak PhotoCD Workstation at three resolutions: 300K, 1MB, and 4.5MG. Photoshop and Debabilizer software is used for color-correction and cropping. Both entire and detail views are available. Both individual images and sets are available for multiuse.

The digital images are site-licensed for campus use, which restricts access to current students, faculty, and staff. Digital images may not be transferred to another institution, copied, or reproduced in any form without permission from Art on File, Inc. Digital images are licensed through a signed site license agreement. Art on File has a standard form for this purpose. Orders are filled within one week if the images have been previously scanned and corrected. A shipping and handling charge of $6.00 is added to each order. Rush development of image orders can be handled as the inventory of contemporary public slides permit.

Other Products: A CD-ROM product called Public Art: Seattle contains several hundred Art on File images sponsored and funded by the Seattle Arts Commission and the National Endowment of the Arts.

Expansion Plans: Plans include the documentation of a number of new projects in Spain, Germany, and England and other locations in North America. Suggestions for projects to document are always encouraged. The library of QTVR panoramas will document important historical and contemporary projects around the world. The first version will be released sometime in late 1998. This product will enable educators and students to explore in 360-degree space noteworthy buildings, site-specific artworks, urban spaces, and landscapes. QTVR is the most effective new media available for the exploration of natural or built space. Art on File is currently investing in a higher production level for new photography, a streamlined ordering process through the World Wide Web, and the creation of new media resources such as QTVR.

Evaluation: Quality, 4; documentation, 3 to 4; service, 3 to 4.

029   Art Resource Inc.

65 Bleecker St. (Ninth Floor)
New York, NY 10012
Telephone: (212) 505-8700 or
(212) 673-4988
FAX: (212) 420-9286
Attn: Theodore Feder

Profile: Entry reprinted from 6th ed. Art Resource, by its own account, is the world's largest photo archive of works of painting, sculpture, architecture, and the minor arts. Large-format photographs, black-and-white and color, available for reproduction in books, magazines, posters, television, film, and publicity. Additional sets have been developed by Art Resource from the holdings of ESM Documentations, New York. A set of more than 100 slides available to accompany the study guide and faculty guide for the "Art of the Western World" television course (PBS, nine segments). Some small sets produced for U.S. museums that are sold exclusively by the museums.

Photography: Most originals are large-format transparencies shot by professional photographers.

Production: No slides printed on unstable film for several years. Now uses Eastmancolor #5384.

Documentation: Brochures or news sheets issued approximately yearly, listing set titles and prices. Contents lists for particular sets sent free of charge on request. Same lists accompany slides. Art Resource sets less completely documented. ESM sets lack information about present locations of works photographed in galleries several decades ago.

Purchasing: Slides sold in sets only. Prices based on per-slide cost of $1.95. Postage added. Television course slide set priced $96.50, postpaid. Purchase orders accepted from institutions. Time interval between receipt of order and shipment is usually four to six weeks. Rush orders accepted; usually no surcharge. Slides not sent on approval, but "we will accept returns for exchange if the client is not satisfied with the quality of the slide set."

Other Products: 4" x 5" transparencies and black-and-white prints.

Evaluation: Quality, 2 to 4; documentation, 2; service, 2.

029a   Arts of the United States
See under Digital Section

030   Asian Art Photographic Distribution (AAPD)

Department of the History of Art
University of Michigan
Ann Arbor, MI 48109-1357
Telephone: (734) 634-5555
FAX: (734) 647-4121
Attn: Wendy Holden
E-mail: wholden@umich.edu
URL: http://www.umich.edu/~hartspc/aapd/
index.html

Profile: This resource was established in 1970 as an outgrowth of photography at the National Palace Museum, Taiwan. Following the successful completion of the distribution of materials from other important collections, Asian Art Photographic Distribution (AAPD) was established. In 1978, AAPD broadened its scope to include the documentation of Japanese paintings in traveling exhibitions, and private and public collections. In addition, some sets of slides have been produced as the result of temporary loans, such as "Paintings from Collections in the People's Republic of China," or permanent loans of materials to the project such as "The New Chinese Painting: 1949–1986" and "Nora Ehon: Illustrated Literature from Medieval and Early Modern Japan." Generally one issue of a collection of photographic materials is made. Current projects are announced and orders solicited. After the closing date for the placement of orders, the sets are made to satisfy the demand. A limited number of uncommitted sets may be available. Future issues are not guaranteed. Orders not placed at the time of the original announcement will be filled as requests are received, as long as the sets are in stock.

Photography: All slide originals are photographed by University of Michigan staff. The team includes head photographer Pat Young, assistant Jeri Hollister, and AAPD project coordinator Wendy Holden. Extensive tests on the film are made prior to shooting, and all original slides are made on film of the same emulsion number.

Production: The color slide duplicates are made on Ektachrome #5071 for the highest quality and color.

Purchasing: Both individual slides and sets are available. Individual slides are priced at $3.00 (minimum order $9.00). Postage costs on special requests are extra. Overseas orders are sent foreign parcel post at a cost of $7.50 per set; Canada $5.00 shipping and handling. Invoices are mailed the day the slides are shipped. Payment is not due, however, until the goods have been received. Checks should be made payable in U.S. currency to Asian Art Photographic Distribution.

Documentation: A catalog is available upon request and also at the website. All sets of educational materials are accompanied by a full identification list that includes artist, dates, format, media, and dimensions.

Other Products: Exhibition catalogs available only if specifically advertised. Islamic Art Archives of black-and-white prints.

Evaluation: Quality, 3 to 4; documentation, 3 to 4; service, 3 to 4.

031   Barnes, James

1378 Massachusetts Ave., Apt. #2
Arlington, MA 02174
Telephone: (617) 648-0407

Profile: Entry reprinted from 6th ed. Approximately 8,000 to 10,000 color slide titles offered of architecture in the United States, Great Britain, Ireland, and Italy. Public art also available. Roman sites in Italy and Great Britain included. Sites in Massachusetts extensively covered.

Photography: Original slides shot by James Barnes using Pentax equipment, perspective-correcting lens when appropriate, and Kodachrome film.

Production: Duplicated by Subtractive Technology, Boston, Massachusetts, on Ektachrome #5071. Mounted in plastic.

Documentation: No catalog. Lists on specific sites sent on request. Slides keyed to lists of identification, including architect, building name, location, dates of construction, and description of view. Orientation not marked.

Purchasing: Slides sold singly or as sets. Originals priced $3.15 each, duplicates $2.50. Discount given on orders of 500 or more duplicates. Postage added. Purchase orders accepted from institutions. Prepayment required from individuals. Duplicates made to order and shipped within two weeks. Requests considered to shoot original slides on commission within New England. Slides not sent

on approval, but several samples may be requested prior to ordering. Returns accepted only by negotiation.

Evaluation: Quality, 4; documentation, 1 to 2; service, 2. (Evaluation by a single committee member.)

032   Baron, Robert A.

P.O. Box 93
Larchmont, NY 10538
Telephone: (914) 834-0233
FAX: (914) 834-0284
E-mail: rabaron@pipeline.com
URL: http://www.pipeline.com/~rabaron/
SLIDES.htm

Profile: Robert Baron is a museum consultant who also has a small collection of slides for sale. The collection includes some Gaudi from Barcelona, the monastery of St. Martin du Canigou in the Pyrenees, the Chateau de Peyrepertuse, and scenes from Oradour, Chateaux of the Loire. Uncatalogued projects include Neolithic Brittany, p-scale domestic architecture in southern Florida, and the white churches from Cape Cod.

Other: The website contains documents relating to various topics of interest to visual resources professionals and others in the visual arts community.

*033   Biblical Archaeology Society

4710 41st St.
Washington, DC 20016
Telephone: (800) 221-4644
FAX: (202) 364-2636
E-mail: basedit@clark.net
URL: http://www.bib-arch.org

Profile: Ten sets of slides offered as follows: Biblical Archaeology (134 slides), Dead Sea Scrolls, New Testament Archaeology (180 slides), Supplemental New Testament Archaeology (105 slides), Jerusalem Archaeology (141 slides), Galilee Archaeology (140 slides), Egypt-Sinai-Negev (142 slides), Archaeology and Religion (141 slides), Mesopotamian Archaeology (140 slides), and Ancient Near East Inscriptions (140 slides). The society is planning to put images on the website.

Documentation: Each set accompanied by a booklet (about 35 to 50 pages) containing brief title list of individual slides, source/photographer list, bibliography of related articles in *Biblical Archaeology*

Review and *Bible Review*, introductory text, and commentaries on each slide (32 pages to 180 pages each).

Purchasing: Sets priced from $99.50 to $159.50.

Other Products: Books, video tapes, *Biblical Archaeology Review* magazine.

Evaluation: Reprinted from 6th ed. Quality, 3; documentation, 3; service, 3.

034 Bicoastal Productions

76 N. Fullerton Ave.
Montclair, NJ 07042
Telephone: (973) 746-6291
Attn: F. Dewey Webster

Price Range: $3.00 per slide for one-time-only reproduction right.

Profile: Started in 1984 with slides of Chinese and Japanese architecture and gardens. Collections modestly expanded; very little contemporary (1990s) work. Most recent work has been traditional and vernacular Chinese, Mongolia, and Pakistan. Originals are sent; customer duplicates desired slide and returns originals, plus $3.00 per dupe.

Photography: Original slides photographed by Dewey Webster, primarily Fujichrome 100 ASA, hand-held, with PC lens for buildings; often 28mm for gardens.

Production: Duplication is up to customer.

Documentation: Catalog of titles is available. Original slides are captioned. Buyers usually photocopy slide mounts before returning originals. This expanded information may be requested prior to ordering by using as reference the code numbers in the catalog. Slides keyed to information on list. Orientation not marked.

Purchasing: Slides sent for buyer's duplication. No minimum order. Single slides priced $3.00 each for one-time reproduction right. Postage added at 10%. Purchase orders accepted from institutions. Payment accepted in U.S. dollars.

Evaluation: Reprinted from 6th ed. Four samples submitted (originals): quality, 4; documentation, 3. "Very good service. Excellent resource for Japanese architecture" (Christine Sundt).

035 Calderca Inc.

10709 Cleary Blvd., #202
Plantation, FL 33324
Telephone: (954) 452-2699
Attn: Jose Luis Colmenares
E-mail: CALDERCA@aol.com

This vendor also provides digital products and is listed in the digital section of the directory.

Profile: Collection of around 30,000 slides of architecture, developed over 20 years by Professor Jose Luis Colmenares. A graduate of the University of Texas at Austin, with several architectural degrees, Professor Colmenares has taught for 17 years and lectured widely in Europe, the United States, and Latin America. He offers 188 sets, ranging from 10 to 150 slides per set of architecture in situ, with a brief essay on the subject of each set. Sets include a wide range of thematic subjects, such as gothic architecture, neoclassical architecture in France, and high-tech architecture, and sets on individual architects. Sets include European, North American, and Latin American architects. Contact Professor Colmenares for a list of sets.

Photography: All the slides were photographed by Professor Jose Colmenares, in situ, over a period of 20 years. Because the collection consists of 30,000 slides, several types of film have been used, but mainly Kodachrome 64, Ektachrome 64, and Fujichrome 50.

Production: Slide sets are duplicated on Ektachrome 64 film and mounted in plastic.

Documentation: Each slide is numbered and individually identified, including: name of building, architect, date, location, and point of view. Accompanying texts are explanations and critical reviews that could be used as lecture notes.

Purchasing: Slides are sold in sets, ranging from set of 10 priced at $30 to set of 150 priced at $450. Set prices do not include shipping. Place order by listing set numbers. If the order is for less than $180 (U.S.), the order can be placed by E-mail or telephone and the purchaser will be billed later. For orders totaling more than $180 (U.S.), send a check payable to CALDERCA Inc. Allow three to four weeks for delivery. Special requests are available if groups of slides are needed for a particular academic course.

Digital Products: Slides can be ordered in CD format. Contact Professor Colmenares for details.

036 Calumet Photographic, Inc.

890 Supreme Dr.
Bensenville, IL 60106
Telephone: (888) 367-2781 (orders)
(Toll Free in U.S., 8 A.M. to 6 P.M., CST, M-F)
or (800) 453-2550
(Customer Service)
FAX: (800) 577-3686 (orders) or
(630) 860-7089
E-mail: custserv@calumetphoto.com
URL: http://www.calumetphoto.com

Profile: Information from website. Calumet Photographic, Inc., has been in business for 60 years and primarily sells photographic equipment and supplies, but does offer three slide sets on photography.

Documentation: Website provides content description and pricing for each slide set. "Survey of the History of Photography" includes 250 toned black-and-white slides, with biographical data and checklist, mounted in plastic, for $425. "Photography During the 19th Century" includes 225 toned black-and-white slides, with catalog and bibliography, mounted in plastic for $385.

"Farm Security Administration," 2d ed., includes 80 black-and-white slides, mounted in plastic, with checklist, for $165. (All prices are U.S. dollars.) A sample image is included for each set at the website. (Type SLIDE SET into the product speed search at the top of the home page.) A printed catalog is available on request but duplicates the information available at the website.

Purchasing: Orders can be placed online, by phone, by fax, and by mail. Credit cards are accepted.

037 Chicago Historical Society

Clark St. at North Ave.
Chicago, IL 60614-6099
Telephone: (312) 642-4600
FAX: (312) 266-2077
Attn: Photoduplication services
URL: http://www.chicagohs.org/

Price Range: $5.00 per slide for educational use.
Profile: Paintings and sculptures documenting Chicago's history. There are 1.5 million prints and photographs relating to the history of the city. The Architectural Study Center documents Chicago's built environment. The Decorative and Industrial Arts Collection contains objects relating to the city's growth. A Costume Center contains 50,000 pieces.

Other Products: 4" x 5" transparencies, negatives, photographic prints, photocopies.

038 Chronicle Books/Eden Interactive
See under Digital Section

*039 Cirrus

542 S. Alameda St.
Los Angeles, CA 90013
Telephone: (213) 680-3473
FAX: (213) 680-0930
Attn: Cameron Whiteman or Jean Milant
E-mail: CCirrus@aol.com
URL: http://www.LACN.org

This vendor also provides digital products and is listed in the digital section of the directory.

Price Range: $.50/slide to $25.00 for Cirrus CD-ROM. Digital images to be downloaded from website as of January 2, 1998.

Profile: Jean R. Milant founded Cirrus Editions, originally located in Hollywood, in 1970. From the beginning, it was a publisher of original graphics and multiples by Southern California artists. The fully equipped workshop produces fine prints (using lithography, silkscreen, and etching) by such contemporary artists as Peter Alexander, John Baldessari, Vija Celmins, Ed Moses, Bruce Nauman, Joan Nelson, Lari Pittman, and Ed Ruscha. Cirrus Gallery was established in 1971 and from that time, it became a major contemporary art gallery exhibiting new and exciting Southern California artists.

Cirrus is a participant in "Faces of LA," which is a project of the Getty's LA Culture Net. This promotes access to cultural resources through online networks. A consortium of Los Angeles museums, libraries, and Cirrus has created a virtual database composed of digital materials from their collections that illustrate the places, monuments, events, culture, and history of the peoples of Southern California, and that represent themselves as local cultural institutions. Cirrus has included 1,000 images that will be accessible through this website. In addition to the digital images, Cirrus offers slides photographed professionally from the original works of art.

Photography: Original works photographed by a professional photographer.

Production: Generally, the slides are duplicated by an outside vendor from 35mm originals to high-quality 35mm duplicates.

Documentation: The Los Angeles County Museum of Art published a catalogue raisonné of the Cirrus Editions archive. This includes 60 color and 400 duotone reproductions. It is available from Cirrus for $65. Key text fields will be available with digital images on website.

Purchasing: Slides are priced at $.50 each, individually or in sets. Discounts for volume purchases and for educational institutions. Payment or large institution purchase order is required with the order, and orders are filled each week. Shipping charges are additional.

Digital Products: The Getty Information Institute contracted with Luna Imaging, Inc., a well-regarded service bureau in Venice, CA, to scan Cirrus master slides and provide digital image files. These are now available in most formats and in a range of resolutions. Luna has corrected the original images for color distortions. Complete views of the Cirrus work of art is available with zoom detail available.

040 Clearvue/eav
See under Digital Section

041 Columbus Area Chamber of Commerce

506 Fifth St.
Columbus, IN 47201
Telephone: (812) 372-1954
Attn: Director, Visitors' Center

Profile: Entry reprinted from 6th ed. Slides offered of exteriors and interiors of buildings in Columbus,

IN, which were designed by major architects of the twentieth century. Most sales are on site, but mail order sales are possible if slides of specific buildings are requested.

Photography: Original slides shot by independent professional photographer.

Documentation: No catalog. Slides labeled with name of architect, architect's dates, building name, and dates of construction.

Purchasing: Slides sold singly or in sets. Please inquire in writing or by telephone.

042 Cosanti Foundation

6433 E. Doubletree Rd.
Scottsdale, AZ 85253
Telephone: (602) 948-6145
Attn: Ivan Pintar

Profile: Six sets of duplicate color slides offered of the work of Paolo Soleri: Arcosanti, Cosanti, and Arcology projects. Objects owned and exhibited by the Cosanti Foundation featured.

Photography: Original slides shot by Ivan Pintar on Kodachrome ASA 25.

Production: Originals duplicated by a Kodak laboratory, Los Angeles. Mounted in cardboard.

Documentation: Free brochure. Slides labeled. Orientation not marked. Twelve-minute audiocassette included with "Two Suns Arcology" set. Set also accompanied by printed transcript and booklet.

Purchasing: Slides sold singly or in sets. No minimum order. Sets of 36 slides priced $36.00. Single slides $1.00 each. Larger set of 80 slides, "Soleri: Two Suns Arcology," priced $100.00. Postage added. Make checks payable to Ivan Pintar. Purchase orders accepted from institutions. Duplicates kept in stock and mailed within two weeks. Rush orders accepted. Slides sent on approval; returns accepted for exchange.

Rental: "Two Suns Arcology" set loaned for one week, $20 prepaid or $25 C.O.D. rush.

Evaluation: Reprinted from 6th ed. Quality variable, including some very good slides; documentation, 3; service, 3. Focus problems related to depth of field noted on slides of models. Some drawings tinted overall blue or green.

043 Creative Concepts of California

P.O. Box 649
Carlsbad, CA 92008-9998
Telephone: (619) 273-2555
FAX: (619) 270-6138
Attn: Robert L. Goddard
E-mail: slidesets@aol.com
URL: http://simpworld.com/creative

Profile: Creative Concepts started in 1969 and has now been in business for 28 years.

Photography: Robert L. Goddard travels throughout the world and takes all the photos of architecture on slide film. The originals are on 35mm film. The slide sets are duped from the original slides using Fuji film, with the dupes mounted in plastic mounts. Duplication may switch back to Kodak film depending on price.

Documentation: Catalog sent to mailing once each year.

Purchasing: Slide sets are offered in units of 5, 10, 15, 20, 25, 30, and 40 slides per set at $3.00 for each slide in the set, with 20% discount when purchasing 100 or more slides. Purchase orders or checks accepted with order. Orders from outside the United States must be prepaid before shipping.

Expansion Plans: More travel to Thailand, Singapore, more temples, Eastern Europe, Egypt, and all around the U.S. next year. Mr. Goddard is considering a move into digital images in the near future.

Evaluation: Quality, 2 to 4; documentation, 2 to 3; service, 2 to 3.

044 CrisMark Slides

6802 Amethyst Ct. S.W.
Tacoma, WA 98498-6400
Telephone: (253) 589-2188
FAX: (253) 589-2350
Attn: R. Sidney Cloud
E-mail: RSIDNEYCLOUD@MSN.COM

Price Range: $3.20 to $4.00 per slide.

Profile: CrisMark Slides has 35mm slides of American architecture, with the vast majority having been taken within the last five years. The first catalog was issued in March 1996 and a second catalog was planned for March 1998. CrisMark provides images of architecture, elevations, and details for use as educational tools. The collection is being continually expanded. There are plans to offer digitized images and an online catalog.

Photography: Originals are photographed on location using tripods and various lenses with available light. Original photograph is taken on Kodachrome 64 to 200.

Production: Duplicating is done by "The Slide Company," in Seattle, WA, with film of their choice.

Documentation: Catalog is sent to mailing list. Each slide is identified with first name of building (current name, if available), city and state, architect, year, view, and detail information.

Purchasing: Slides are priced at $4.00 per slide with discounts of 5% for 25 or more slides; 10% for 50 or more; and 20% for orders of more than 100 slides. Periodic sales are offered to customers on specific slides and sets. Check or university purchase orders accepted. Slides are mailed by priority mail within two to three weeks with shipping paid by CrisMark.

Evaluation: Quality, 2 to 4; documentation, 2 to 4. (Evaluation of samples.)

045 Crystal Productions

1812 Johns Dr., P.O. Box 2159
Glenview, IL 60025
Telephone: (800) 255-8629 (Outside United States and Canada 1-708-657-8144)
FAX: (800) 657-8149 (Outside United States and Canada 1-708-657-8149)
E-mail: custserv@crystalproductions.com
URL: http://www.crystalproductions.com

This vendor also provides digital products and is listed in the digital section of the directory.

Profile: Information from catalog and web page. Company sells CD-ROMs, videodiscs, videotapes, posters, art prints (Shorewood Prints and New York Graphic Society Prints), books, games, filmstrips, and slide sets, including sets from the American Craft Council. Selected CD-ROM titles include *History Through Art, The Hermitage, Exploring Modern Art* (Tate Gallery), *Microsoft Art Gallery* (National Gallery, London), *Renaissance, Impressionism, The Ultimate Frank Lloyd Wright, American Visions: 20th Century Art from the Roy R. Neuberger Collection, Survey of Western Art,* and *The Electronic Library of*

Art: European and American Art. The company also sells timelines and color wheels. Topics include art, art history, architecture, and multicultural series. Products are suitable for elementary to college-age audiences with intended audience noted in catalog.

Documentation: Catalog available on request and sent to mailing list annually. Format and hardware requirements are noted in catalog. Most CD-ROMs listed in recent catalog are available in both Windows and MAC formats.

Purchasing: Purchase orders, credit cards, and checks are accepted. All payments must be in U.S. funds. Material can be returned within 30 days if not satisfactory. Preview period of 30 days on all products except books and CD-ROMs. Preview requests should be made on institutional letterhead or purchase order. Shipping charges additional (7% of total or minimum of $3.50). Order shipped within 7 to 10 days of receipt of order. Rush shipping available for additional charge.

046   The Cultural Landscape

Slide Images for Teaching and Publication
121 Applewood Ln.
Spartanburg, SC 29307
Telephone: (864) 597-4599
Attn: Peter L. Schmunk

Profile: Slides photographed by a professional art historian with the aim of providing vivid cultural documentation for teaching and publication. Focusing on significant works of architecture and urban design in Europe and North America, individual images depict subjects ranging from full buildings in their urban context to structural techniques and column and molding details.

Production: Duplicate slides, made directly from the original transparencies, are available individually or in sets.

Documentation: Catalog available upon request.

*047   Davis Art Slides

(formerly Rosenthal Art Slides, also U.S. and Canadian distributor for Scala)
50 Portland St.
Worcester, MA 01608
Telephone: (800) 533-2847
FAX: (508) 831-9260

Attn: Karl Cole, Curator or Helen Ronan, Editorial Director
E-mail: rb-davis@ma.ultranet.com or davispub@aol.com
URL: http://www.davis-art.com

Profile: Founded late 1940s by Julius Rosenthal, run by John Rosenthal from 1960s to 1995. Became a division of Davis Publications in 1995. The collection covers from prehistoric to contemporary (1990s) in all art forms. Collection of more than 40,000 slides. U.S. and Canadian distributor for Scala Slide Books (sets).

Photography: The original photography is a combination of that done by art historians and photographers on-site (architecture) and original photography provided by museums.

Production: Ektachrome E6 duplicating film.

Documentation: A catalog is available. Slides are completely labeled. Brochures of Scala Slide sets are mailed to mailing list or on request. Detailed listing of contents of sets available on request.

Purchasing: Individual slides are priced as follows depending on quantity ordered: 1-24 slides, $3.25 each; 25-49 slides, $3.00 each; 50-299 slides, $2.75 each; and 300-999 slides, $2.50 each. Prices are in U.S. currency and are subject to change without notice. Prepayment is preferred by P.O., check, or charge card. Orders are processed within a week of receipt; only foreign orders are charged for shipping except that domestic shipping is charged to the customer if special (overnight or second day) delivery is requested.

Evaluation: Quality, 3 to 4; documentation, 3 to 4; service, 3 to 4. (Ratings of Rosenthal images.)

048   DeMarco, Nicholas

9 Vassar Lake Dr.
Poughkeepsie, NY 12603
Telephone: (914) 437-7000
E-mail: DeMarco@Vassar.edu

Profile: Entry reprinted from 6th edition at request of image provider. Duplicate color slides offered of originals shot by slide curator while traveling in Europe, covering architecture, sculpture, and painting from ancient Greek and Roman to modern. Many views available of sculpture in the Pergamon Museum, East Berlin. Some works in the Kunsthistorisches Museum, Vienna, documented. Architecture in Chicago and Minneapolis also offered. Slides available of Versailles exteriors and gardens, including fountains photographed while turned on. New slides continually added.

Photography: Original slides shot by N. DeMarco with Nikon camera, using 55mm and 50mm lenses and occasionally a 26mm wide-angle lens. Films used include Kodachrome ASA 25 and 64 and Ektachrome ASA 400 and 160 tungsten.

Production: Duplicated by Kodak laboratory at Fair Lawn, New Jersey.

Documentation: Computer-generated list available of subjects covered. Views of architecture not specifically described.

Purchasing: Groups of original slides sent on approval for selection of desired views. Orders usually filled within two weeks.

Evaluation: Reprinted from 6th ed. Quality variable, including some excellent slides. Documentation sketchy. Quality, 3; documentation, 3; service, 3. (Evaluation by a single committee member.)

049   DeMartini Associates

414 Fourth Ave.
Haddon Heights, NJ 08035
Telephone: (609) 547-2800
Attn: Alfred DeMartini
E-mail: unavoce@aol.com but prefers mail

Profile: Audiovisual programs, chiefly sound film-strips, produced for secondary and college levels. 100,000 color slide titles offered. "Silkscreen" set available in slide format for $695, illustrating works by 100 artists whose prints are in the collection of the Philadelphia Museum of Art (960 frames). Other works in the Philadelphia Museum of Art and other museums and galleries also represented in archives Approximately 1,000 new slide titles added annually.

Photography: Slides and Ektacolor negatives shot by A. DeMartini and a staff photographer using Nikon equipment.

Production: Copies made by VI-TECH laboratory in Camden, New Jersey, and Kodak in Rockville, Maryland. Color-corrected and contrast-controlled. Mounted in cardboard or plastic.

Documentation: Free brochures. No catalog available. Slides keyed to identification lists. Artist name, nationality, and dates given, plus title of work. Orientation not marked. "Silkscreen" set accompanied by teacher's manual, with brief commentary for most frames.

Purchasing: Slides sold singly. Quotations made for quantity purchases. Minimum order $25. Some slides kept in stock, but duplicates usually made to order and shipped within five days to two weeks. No returns accepted.

Other Products: Transferring filmstrips to videotapes.

050   Dick Blick Co.

P.O. Box 1267
Galesburg, IL 61501
Telephone: (800) 447-8192 (orders only)
or (800) 723-2787 (customer service)
FAX: (800) 621-8293
E-mail: info@dickblick.com
URL: http://www.dickblick.com

This vendor also sells digital products and is listed in the digital section of the directory.

Profile: Company sells CD-ROMs, videotapes, and art and educational supplies. Offers more than 200 slide sets. Art and architecture covered from prehistory to the present. Several sets offered that are coordinated with textbooks. Very large survey set also available, 800 slides for $1,049.90. Selected CD-ROM titles include *Van Gogh, Michelangelo, Leonardo* and *History Through Art Series* (nine CD-ROMs).

Production: Most sets produced by Universal Color Slides (90%, according to Universal).

Documentation: Slide sets listed in general catalog ($3.00). New catalog issued annually. Identification of individual slides not provided in catalog, but slides themselves are labeled.

Purchasing: Order form included in catalog. Slides sold in sets only, ranging in size from 10 slides to 800 slides. Quantity discounts figured into price structure, with per-slide cost about $2.00 in small sets. Postage added (10% on prepaid orders). Special prices quoted for very large orders. Minimum charge card order $10.00. Prepayment required except from institutions or companies with Dun & Bradstreet rating. Credit card charges accepted. Slides kept in stock and shipped within two to three weeks, usually via UPS. Rush orders filled within one week; no surcharge. Returns accepted for refund within 10 days. "All sales guaranteed."

Digital Products: CD-ROMs on individual artists (Van Gogh, Michelangelo, da Vinci) and History Through Art series (nine CD-ROMs). The individual artist CD-ROMs are priced at $49.95 each, and the price of each CD-ROM in the History Through Art series is $75.00; the entire set can be purchased for $600.00. All prices are in U.S. dollars.

Other Sources: Mail orders should be sent to the nearest office. Besides the central office listed above, orders may be addressed to one of the following:

Dick Blick East
P.O. Box 26
Allentown, PA 18105
Telephone:
(215) 965-6051
FAX: (215) 965-4026

Dick Blick West
P.O. Box 521
Henderson, NV 89015
Telephone:
(702) 451-7662
FAX: (702) 451-8196

Also, retail stores located in 10 U.S. cities.
Other Products: Videotapes.
Evaluation: See Universal Color slides **(095)**.

051   Digital Arts & Sciences
See under Digital Section

052   Dupuy Art Images

385 Knowlton St.
Stratford, CT 06615
Telephone: (888) 413-8789 (toll-free) or
(203) 380-1943
FAX: (203) 380-1125
Attn: Pierre Dupuy
E-mail: dupuy@sprintmail.com
URL: dupuy-artimages.com

Profile: Distributor of art-related slides, CD-ROMs, videos and, books for art education. These products are produced by foreign and domestic companies. Dupuy is now the exclusive distributor in the USA and Canada for slides produced by Visual Publications in England. Dupuy is also liquidating Sandak's remaining inventory of Scala slide sets and art books, and some individual slides, while supplies last. Catalog available upon request or visit the website.

053   Educational Resource

McGraw-Hill Book Co.
P.O. Box 408
Hightstown, NJ 08520
Telephone: (800) 843-8855

Profile: Entry reprinted from 6th ed. Formerly known as Educational Dimensions Group. Educational filmstrip company in business for more than 20 years, oriented toward high school and college audiences.

Promised catalog was never received by editor. Archive of 300,000 color slides available, "mostly outtakes shot for our filmstrips." Sets of slides packaged in carousels. Individual slides sold as "stock photos" for reproduction. Art and architecture covered among other subjects. Techniques, art appreciation, and art historical survey emphasized. Works in New York museums and galleries represented. New titles continually added.

Photography: Originals (slides and some large-format transparencies) shot by staff photographers on Kodachrome and Ektachrome using Nikon equipment.

Production: Duplicates on Kodachrome ASA 25 with Bowens Illumitran. Color-corrected and contrast-controlled. Packaged in carousels or sleeves.

Documentation: Mailing list kept. Free catalog of filmstrips issued annually; slide sets included. Sets accompanied by teacher's guides and sometimes by audiocassettes. Some slides labeled, others keyed to booklet. Orientation not routinely marked but may be requested on stock photo orders.

Purchasing: Toll-free number available for placing orders; order form included in catalog. Sets sent on approval to institutions for 30-day preview. Prepayment required from individuals and businesses. Shipping covered on prepaid orders or added to invoices. Twenty-slide sets $36.50. Sets in carousels approximately $1.00 per slide; two sizes offered, 160 and 320 slides (i.e., two or four carousel trays). Guarantee: "You may replace absolutely free any component of your . . . slide set if it becomes damaged or defective." Stock photo orders sold according to ASUP (American Society of Magazine Photographers) price list. Originals can be mailed out on day of request. Picture researchers invited to visit archive by appointment.

Other Products: Black-and-white prints made from slides on request.

054   Engelmann, Ted

P.O. Box 6832
Denver, CO 80206
Telephone: (303) 377-6551

Profile: Entry reprinted from 6th ed. Entry based on letter received in May, 1989; no answer to questionnaire sent subsequently. Mr. Engelmann is an educational consultant and photojournalist who has compiled an archive of images of Southeast Asia and Australia, as well as of the United States as relevant to the Vietnam War. Architectural design documented in addition to people and landscapes. More than 4,000 images of Vietnam and Thailand shot in early 1989, mostly as color slides.

Photography: Original slides shot on Ektachrome ASA 100 plus. Black-and-white negatives shot on T-MAX ASA 400.

Other Products: Videocassettes in preparation, transferred from slide programs, intended for use by secondary school teachers. Black-and-white photographic prints available.

055   European Access
See under Digital Section

056   Films for the Humanities & Sciences
See under Digital Section

057   Foundation for Latin American Anthropological Research (FLAAR)

Photo Archive of Maya Art, Architecture, and Archaeology
5 Conway Ln.
St. Louis, MO 63124
Attn: Dr. Nicholas Hellmuth, Director
http://maya-art-books.org/html/nickspage.
Html (Dr. Hellmuth's home page)
E-mail: flaar_maya@yahoo.com

Websites: http://maya-art-books.org/html/2PhotoArch.html, http://maya-archaeology.org/ and http://www.digital-photography.org/

Profile: Holdings include 40,000 images of Mayan Art in Mexico and Japan. FLAAR accepts requests only for very large orders and is willing to work with museums and universities to make images available for educational use. FLAAR does not wish to become a commercial source. Selected images and information about FLAAR can be viewed at the websites listed above. Contact Dr. Hellmuth for further information about images for education use.

058   G. K. Hall
See under Digital Section

059   Hart Slides World Wide

278 Roosevelt Way
San Francisco, CA 94114-1432
Telephone: (415) 863-8747
Attn: Neil Hart
E-mail: neilhart@aol.com

Profile: Established 1975. More than 7,000 color slide titles offered that were taken in Iran, Afghanistan, Pakistan, India, Malaysia, Thailand, Japan, Greece, Turkey, Spain, Latin America, and elsewhere "to document architectural and historical subjects, urban settlements, and the relation of public space to public life." New slides continually added.

Photography: Original slides shot by Neil Hart, architect and urban designer, on Kodachrome (and in the past occasionally on Agfachrome and Ektachrome), using a hand-held 35mm camera, natural light, and various lenses, including wide-angle and telephoto.

Production: Duplicated at Faulkner Color Lab on Ektachrome #5071. Color-corrected and contrast-controlled. Mounted in cardboard.

Documentation: Mailing list kept. Computer-generated catalog (1981), $8.00, deductible from first order. Identification consists of site, building name, view description, date, and references to subject index. For contemporary buildings, name of architect provided. Supplements issued as new slides become available. Slides keyed to catalog or supplementary lists. Orientation marked by index number at top.

Purchasing: Order form included in catalog. Slides sold singly and in sets. Sets limited to Barcelona and Gaudi. Single slides priced $4.50 each. Per slide cost in sets discounted. A discount of 10% applies to orders of more than 100 slides. Postage and handling charged at 10% to maximum of $10.00. Minimum order $50.00. Prepayment required from individuals and foreign accounts. Purchase order required from institutions. Make checks payable to Neil Hart. Slides duplicated to order and shipped within three to four weeks. Sets (only) sent on approval. Returns accepted within five days for exchange or refund. Requests considered for slides shot to order.

Evaluation: Quality, 2 to 4; documentation, 3; service, 3 to 4. (Reprinted from 6th edition: Catalog well organized and easy to use.)

060   Heaton-Sessions Inc.

222 Glade Hill Rd.
Grahamsville, NY 12740
Telephone: (914) 985-0231
FAX: (914) 985-0231
Attn: Adria Heaton-Sessions-Picard

Profile: Since 1951 Heaton-Sessions has been providing slides at low prices to Art History and Humanities Departments and individual slides to art history professors and collectors. Rex Heaton-Sessions was the original owner and professional photographer of the business. In 1979, his daughter, Adria Heaton-Sessions-Picard, took over the slide business. In 1994 Heaton-Sessions became incorporated. Edward Picard is the primary photographer and Adria Heaton-Sessions-Picard is the office manager.

Heaton-Sessions offers color slides only to accompany various History of Art textbooks and has approximately 3,000 slide titles. In 1998 the company is adding digital images and CDs for IBM-PC compatible computers.

Photography: Original photography is by Ed Picard, professional photographer, with 35mm SLR Nikon and tripod in existing conditions with interior Kodak Ektachrome tungsten 160 film and exterior Kodak Ektachrome 200 film.

Production: Original slides (known as master slides) shot with Kodak 200 professional film and tungsten 160. Duplicate slides shot with Kodak slide duplicating film with tungsten bulb and developed by using E6 chemistry. Slides are bound in cardboard, or in anti-newton ring glass and labeled individually by number in accordance with textbook.

Documentation: A catalog is available. Identification of slide by textbook identification, illustration number only. Our slides are labeled to accompany illustrations in corresponding textbooks—packed in boxes and labeled in sequence.

Purchasing: Both individual slides and sets are offered with a minimum order of 10 slides. Individual slides are priced at $2.50 each mounted in cardboard or $3.15 each mounted in glass with a 10% discount on orders over $1,000.00 total. Sets are priced from $199.60 to $1,318.65 mounted in cardboard and from $322.94 to $2,132.85 for slides mounted in glass. Slides are made on order only. Orders must be prepaid or purchase order number included. Shipping and packing charges for sets only are 8% of list price for glass; 7% of list price for cardboard. Shipping and packing charges for individual slides are: up to $25.00, $6.00; $25.01 to $50.00, $8.00; $50.01 to $100.00, $10.00. More than $100.00, add 10% to the order. Orders from foreign countries must include all shipping instructions and check for 100% of catalog price in U.S. dollars. The cost of shipping plus 5% of catalog price will be added to invoice for packing. Allow three to four weeks for shipment after receipt of payment. Rush orders filled within one to two weeks depending on size of orders.

Expansion Plans: Plan to join World Wide Web in 1999.

Evaluation: Quality, 1 to 2; documentation, 1 to 2; service, 2.

061   Hedrich-Blessing Photography

11 W. Illinois St.
Chicago, IL 60607
Telephone: (312) 321-1151
FAX: (312) 321-1165
Attn: Michael Houlahan or Bob Shimer
E-mail: hedrich@hedrich-blessing.com
URL: http://www.hedrich-blessing.com/

This image provider also provides digital products and is listed in the digital section of the directory.

Profile: Hedrich-Blessing specializes in architectural and interior design photography, so the images are limited to that area. All the material that is sold is created from assignments that were completed for clients. Images are sold individually.

062 Image Directory
See under Digital Section

063 Insight Media
See under Digital Section

064 Instructional Resources Corporation
See under Digital Section

065 Islamic Perspectives

42 Monument St.
West Medford, MA 02155
Telephone: (617) 354-1229
Attn: Kendall Dudley

Profile: Reprinted from 6th ed. Approximately 7,000 color slide titles offered of Islamic architecture, cities, villages, and aspects of daily life. Iran, Turkey, India, and Spain featured in current holdings. A few museum objects represented. New titles added occasionally.

Photography: Original slides shot by K. Dudley (70%) and independent professionals (30%). Kodachrome used for 90% of originals; remainder shot on Agfachrome ASA 125. Nikon cameras used with variety of lenses. Tripod used wherever possible and necessary. Flash used where permitted. Vast majority of slides and black-and-white negatives were taken with available light.

Production: Duplicated by Kodak at Rochester or Fair Lawn, depending on client's preference. No color-correction or contrast-control attempted. Mounted in cardboard.

Documentation: Mailing list kept. Free catalog of sites and sets, including price list. Comprehensive catalog listing all slides $6.00, deductible from first order. Catalog revised as necessary. Slides keyed to catalog. Orientation marked only as necessary.

Purchasing: Slides sold singly or in sets. Single slides $2.95 each. Per-slide cost in sets approximately $1.75. Special prices quoted on large orders

of single slides and on combinations of sets. Postage added. Minimum order five slides. Duplicated to order and shipped within two weeks. Rush orders filled in two days (local laboratory) or one week (Kodak); possible surcharge on small orders. Prepayment requested on large orders: 50% on U.S. orders, 100% from overseas customers. Sample slides sent on request, but slides duplicated to orders not sent on approval. Returns accepted for exchange "if slide is defective or poorly exposed." Requests considered for slides shot to order. Also, documentation of New England architecture arranged at hourly rate of $60.00, "total cost subject to negotiation."

Other Products: Black-and-white prints also supplied.

Evaluation: Quality, 3; documentation, 3 to 4; service, 4. (Evaluation by a single committee member.)

*066 Jacoby, Trudy (formerly Trinity College Slide Exchange)

Trinity College, Hallden Hall
300 Summit St.
Hartford, CT 16106-3100
Telephone: (860) 297-2194
FAX: (860) 297-5349
Attn: Trudy Jacoby
E-mail: Trudy.Jacoby@Trincoll.edu

Profile: Trudy Jacoby has been photographing architecture and works of art for more than 15 years for the Trinity College Slide Collection, sales, and lectures. Slides are shot with Nikon equipment including perspective control lenses, mostly on Kodachrome slide film. Slides have been sold for more than 10 years, and a catalog of monuments is being completed. Several thousand slides are offered of buildings in the United States, Germany, the Netherlands, and other countries. While the concentration is on architecture, there is also coverage of works of art and gardens. The purchaser may request slides by building. A group of original slides is sent on, and the purchaser then makes their own duplicates. Will permit digitization on limited basis.

Photography: Slides are photographed on site with Nikon equipment, mostly using Kodachrome slide film. Perspective correction lenses are used. Museum photography is done with available light.

Production: The purchaser is responsible for the duplication of the original slides. Thus they have the choice of duplicating process and film. In addition to Kodachrome 64, some slides, particularly interiors, have been photographed on Kodachrome 200 or Ektachrome film. Fujichrome is also used.

Documentation: Information is sent on request. Updated list created in August 1998. Full documentation is supplied with slides (creator, location, title, repository, date, view, etc.).

Purchasing: Individual slides are priced at $1.50 usage fee per image duplicated (in addition to purchaser's duplicating cost). Purchase order required from institutions. Shipping added to duplication fees. Original slides expected back within one month. Approval plans available; catalog in preparation.

Digital Products: Will negotiate fees for digitization. Digitizing is allowed only for limited campus use, and appropriate copyright notice must be given.

Textbooks: Not yet available. Plan to compile lists illustrating *Gardner's Art Through the Ages.*

Evaluation: Quality, 3 to 4; documentation, 4; service, 4.

dates, location, name, artist, architect, if known, etc. Slide lecture series for Ibero-American Architectural History available that provides texts and two semesters of lectures keyed to slides.

Purchasing: Both individual slides and sets are available with prices ranging from $5.00 to $10.00 depending on how many are ordered. Always willing to discuss discounts for large orders. All slides are custom made per order. Prefer one-half of total order price before processing and one-half on delivery. Thirty-day accounts less likely to be offered discounted price. No interest in accounts requiring more than 30 days for settlement.

Rental: No rental, but willing to consider requests from Ph.D. candidates.

Expansion Plans: Series of CD-based illustrated lectures and readings.

Evaluation: Quality, 3; documentation, 2; service, 2. (Evaluation by a single committee member.)

067   Jericho World Images (Inter-American Institute)

P.O. Box 93
Free Union, VA 22940-0093
Telephone: (804) 973-6253
Attn: Dr. James B. Kiracofe

Price Range: $5.00 to $10.00 per slide depending on quantity.

Profile: Dr. James B. Kiracofe began archive of images while a graduate student in Architecture; History of Mexico, but the archive has grown over time to include a wider scope. Currently includes more than 20,000 images, mostly related to Latin America, Art and Architectural History, with a special focus on cultural transmission through arts of late medieval and early Renaissance Europe into late post-classic Mesoamerica. While at Virginia Tech, Dr. Kiracofe developed a prototype for an interactive CD database for Latin American Studies.

Photography: Dr. Kiracofe is principal photographer and uses a Nikon 35mm cameras and Nikon lenses with mostly Fujichrome film ASA 50 and ASA 100, but uses faster films when required for interiors. Natural light is used with no manipulation by filtration, and a tripod is used where needed.

Production: Original 35mm slide duped by Professional Labs in Charlottesville, VA. Other formats are possible by request.

Documentation: Catalog available. All slides are numbered with catalog number. Catalog gives

068   Johnson Architectural Images

2877 Glacier Valley Rd.
Madison, WI 53711
Telephone: (608) 278-0934 or
(888) 800-7942, x7970
FAX: (608) 278-1574
Attn: Don Johnson
E-mail: jai@jfam.com

Profile: Reprinted entry from 6th ed. More than 1,800 color slide titles offered in 46 sets of architecture from Roman times to the present. Work of several individual architects featured: Thomas Jefferson, Robert Maillart, Pier Luigi Nervi, Fillippo Brunelleschi, V. Horta, H. P. Berlage, and Willem M. Dudok. Large set on Chicago architecture available. New slide sets occasionally added.

Photography: Slides shot by Don Johnson using Nikon camera, perspective-correcting lens, zoom lens, and tripod. Kodachrome ASA 25 and 64 used in available light. Most shots composed in horizontal format because Mr. Johnson believes that is the preference of most of his customers. Tall buildings in urban areas may be cropped.

Production: Duplicated on Ektachrome #5071 or #5038 in a California laboratory. Color-corrected, contrast-controlled "when possible." Mounted in cardboard or plastic.

Documentation: Mailing list kept. Free catalog, revised annually. Selection of available sets described in catalog. Slides keyed to identification list accompanying set. Orientation marked by label position.

Purchasing: Slides sold in sets, which by request will be sent on approval for a 21-day review period. Sets may no longer be broken, but singles can be duplicated to order from list compiled by customer while previewing set. Single slides priced $3.50 each. Per-slide cost discounted in sets; no further discounts offered. Orders mailed to schools within the United States sent postpaid. Postage added at 3% on Canadian and overseas orders ($5.00 minimum). Prepayment required from individuals. Sets kept in stock and shipped within one to two days. If customer dissatisfied, return of part or all of order accepted for exchange or refund.

Evaluation: Quality, 2; documentation, 2; service, 3. (Evaluation by a single committee member.)

069 Kautsch, Capt. Thomas N.
The Master's Tripod
955 Alla Ave.
Concord, CA 94518-3010
Telephone: (415) 682-8738
E-mail: tripodm@aol.com

Profile: Some information reprinted from 6th ed. Continuation of slide sales confirmed. More than 20,000 color slide titles offered of architecture, emphasizing cities, ruins, and temples. The countries documented include Burma, Cambodia, Egypt, India, Italy, Japan, Sri Lanka, Taiwan, Thailand, and Petra. Angkor Wat covered extensively. Objects in New York's Metropolitan Museum of Art represented. New titles continually added.

Photography: Original slides shot by Captain Kautsch on Kodachrome. Negatives also shot, on Kodacolor ASA 64 and Plus-X. Tripod used for most photography.

Production: Copies made commercially in several laboratories. Film type unknown but not Eastmancolor. Mounted in cardboard.

Documentation: Mailing list kept. Free single sheet listing sites. Slides keyed to information provided. Orientation marked.

Purchasing: Slides sold singly. Some are originals. No minimum order. "Market price." Duplicates made to order and shipped within one week.

Slides sometimes sent on approval. Returns accepted for exchange only.

Other Products: Photographic prints may also be ordered.

070 The Lace Merchant
P.O. Box 222
Plainwell, MI 49080
Telephone: (616) 685-9792
Attn: Elizabeth Kurella
E-mail: ekurella@accn.org
URL: http://www.tias.com/stores/lace/

Profile: Some information reprinted from 6th ed. Several hundred slide titles offered of antique lace and whitework embroidery. Approximately 10% of holdings are black-and-white. New slides continually added. Slide programs (larger sets: 50 to 70 slides each) include "Analyzing Lace," "Evaluating Lace," and "Lace in Victorian Times." Further coverage planned of lace in fashion.

Photography: Original slides shot by Elizabeth Kurella, a lace collector and dealer (80%), and independent professional photographers (20%), using various extenders and micro lenses. 95% of originals shot on Kodak Ektachrome EPY ASA 50. Coins included in some views to provide scale.

Production: Duplicated on Ektachrome #5071 by Allied Labs, Grand Rapids, MI. Contrast-controlled. Mounted in plastic and sleeved for shipment.

Documentation: See website. Printed script provided with slide sets. Slides also labeled. Orientation marked only when necessary.

Purchasing: Slides sold singly and in sets. Sets are $125, $135, and $150. Minimum order $10. Order form included on website. Postage added. Payment in U.S. dollars requested. VISA and MasterCard charges accepted. Slides sent on approval. Rush orders accommodated.

Other Products: Conversion of slide sets to videotapes is planned.

Evaluation: Reprinted from 6th ed. No samples available, but tipped-in color reproductions in catalog indicate good quality. Well-designed catalog contains information about individual slides. No information available about documentation accompanying slides or about service.

071 Landslides

35 Richdale Ave.
Cambridge, MA 02149
Telephone: (617) 497-9400
FAX: (617) 491-9116
Attn: Alex S. MacLean
E-mail: maclean@tiac.net

Profile: Description reprinted from 6th ed. Company founded 1975. Archive accumulated of 140,000 original color slides of aerial views of sites in the United States. Duplicate slides of urban and rural subjects offered, useful for teaching about architecture, urban planning, land use, environmental issues, geology, and so forth. Sites and cities from 40 states represented. Approximately 10,000 slides added annually to archives. New sets offered periodically.

Photography: 98% of original slides shot by Alex MacLean on Kodachrome ASA 64 from either fixed-wing planes or helicopters using Nikon and Canon 35-mm equipment and a Kenyon KS4 Gyro Stabilizer. Pre-1975 slides shot on Agfachrome.

Production: Duplicated in-house on Ektachrome #5071; E6 processed at Boris Master Color, Boston, MA. Color-corrected and contrast-controlled. Mounted in plastic.

Documentation: Mailing list kept. Computer-generated catalog available in several volumes, $5.00 each. Slides labeled with brief information and also keyed to list and/or catalog.

Purchasing: Slides sold singly or in sets. Prices for educational institutions $3.00 per slide in sets, $5.00 per single slide. Minimum order $25.00. Some slides kept in stock; if necessary, slides duplicated to order. Shipped within three to four weeks. Rush orders filled within two days; surcharge of 100%. Slides sent on approval for five days; returns accepted for exchange if defective.

Evaluation: Quality, 4; documentation, 3; service, 3.

072 Malcolm Lubliner Photography

1822 Shasta St.
Richmond, CA 94804
Telephone: (510) 530-3100
FAX: (510) 530-3355
E-mail: mlp@cityvisions.com
URL: http://www.cityvisions.com

Photography: Slides are photographed from prints using Ektachrome E100S.

Documentation: Slide sets come with photocopies of images with titles and dates.

Purchasing: Slides are available only in sets, priced at $75.00-$105.00 per set. Prepayment or purchase order only. All funds must be in U.S. currency. No returns accepted: Please return defective slides for replacement. Orders are filled 10 days after they are received. Shipping and handling is U.S./Canada $6.50 and elsewhere $10.00.

*073 Media for the Arts (formerly Budek)

360 Thames St., Suite 2N
P.O. Box 1011
Newport, RI 02840-6631
Telephone: (800) 554-6008 or
(401) 845-9600
FAX: (401) 846-6580
Attn: Elizabeth Allen, Director
E-mail: artmfa@art-history.com
URL: http://www.art-history.com

This vendor also offers digital products and is listed in the digital section of the directory.

Profile: In the business since 1948. Company has 30,000 color slides on architecture, sculpture, painting, and archaeology. Slides are sold in sets only.

Documentation: Annual catalog sent to mailing list.

Purchasing: The price for each slide set depends upon the mount selected and the size of the slide set. The number of slides is indicated in parentheses. Standard sets average 10 slides. Super Sets, designated by catalog number ending in -4, average 40 slides. Standard sets are priced at $15.00 (cardboard mounts) and $19.00 (Gepe glass mounts), and Super Sets (-4) are priced at $59.00 (cardboard mounts) and $76.00 (Gepe glass mounts). Any other special pricing is denoted in catalog. All prices are subject to change without notice. Quantity discounts are offered. Contact vendor for details. All prices are FOB Newport, RI, 30 days NET. Please add 7% to the total of your order to cover postage/handling insurance for U.S. and Canadian shipments. There is a $6.00 minimum shipping charge. On overseas orders, please state shipping preference. Shipping and Receiving claims must be made within 10 days of receipt of order. There is a 10% surcharge for any orders needed prior to the normal 14-day ARO.

Please allow enough delivery time when ordering. Videos may take three weeks for delivery. Only firm orders are accepted for videos and CD-ROMs. They are not available for preview. There are no returns except for manufacturer's guarantee. Slide sets are available for 30-day approval privileges. Institutional purchase orders are accepted. Orders from individuals must be prepaid either by check or credit card (MasterCard and VISA accepted).

Digital Products: CD-ROMs in both Windows and MAC formats. Laserdiscs. Selected titles include: The Art Historian (Ancient to Medieval $49.95 and Renaissance to Modern $49.95); History Through Art: Series of nine titles $675.00 (individual titles $75.00 or Lab packs of five CDs $225.00); Early American History Through Art: $75.00 (Lab packs of five CDs $225.00); Art of the Western Art (Laserdisc) 10 titles 1-9: $100.00 each.

Other Products: VHS videotapes.

Evaluation: Quality, 1 to 3; documentation, 1 to 3; service, 2 to 3.

074   Media Loft, Inc.

10720 40th Ave. N.
Minneapolis, MN 55441
Telephone: (612) 375-1086

Profile: Entry reprinted from 6th ed. More than 1,700 color slide titles in 21 sets offered of photo communications: art, documentary photography, photojournalism, commercial photography, and illustration. Works of an individual photographer featured in some sets. Photographic techniques documented in other sets. New titles continually added.

Photography: Slides shot by more than 50 different photographers on various films.

Production: Copies made by Allied Lab, Chicago, or Color Film Corporation. "In many cases we do our own master set from the original and another laboratory does the duplications from our master." Color-corrected and contrast-controlled. Mounted in plastic or cardboard. Packaged in carousels, oriented correctly.

Documentation: Free catalog issued annually. The series was conceived and produced by R. Smith Schuneman, B.F.A., M.F.A., Ph.D. Audiocassette (18-30 minutes) included with each set. Printed information provided as well (biographies, and so on).

Purchasing: Slides sold in sets only, consisting of 80 to 120 slides. Minimum order one set. Eighty-slide sets priced $125.00 each. Postage included for United States orders; from Canada, add $5.00. Discount of 5% given on orders more than $400.00, 10% on orders more than $600.00. Payment accepted in U.S. currency only, by way of check, money order, or credit card. Purchase order with 30-day term also accepted. Prepayment required from new individual customers unaffiliated with a college and from any customer who has previously been delinquent in paying. Copies kept in stock and shipped within two weeks. Rush orders filled next day if possible; no surcharge. Slides sent on two-week approval; returns accepted for exchange or refund.

Evaluation: Quality, 2 to 3; documentation, 3; service, 3. (Evaluation by a single committee member.)

075   Michel Studio, Inc.

2710 Oxford Rd.
Lawrence, KS 66044
Telephone: (913) 842-4664
Attn: Lou Michel

Profile: Entry reprinted from 6th ed. More than 5,000 duplicate color slide titles offered of architecture and sculpture in Europe, North Africa, and the United States, from ancient through modern times, including images appropriate for urban studies. Company founded 1964 by Lou Michel, Professor of Architecture at the University of Kansas. New titles continually added. Archive of approximately 22,000 slides accumulated that are not listed in catalogs.

Photography: Original slides shot on Kodachrome ASA 64 by Lou Michel using Nikon equipment on a tripod. About 2% of holdings shot on Ektachrome ASA 100. Slides shot under ideal natural lighting whenever possible. Perspective-correcting and telephoto lenses used when appropriate.

Production: Duplicated on Ektachrome #5071 by Custom Color Corporation, Kansas City, Missouri. Color-corrected and contrast-controlled. Flashing technique used to prevent loss of detail in shadow areas of high-contrast slides. Mounted in plastic.

Documentation: Mailing list kept. Three-volume catalog available for $4.00 per volume. Full identifications given. Slides listed in sequence to approximate experience of walking through a space. Supplements to catalog issued approximately every three years. Slides keyed to catalog. Orientation marked.

Purchasing: Slides sold singly, $2.50 each. Minimum order 10 slides. Discount of 10% given on purchase of more than 100 slides if invoice paid within 30 days. Shipping charges added. Prepaid orders sent postpaid. Prepayment required from individuals. Slides duplicated to order and sent within two weeks. No rush orders accepted. Orders sent on approval for 30-day review period. Returns accepted for refund (institutions only) or exchange. Requests considered for slides shot to order; travel and expenses to be covered by client.

Evaluation: Reprinted from 6th ed. Quality, 3 to 4; documentation, 3; service, 3 to 4.

*076   Mini-Aids

Mini-Aids ceased business as of December 31, 1998. Contact Ancient World Slides/Canyon Lights **(023)** for some images previously distributed by Mini-Aids.

077   Miranda, Dan

P.O. Box 145
Brookline, MA 02146
Telephone: (617) 739-1306

Profile: Antique picture postcards (1890–1930) in the personal collection of Dan Miranda reproduced as slide sets. Subjects include "Anti-Semitic Picture Postcards, 1890–1920"; "Black Stereotypes, 1900–1920"; "Stereotypes of Women, 1890–1930"; and "Boston, 1900–1920." In all, more than 850 color slide titles offered in seven sets.

Photography: Slides shot on copystand with photo floods by Dan Miranda using Ektachrome tungsten ASA 50 professional film #5018. Processed by a commercial laboratory.

Production: Most slides sold are originals. Occasionally duplicated on Ektachrome #5071 by Subtractive Technology, Boston. Color-corrected and contrast-controlled. Mounted in plastic.

Documentation: Mailing list kept. Free brochure describing sets. Slides keyed to "full descriptive information" supplied with each set. Orientation marked by copyright name and date at top on front side.

Purchasing: Slides sold in sets only. Most are originals, 2% duplicates. Slides kept in stock and shipped within three days. Priced from $1.11 to $2.60 per slide, with the majority $1.60. Prepayment required. Quantity discounts. Shipping, handling, and insurance included in prices. Rush orders filled in three days; no surcharge. Slides made to order within three days. Sample slides (only) sent on approval. No exchanges or refunds permitted.

Evaluation: Reprinted from 6th ed. Quality, 4; based on two samples submitted in 1984: good color and sharpness; lighting uneven, noticeable mainly in background framing the postcard.

*078   Moorhead/Schmidt Slide Collection

1842 Marshall St.
Houston, TX 77098
Telephone: (713) 529-6905
FAX: (713) 529-6905
Attn: Gerald Moorhead

Price Range: $2.50/slide (1 Dec 1997).

Profile: Moorhead and Schmidt are practicing architects who have provided photography of architectural subjects for professional education since 1970. Approximately 20,000 images are available of architectural subjects from all periods, Egyptian to Modern, including gardens and cityscapes.

Photography: Originals are photographed by a semiprofessional photographer using Nikon/Leica Contac equipment with PC lens, and Kodachrome 64 and Fuji Velvia film.

Production: Duplicates made on Ektachrome #5071 film can be ordered from the company. Full payment is expected upon receipt of slides. Orders must be accompanied by purchase order. Orders usually filled within two weeks. Shipping cost (Federal Express or UPS) added. Duplicates can also be made by the purchaser from originals owned by the vendor with payment of a one-time-use fee per slide. Purchaser pays use fee only for slides duplicated. Orders can also be filled with preselected sets from catalog.

Documentation: Catalog is sent to mailing list or on request. Slide documentation includes building name, location, date, and architect. Duplicate slides ordered from company are in plastic mounts with typed labels.

Expansion Plans: Usually one major study trip per year (Greece in 1998).

Evaluation: Quality, (1) 3 to 4; documentation, 2 to 4; service, 2 to 4. (All but one evaluator rated quality at 3 to 4.)

079 Murvin, H. L., AIA

Architectural Books, Slides & Seminars
500 Vernon St.
Oakland, CA 94610
Telephone: (510) 658-7517
Attn: Hank Murvin

Profile: Entry reprinted from 6th edition at request of the image provider. Approximately 5,000 duplicate color slide titles offered of Pre-Columbian architecture, architecture in Europe and the Americas, indigenous architecture, and markets and people. Forty-eight Pre-Columbian sites in Mesoamerica represented, 37 in South America, 23 in North America. Twenty-two sets available of European architecture, Greek to modern, and another 22 sets of architecture in North and South America. New titles continually added. Some 2,000 items available that are not listed in catalog. Five hundred new slides of postmodern architecture added in 1989.

Photography: Original slides shot by H. L. Murvin on Kodachrome ASA 64. Tripod used.

Production: Duplicated from originals at the Kodak laboratory in Palo Alto, California. Color-corrected and contrast-controlled.

Documentation: Mailing list kept. Catalog (second edition) $3.95, deductible from first order. Supplements issued annually. Full information provided in catalog. Slides not labeled but keyed to catalog. Orientation marked by number placement (upper left corner).

Purchasing: Slides sold singly or in sets. Minimum order 50 slides. Per-slide cost to institutions $2.45 in sets, $2.95 as single slides. Per-slide cost to individuals or private firms $5.00. Postage added. Purchase orders required from institutions, prepayment from individuals and companies. Slides duplicated to order and shipped within three weeks. Rush orders filled within 10 days; 15% surcharge. Returns accepted for exchange only; no refunds. Slides sent on approval upon special arrangement; shipping and insurance costs paid by institution. Mr. Murvin visits seven to ten major metropolitan areas each year to allow customers to view his slides by appointment.

Other Products: Transparencies sold of forms and documents for architectural education (AIA documents and others).

Evaluation: Reprinted from 6th ed. Forty samples sent, mostly of Pre-Columbian architecture and sculpture: quality, 3 to 4. Many excellent details included. A few slides among them were high in contrast, and one was overexposed. Four samples of miscellaneous other architecture were less sharp and the colors less vibrant. One evaluator who had purchased slides in 1987 rated this vendor 2 on quality, 2 on documentation, and 2 on service.

080 National Archives and Records Administration

General Services Administration
5825 Port Royal Rd.
Springfield, VA 22161
Telephone: (703) 487-4650
Attn: National Technical Information Service
URL: http://www.nara.gov/nara/nail.html

Note: NARA Archival Information Locator database at website.

Profile: Sells slide sets only. Sets include "Pictures of the American City," "Pictures of the Harmon Foundation Artwork and Art Activities," "Pictures of Contemporary African Art from the Harmon Foundation," and "Pictures of Indians in the United States."

Purchasing: Slide sets average less than $.50 per slide. Check, money order, or charge card accepted.

081 Pictures of Record, Inc.

119 Kettle Creek Rd.
Weston, CT 06883
Telephone: (203) 227-3387
FAX: (203) 222-9673
Attn: Nancy Hammerslough, President
E-mail: por@webquill.com
URL: http://www.picturesofrecord.com/

Profile: Pictures of Record, Inc. publishes slide sets of archaeological sites and artifacts, techniques of archaeology, and ethnographic subjects, as well as reproductions of stone tools. In most cases, Pictures of Record slide sets are the only slides available for study of a site, culture, or archaeological technique.

Two Mesoamerican surveys available. Sets also offered in the following series: North American, Mexican, Maya, South American, Near East, and Aegean. One exhibition at the Metropolitan Museum of Art, NY, documented "Art of the Taino." Museum and private collections worldwide represented. New slides continually added.

Photography: Designed for classroom and archival use by museums and universities, these color slides are photographed, edited, and annotated in detail by professional photographers and distinguished anthropologists, archaeologists, and art historians. Most slides shot on Kodachrome ASA 64; ASA 400 film used when necessary. Tripod always used when possible. Variety of lenses and lighting techniques employed.

Production: Slides are printed on Eastmancolor print film and are packaged in 8.5" x 11" looseleaf binders for bookshelf storage.

Documentation: Documentation includes an introduction, bibliography, and extensive notes for each slide.

Purchasing: The slides and tools are sold only in sets. Sets or kits are not sent out for preview; however, if not fully satisfied, the materials may be returned in good condition within 10 days for a full refund or credit. Orders may be charged to Master-Card and VISA. Delivery may be expected within 30 days of receipt of the order. Shipping and handling charges within the contiguous United States are $5.00 per set of slides and $10.00 per tool kit. Where possible, slides are shipped by UPS and need a street address or university building, not a box number. Orders to Puerto Rico, Alaska, and Hawaii will be billed at actual shipping and handling costs. For orders of three or more sets, deduct 10% of the subtotal. Foreign Orders: *Canada and Mexico.* The cost of shipping and handling will be added to the bill.

If a credit card is not used, payment must be made in U.S. funds, payable through a U.S. bank. *All other countries.* Unless a credit card is used, payment in U.S. funds, payable through a U.S. bank, is required in advance. When the order is placed, indicate choice of shipping, e.g., surface mail, air parcel post, UPS where available, etc. To reduce shipping weight, sets may be sent without binders. The customer can request a pro forma invoice. When ordering by E-mail, please include name, address, and telephone or fax number, as well as planned method of payment. Customer will be contacted by telephone or fax within two business days to confirm the order. Please do NOT include a credit card number.

Evaluation: Quality, 2 to 4; documentation, 1 to 4; service, 2 to 4.

082   Larry Qualls

141 Wooster St.
New York, NY 10012
Telephone: (212) 473-6695
FAX: (212) 473-6695
Attn: Larry Qualls
E-mail: lqualls-dchin@worldnet.att.net

Profile: Coverage of contemporary art and architecture, including film, video, installations, performance, architecture history, theater history.

Photography: Originals shot by various photographers. Architecture slides by John Pile, except as noted (sets by Sergey Ozhegov and Bradford Ensminger). Dr. Pile shoots exclusively on Kodachrome 25; Dr. Ozhegov uses various European films for his architecture sets. Art slides are made on the appropriate film, depending on location (indoors, outdoors, etc.).

Production: All duplicates are on Ektachrome slide duplicating film #5071 unless another film is requested.

Documentation: Available slide lists are sent quarterly, sometimes more often, to mailing list. All art slides come with complete cataloging information as supplied by artist or gallery; proprietary information is not included. All information is also included on computer disks, free of charge, if requested.

Purchasing: Individual slide price varies according to type, and set price varies with number of slides in set. University purchase orders accepted. Orders are shipped generally with 10 days of receipt. Orders are shipped only by U.S. mail, with charges added to invoice.

Evaluation: Quality, 1 to 2; documentation, 2 to 3; service, 1 to 3. (Samples rated quality, 2 to 4; documentation, 2 to 4.)

*083   Oliver Radford Architectural Slides

24 Cambridge Terrace
Cambridge, MA 02140
Telephone: (617) 547-4723
FAX: (617) 547-4724
Attn: Oliver Radford
E-mail: oradford@aol.com

Profile: More than 13,000 color slides offered of architecture in Europe, the United States, and Japan, from Greek temples to contemporary work. Slides available are mostly exterior views and details. New slides are continually added.

Photography: Original slides shot by Oliver Radford, Architect, on Kodachrome (95%) and Ektachrome (5%). Various lenses used, including telephoto, wide-angle, and perspective-correcting. All slides shot with available light only (no flash).

Production: Slides will be lent for three to four weeks to institutions for duplication by a lab of the institution's choice, at the institution's expense. If preferred, Radford will arrange for duplication by Zona labs in Cambridge, MA.

Documentation: Slides labeled with full information (except birth and death dates of architect). Names and places and buildings usually given in original languages. If originals are borrowed for duplication, it is the responsibility of the purchaser to record identifications from labels on the original slides. For all the material since 1992, identifications available in database format on diskette, upon request.

Purchasing: Slides sold singly. No minimum order. $1.75 each if duplication cost is borne by the purchaser; $3.00 each if duplicated by Radford. No prepayment or purchase order required. Payment in U.S. dollars requested. Minimum order approximately 75 slides for shipment. Rush orders accommodated to the extent possible. Slides sent on approval. Sample slide and brochures sent on request.

Other: Slides are generally available for digitization by purchaser. Each such request considered individually. Contact Radford.

Evaluation: Quality, 4; documentation, 3 to 4; service, 4. Editors' note: Recommended by several visual resources professionals at architectural institutions on the VRA listserv in 1997–1998.

084 Reindeer Company
See under Digital Section

085 Rogala Studio/Outerpretation
1524 S. Peoria
Chicago, IL 60608
Attn: Miroslaw Rogala (312) 243-2952 or
Joel Botfeld (312) 743-8735

Profile: Entry reprinted from 6th ed. No response to questionnaire. Entry based on information from the Fall 1988 "Slide Market News" column in the *VRA Bulletin*. Duplicate color slides offered by Miroslaw Rogala, a video and multimedia artist who has exhibited internationally, of his own work. "My primary accomplishments" he states, "have been video installation/performance works which incorporate synchronized multi-channel video and electronic sound with original live music, dance, performance, and slide projections. In addition, I have specialized in graphic works, painting, and laser photography."

Photography: Originals shot by independent professional photographers, including the artist.

Production: Duplicated on Ektachrome. Color-corrected and contrast-controlled.

Documentation: Sample slides fully labeled.

Purchasing: Slides sold singly and in sets.

Evaluation: Reprinted from 6th ed. Twenty samples sent in 1988: quality, 3; documentation, 3. No information available on service.

*086 Saskia, Ltd. Cultural Documentation
5 Horizon Ln.
Freeport, ME 04032
Telephone: (877) SASKIA2 or
(877) 727-5422
Attn: Renate Wiedenhoeft
E-mail: info@saskia.com
URL: http://www.saskia.com

This vendor also offers digital products and is listed in the digital section of the directory.

Profile: Approximately 20,000 color slide titles offered of art and architecture of Western Europe, dating from Ancient Greece through the early twentieth century, with emphasis on the Italian Renaissance, Italian and northern Baroque painting, and nineteenth-century French and German painting. This company has more than 30 years of experience documenting museum objects. Color slides offered as originals and some as duplicates. New slides continually added. For more than 30 years, Saskia has documented the history of Western art in Europe—working in the major repositories of France, Italy, Germany, Austria, Greece, Turkey, and Scandinavia from Ancient Greece to the beginning of the twentieth century. The company has already incorporated the most advanced technologies: digital images, interactive website browsing, online ordering and searching, and credit card purchases. Museum collections documented selectively as follows:

◆ AUSTRIA

    Gemäldegalerie der Akademie der Bildenden Künste, Vienna

    Historisches Museum (Museum der Stadt Wien), Vienna

    Kunsthistorisches Museum, Vienna

    Österreichische Galerie im Belvedere, Vienna

    Schatzkammer, Vienna

◆ BELGIUM

    Musées Royaux des Beaux-Arts de Belgique, Brussels

◆ DENMARK

    Thorvaldsen Museum, Copenhagen

◆ FINLAND

    Finnish Architecture Museum, Helsinki

◆ FRANCE

    Musée du Louvre, Paris

◆ GREECE

    Acropolis Museum, Athens

    Archaeological Museum, Delphi

    Archaeological Museum, Olympia

    National Archaeological Museum, Athens

◆ GERMANY

    Alte Pinakothek, Munich

    Germanisches Nationalmuseum, Nuremberg

    Glyptothek, Munich

    Schloss Charlottenburg, Berlin

    Staatliche Museum zu Berlin, East Berlin

    Staatsgalerie, Stuttgart

    Städelsches Kunstinstitut, Frankfurt-am-Main

    Stiftung Preussischer Kulturbesitz, Berlin (Gemäldegalerie, Kupferstichkabinett, Nationalgalerie, and Schloss Grünewald)

    Suermondt-Ludwig Museum, Aachen

    Wallraf-Richartz Museum and Museum Ludwig, Cologne

◆ HUNGARY

    Museum of Fine Arts, Budapest

◆ ITALY

    Galleria Borghese, Villa Borghese, Rome

    Galleria degli Uffizi, Florence

    Galleria dell'Accademia, Florence

    Galleria dell'Accademia, Venice

    Galleria Doria Pamphili, Rome

    Galleria Nazionale d'Arte Antica, Rome (Palazzo Barberini & Palazzo Corsini)

    Galleria Palatina, Palazzo Pitti, Florence

    Galleria Spada, Rome

    Museo Archeologico Nazionale, Naples

    Museo Campano, Capua

    Museo Capitolino, Rome

    Museo del Duomo, Florence

    Museo del Duomo, Siena

    Museo di Palazzo Venezia, Rome

    Museo e Gallerie Nazionale di Capodimonte, Naples

    Museo Nazionale del Bargello, Florence

    Palazzo Rosso, Genoa

    Pinacoteca di Brera, Milan

    Pinacoteca Nazionale, Bologna

    Pinacoteca Nazionale, Siena

◆ NETHERLANDS

    Centraal Museum, Utrecht

◆ NORWAY

    Bergen Billedgalleri Permanenten, Bergen

    Historisk Museum, University of Bergen, Bergen

    Nasjonalgalleriet, Oslo

    Rasmus Meyers Samlinger, Bergen

◆ SPAIN

    Madrid, Prado

◆ SWEDEN

    Goteborgs Konstmuseum, Gothenburg

Nationalmuseum, Stockholm

Uppsala Universitets Konstsamling, Uppsala

◆ SWITZERLAND

Offentliche Kunstsammlung-Kunstmuseum, Basel

◆ UNITED STATES

California Palace of the Legion of Honor, San Francisco, CA

Cleveland Museum of Art, Cleveland, OH

Denver Art Museum, Denver, CO

M. H. DeYoung Memorial Museum, San Francisco, CA

Metropolitan Museum of Art, New York, NY

Nelson-Atkins Museum of Art, Kansas City, MO

North Carolina Museum of Art, Raleigh, NC

Photography: Museum photography conducted at times when collections are closed to the public. Kodak color scale often photographed with work of art. Background cloth usually hung in galleries when photographing freestanding objects. Professional studio equipment used. Art works are photographed by a professional art historian/photographer using Kodak and Fuji film under controlled conditions using constantly upgraded professional equipment. Original 35mm slides (4" x 5" in some cases) are photographed directly in front of the work of art on Kodak EPT 5037 and Fuji film.

Production: Duplicates printed on standard Kodak duplicating film #5071. Originals inserted in window of 3" x 5" index cards or (formerly) mounted in thin paper masks. Duplicates color-corrected and mounted in cardboard or plastic. Frames not masked prior to duplication.

Documentation: Mailing list kept. Free catalog available, and updated catalogs regularly sent to mailing list. Slides accompanied by full identifications imprinted on mounts or index cards. Documentation is obtained from museums and does not always reflect scholarly disagreements about attributions. Orientation not marked.

Purchasing: See website and/or catalog. Slides are priced at $3.25 each for duplicates; $6.75 each for originals; and $7.50 each for limited-edition originals. Discounts: 5% for 20 slides or more; 10% for 50 slides or more; 15% for 100 slides or more. University purchase orders accepted; pre-

payment required (including credit cards) for individuals. Orders filled in three to ten days.

Digital Products: Saskia offers digital images and licenses for networked use. (See entry in digital section of this directory for information on digital products.)

Other Products: Black-and-white 8" x 10" photographic prints of items in St. Peter's Basilica, Rome.

Expansion Plans: Saskia is on a continuous and systematic program to digitize the archive of original color slides (overall views as well as details). Close to 3,000 images are available at the end of 1997, including most of the works offered in Italian Renaissance and Ancient Art. Documentation of new collections will depend upon the interest and sale of existing slides. Saskia states they have assembled a very rich and diverse archive with which to teach art history and plan to make wider use of it through modern technology.

Textbooks: Lists available for images to accompany textbooks including Tansey and Kleiner's *Gardner's Art Through the Ages,* Stokstad's *Art History,* Hartt's *Italian Renaissance Art,* and Gilbert's *Living with Art.*

Evaluation: Quality, 4; documentation, 4; service, 4. Photography of paintings, including well-selected details, especially fine. Valuable coverage of collections in Europe.

087 Slide Presentations Publishers, Inc.

555 Broadway
New York, NY 10012
Telephone: (212) 274-9385
FAX: (212) 274-8224
Attn: Beverly Grossman or Stephen Sbarge

Profile: Company sells two large slide sets: "History of Architecture, Interiors and Furniture" (8 vols., 1,900 slides) and "History of Costume" (6 vols., 1,500 slides). An abridged version of the "History of Costume" (2 vols., 430 slides) also is available.

Photography: Slides shot extensively from secondary sources (book reproductions, etc.). Copystand photography by S. Sbarge using Kodachrome.

Production: Duplicated by Kodak. Slides inserted in sleeves, packaged in looseleaf binders with text.

Documentation: Mailing list kept. Free brochures. Slide-by-slide commentaries provided in texts:

more than 500 pages for architecture set and 350 pages for costume set. Commentaries are quite elementary and do not always provide all the basic facts of identification.

Purchasing: "History of Architecture, Interiors and Furniture" (8 vols.) is $5,143; "History of Costume" (6 vols.) is $4,362; abridged version (2 vols.) is $1,180.

Evaluation: Reprinted from 6th ed. Quality, based on samples viewed in 1984, 2 to 3; documentation, 2 to 3; service, 3. Quality of slides is average for copystand production but not comparable to results obtainable when slides are produced from original transparencies or negatives. Prospective purchasers should be wary of attractive but unnecessary packaging and hyperbolic advertising claims. Costume set rated 2 on quality and 1 to 2 on documentation by Christine Bunting, who received it as a gift in 1989. "[The set] has been a real boon for students studying theater arts and costume design. However, the set is fraught with problems, such as cropping and inaccurate documentation. I would recommend only buying this set for its value to costume history; it isn't worth purchasing as an art historical resource."

Quality, 4; documentation, 4; service, 4. (Evaluation by a single committee member; 6th edition ratings: quality, 2 to 3; documentation, 2 to 3; service, 3.)

088   Slides for Education

22500 Rio Vista
St. Clair Shores, MI 48081
Telephone: (313) 773-5815
Attn: Joseph P. Messana

Profile: Entry reprinted from 6th ed. In business since circa 1964. 100,000 duplicate color slide titles offered of architecture and public art. Subjects extensively covered include the work of Frank Lloyd Wright (more than 1,000 slides), American public sculpture, and churches worldwide. New titles continually added (500 in 1989). Some 5,000 slides available that are not listed in catalog.

Photography: Original slides (and some large-format transparencies) shot by J. Messana using Kodachrome ASA 64 for exteriors and Ektachrome for interiors. Tripod and various lenses, including perspective-correcting, zoom, and wide-angle, employed with Leica, Olympus, and Mamiyaflex equipment. Natural light preferred; flood lights used on some interiors and art objects when necessary.

Production: Duplicated from originals onto Ektachrome #5071 by a private laboratory. Color-corrected and contrast-controlled. Mounted in cardboard or in Wess plastic and glass mounts. Slides on Eastmancolor #5381 no longer stocked.

Documentation: Mailing list kept. Multi-volume catalog $3.00, postpaid in the United States and Canada. Catalog revised every three years. Slides labeled. Orientation marked.

Purchasing: Slides sold singly or in sets. Minimum order 50 slides. Single slide in cardboard mount priced $2.75; in glass mount, $3.75. Postage added. Purchase orders required from institutions. Prepayment required from individuals and foreign customers. Some slides kept in stock, or, usually, duplicates made to order. Slides usually shipped within 30 days. Rush orders filled within two weeks; surcharge of 20%. Slides not sent on approval, and no returns accepted. Requests considered for slides to be shot on commission.

Evaluation: Reprinted from 6th ed. Four samples sent. Quality, 2 to 3 (high contrast noted on all four duplicates); documentation, 2; service, 2 to 3.

089   Southern Graphics Council

c/o Art Department
University of South Carolina
Columbia, SC 29208
Telephone: (803) 777-3500

Profile: Entry reprinted from 6th ed. A limited edition set of 31 original color slides offered representing the works of 30 contemporary Southern printmakers. The set documents the 1986–1988 biennial traveling exhibit of the Southern Graphics Council.

Photography: Original slides shot on Ektachrome ASA 50 by an independent professional photographer.

Production: Duplicates occasionally made from originals, but generally the originals themselves are sold. Processing done by Color Copy, Columbia, South Carolina. Mounted in plastic and packaged in notebook binders.

Documentation: Free brochure. Set supplied with artists' biographies, technical descriptions, and philosophical comments. Slides keyed to list. Full identifications given except for collection, because at the time of the exhibition the works were still owned by the artists.

Purchasing: Set priced $95, postpaid. Prepayment required, or purchase order from institutions.

Orders filled within three weeks. Rush orders accepted. No returns accepted.

Evaluation: Quality, 3; documentation, 3; service, 3. (Evaluation by a single committee member.)

090 Tamarind Institute

University of New Mexico
108 Cornell Dr., S.E.
Albuquerque, NM 87106
Telephone: (505) 277-3901
Attn: Cynthia Barber

Profile: Nine sets (303 duplicate color slides) offered of lithographs by artists associated with the Tamarind Institute or the Tamarind Lithography Workshop, Los Angeles.

Photography: Original slides shot on Kodachrome.

Production: Duplicated onto Ektachrome by University of New Mexico Photo Services. Packaged in plastic sleeves.

Documentation: Free list available of artists included in each series. Catalog no longer available. Full identifications provided with slides.

Purchasing: Slides sold in sets only. Prices provided on request. Prepayment or purchase order required. Sets kept in stock, and orders filled within 10 days.

Evaluation: Reprinted from 6th ed. Four-star rating in the 4th edition.

091 Taurgo Slides

154 E. 82nd St.
New York, NY 10028
Telephone: (212) 879-8555
Attn: Thomas R. Todd

Profile: Entry reprinted from 6th ed. No response to 1989 questionnaire, and information promised during [1989] telephone update not received. Approximately 50,000 color slide titles offered of Western art and architecture from Ancient Greece to the eighteenth century. Some slides available of Egypt, the Near East, and Islamic sites. Company established 1949. Approximately 100,000 black-and-white negatives available from which slides can be made.

Photography: Slides shot by T. R. Todd or staff photographers on Kodachrome. A few (approximately 200) slides shot by others. Flash used where possible, tripod where needed.

Production: Duplicated by Kodak at Rochester or Fair Lawn laboratories. No color-correction or contrast-control attempted. Mounted in cardboard, or glass mounts by request.

Documentation: Mailing list kept. Free series of lists, continually revised. Identifications on lists brief; few dates given. Slides keyed to lists. Orientation marked.

Purchasing: Single slides $1.50 each in cardboard mounts, $2.00 each glass-mounted (1984 prices). Minimum order 10 slides. Postage added. Duplicated to order and shipped within two weeks; glass mounting may require more time. Small rush orders accepted, filled in one week with 10% surcharge. Prepayment required on foreign orders. Slides not sent on approval. Returns accepted for exchange. Slides made to order from books or photographs on request; orders filled within two weeks, and prices charged as above.

Evaluation: Reprinted from 6th ed. No recent samples sent. "Based on one small order of color slides placed ten years ago, quality 1 to 3, documentation 2, service 2" (Norine Cashman).

092 Teitelman, Edward/ Photography

305 Cooper St.
Camden, NJ 08102
Telephone: (609) 966-6093

Profile: Approximately 2,000 color slide tides offered of architecture, covering the United States, Mexico, Great Britain, Europe, and the Soviet Union, with emphasis on the nineteenth and twentieth centuries. Both originals and duplicates sold. All slides produced on color film, although a few are black-and-white images (old photographs, plans, etc.). In business almost 30 years. New titles continually added. Philadelphia material almost all rephotographed in the early 1980s.

Photography: Original slides shot on Kodachrome ASA 25, mostly by E. Teitelman, some by a traveling scholar. Processed by Kodak. Perspective-correcting lens used. Interiors shot with available light when possible.

Production: Duplicated by Atkinson/Stedco, Hollywood, CA, on Ektachrome. Color-corrected and contrast-controlled. Mounted in cardboard.

Documentation: Free catalog, indexed by architect and building type. Supplements issued. Identifications consist of building name, location, architect, and completion date. Slides keyed to catalog. "Supplementary descriptions will be sent with sets involving items not identified fully in the catalog. We are always available to further aid if these identifications do not suffice." Orientation marked by number in upper right corner.

Purchasing: Extra originals sold until exhausted. Slides sent in groups for selection, sold singly at $2.50 each. No minimum order. Postage added to orders under $50.00. Some slides kept in stock; orders filled within 7 to 10 days with no surcharge. Slides sent on approval for 10 days. Returns accepted for exchange or refund.

Other Products: Black-and-white and color prints custom-made on request. Reproduction rights available.

Evaluation: Quality, 3; documentation, 1; service, 1. (Evaluation by a single committee member. 6th edition ratings: quality, 2 to 3; documentation, 3; service, 3.)

093   Tektonica Slides
87 Howard St.
Cambridge, MA 02139
Telephone: (617) 492-0774
FAX: (617) 492-0774
Attn: Brad Bellows

Profile: Founded in 1985. Clients with large holdings of Tektonica slides include Harvard/Fogg Museum, Art Institute of Chicago, Chinese University of Hong Kong, Yale University, Metropolitan Museum, University of Montreal, Wellesley College, and Trinity College. Tektonica provides architectural slides of sites in North America, Europe, India, and Japan. The company is investigating digital technology and expect to offer digital images within the next few years.

Photography: Originals are photographed by Brad Bellows (architect and professor at Rhode Island School of Design) using perspective correction, Nikon equipment, tripod, and available light. Originals are photographed on 35mm Kodachrome film.

Production: Slides are duplicated on 35mm Ektachrome #5071 film.

Purchasing: Slides are priced at $75/set of 20 slides. Purchase orders are accepted, and shipping is via Federal Express.

Evaluation: Quality, 3 to 4; documentation, 3 to 4; service, 3 to 4.

094   Texas Department of Transportation
Photograph Library
Travel and Information Division
P.O. Box 5000
Austin, TX 78763-5000
Telephone: (512) 465-7991
FAX: (512) 465-3090
Attn: Anne L. Cook, Photograph Librarian
E-mail: acook@mailgw.dot.state.tx.us

Profile: The Texas Department of Transportation maintains a Photograph Library containing slides, large-format color transparencies and black-and-white materials concerning highway construction and travel and tourism in Texas. This includes professional photography of Texas landmarks, architecture, and general scenes. Statues and paintings located at the Texas State Capitol are included in the collection.

Purchasing: No user fees or service charges. Copies may be ordered of materials in the collection similar to the LC and NA policies. One of the labs used charges $.90 per slide duplicate, with a minimum $7.00 order. Contact the Photo Librarian for more information.

*095   Universal Color Slide Co.
8450 S. Tamiami Tr.
Sarasota, FL 34238-2936
Telephone: (800) 326-1367
FAX: (800) 487-0250
Attn: Marjorie Crawford
E-mail: ucslide@aol.com
URL: http://www.universalcolorslide.com

This vendor also offers digital products and is listed in the digital section of the directory.

Price Range: $2.25 to $2.90 per individual slide, depending on quantity. Slide sets also available.

Profile: The company has been in business for more than 50 years. The current owners have continually upgraded and added to the slide collection since 1984; VRI Slide Library was recently purchased and is now available. Personal customer service representatives are available to answer questions about the collection.

More than 8,000 different slide images offered. Periods covered are from prehistoric through the twentieth century. More than 850 different slides sets available. More than 50 sets are correlated to books, including the major art history/appreciation texts. Company may make images available on Photo-CD if customers are interested.

Photography: Originals are photographed by professional photographers on staff using Ektachrome ASA 64 professional film (tungsten). Original slides also supplied by artists or galleries. Transparencies supplied by museums.

Production: Originals are duplicated in-house on Ektachrome #5071 and mounted in cardboard mounts. Professional inkjet printing is used for slide information.

Documentation: A catalog is sent to mailing list once or twice each year. Slide number, artist name or period, artist birth and death dates, title of work, date of work, medium, dimensions, location, and asterisk for orientation in projector is printed on slides with high-quality inkjet printer.

Purchasing: Individual slides are priced at $2.25 to $2.90 each, depending on quantity ordered. Slide sets start at $29.55. Call for details; volume discounts available. No minimum order. Schools and universities need to supply purchase orders. A 2% prepayment discount is offered.

Shipping charges prepaid and added to invoice. Call for quote. Special shipping and handling available. International orders must prepay in U.S. dollars. Turnaround time 3 to 21 days depending on quantity.

Digital Products: PhotoCDs available in both Windows and MAC formats.

Other Products: Books, videotapes, reproductions, CD-ROMs, slide cabinets, sorters, projectors, resource sets.

Expansion Plans: Expanding into areas of contemporary art. Slide curriculum guides are becoming available with slide sets at no extra charge.

Textbooks: *History of Art* by H. W. Janson; *History of Art for Young People* by H. W. Janson; *A Basic History of Art* by H. W. Janson; *Gardner's Art Through the Ages* by Tansey and Kleiner; *Art History* by Stokstad; *American Art of the 20th Century* by Hunter and Jacobus; *A History of Western Art* by Schneider Adams; *History of Modern Art* by Arnason; *Discovering Art History* by Brommer; *Art: A History of Painting, Sculpture and Architecture* by Hartt; *Modern Art* by Hunter and Jacobus; *Art Past/Art Present*

by Wilken, Schultz, and Linduff; *Art & Civilization* by Lucie-Smith; *The Visual Experience* by Hobbs and Salome; *Art: The Way It Is* by Adkins Richardson; *Varieties of Visual Experience* by Burke Feldman; *The Story of Art* by Gombrich; *Art Forms* by Preble; and *Women Artists: An Illustrated History* by Heller. Others available by request.

Evaluation: Quality, 1 to 3; documentation, 1 to 3; service, 1 to 3. Newer sets tend to be higher in quality.

*096 University of Michigan Slide Distribution

c/o Department of the History of Art
60 Tappan Hall
519 S. State St.
Ann Arbor, MI 48109-1357
Telephone: (734) 763-5406
FAX: (734) 747-4121
Attn: Jeri Hollister
E-mail: jerih@umich.edu
URL: http://www.umich.edu/~hartspc/umsdp

Profile: The University of Michigan Slide Distribution Project is a not-for-profit organization established by the Department of the History of Art, University of Michigan. Since 1982 the UMSD has functioned as a service to the educational community. The Project concentrates on photographing and distributing, at an affordable price, slides of art objects from exhibitions, distinguished private collections, and the permanent collections of major American and European museums. The Project also photographs and distributes slides of major architectural and sculptural monuments. In 1993 the operation was reorganized to offer our slides for sale in small sets designed by the purchaser. These sets consist of a minimum of 20 slides per set. The ability to purchase individual slides allows the customer to select only those images relevant to their teaching and research needs. Collections that have been selectively photographed are as follows:

Albright-Knox Gallery, Buffalo, NY

Art Institute of Chicago, Chicago, IL

Carnegie Institute, Museum of Art, Pittsburgh, PA

Corcoran Gallery of Art, Washington, DC

Galleria dell'Accademia, Florence, Italy

High Museum of Art, Atlanta, GA

Hunter Museum of Art, Chattanooga, TN

J. B. Speed Art Museum, Louisville, KY

Kimbell Art Museum, Ft. Worth, TX

Kreeger Museum, Washington, DC

Minneapolis Institute of Art, Minneapolis, MN

Nelson-Atkins Museum of Art, Kansas City, MO

Sellars Collection: American Women Artists, Marietta, GA

Pitti Place, Florence, Italy (Andrea del Sarto Exhibition)

Thyssen-Bornemisza Collection, Lugno, Switzerland

Toledo Museum of Art, Toledo, OH

Uffizi Gallery, Florence, Italy

Vatican Library, Vatican City, Italy

Most slides are of paintings; some are sculpture. There are slides of manuscript pages from the Vatican Library. Art Institute of Chicago sets are of prints and drawings only. A set of prints by Frank Stella is offered, as well as several sets of architecture in Italy; one at St. Andrews, Scotland; and one of the Timberline Lodge on Mt. Hood in Oregon. There are two small sets of paintings by Jacopo Pontormo and Rosso Fiorentino. A set of 175 slides of art by American women artists is available, selected from the collection of Louise and Alan Sellars. There are some slides in the inventory that are not offered for individual sale. Small sets such as "The Paintings of Jacopo Pontormo and Rosso Fiorentino," "Jacopo Pontormo's Passion C Cycle from the Certosa del Galluzzo," and "Views of Or San Michele" are specially composed to be of an affordable size. Similarly, the architectural sets from Florence, Siena and Pisa, Venice, St. Andrews, and the Timberline Lodge are designed to provide your institution with a concise record of the location for lecture purposes. Our agreement with the Corcoran Gallery of Art allows sale of those images in set form only.

Photography: Original slides are shot by staff photographers using Nikon equipment on Ektachrome (95%) and Kodachrome slide film. Museum photography is done with studio tungsten lighting, and a tripod is used. Original photography for the Uffizi drawings was done in 4" x 5" transparencies. For architecture, a tripod and perspective-correcting lens are used.

Production: Original slides are duplicated on #5071 film by Precision Photographics, Ann Arbor, Michigan with color and exposure correction for accuracy. Slides are mounted in plastic and shipped inside bubble pack envelopes.

Documentation: Promotional information is sent as new slides are offered. A catalog is available at a cost of $5.00, refunded with first order, or free with order. The catalog is updated as slides are added. The catalog is divided into three sections. Part 1 is a complete listing of our slides offered only in sets. Each set is briefly described, and the complete contents are listed. Part 2 is a complete catalog of the slides offered for individual sale (minimum order 20 slides). The list is organized by media, country, artist, and title. Each title also has an order number. Part 3 is a listing of the same slides offered in set form; the contents of each set are described in a brief paragraph. A detailed list of the slides offered in these large slide sets is available at no charge, upon request. Slides are accompanied by an identification list detailing the artist, title, date, medium, dimensions, and other relevant information. Slides are coded to the list.

Purchasing: Both individual slides and sets are offered. Individual slides are priced at $2.75 to $3.50 each depending on quantity ordered. Discounts are as follows: 25% if all sets are purchased; 20% for orders totaling $3,000 or more; 15% for orders totaling $2,000-$2,999; and 10% for orders totaling $1,000-$1,999. Prepayment in the form of check or purchase order is requested. Orders are generally filled within two weeks of receiving the order. Slides are boxed and shipped via UPS (domestic) in a bubble pack envelope. Foreign orders are sent via the mail. Domestic shipping and handling: $10 for 20-100 slides, $15 for 101-200 slides, and increasing in increments of $5.00 per 100 slides. Foreign shipping and handing: $15 for 20-1,000 slides, and $25 for 101-200 slides, increasing in increments of $10 per 100 slides.

Evaluation: Quality, 3 to 4; documentation, 3 to 4; service, 3 to 4. One of the top sources of quality slides of paintings at a reasonable price.

097   Visual Media for the Arts and Humanities
P.O. Box 737
Cherry Hill, NJ 08003

Profile: Entry reprinted from 6th ed. No response to 1984 or 1989 questionnaires. Perhaps company does not have its own mail-order sales. Slides produced for sale by institutions (the Metropolitan Museum of Art, New York, for instance).

Evaluation: Reprinted from 6th ed. Slides are characteristically very high in contrast and tend to be too green.

098 Wible Language Institute, Inc.

24 S. 8th St.
P.O. Box 870
Allentown, PA 18105

Profile: Entry reprinted from 6th ed. No response to 1989 questionnaire. Entry written from catalog. Company offers various audiovisual products to aid in language instruction. French, German, Italian, Latin, and Spanish materials featured, with 50 other languages represented. Slide sets available that may contain views of art and architecture.

099 Yale University Press
See under Digital Section

Museums

100 Albright-Knox Art Gallery

1285 Elmwood Ave.
Buffalo, NY 14222
Telephone: (716) 882-8700
Attn: Gallery Shop or Slide Library

Profile: Thirty-six slides in three sets offered by Gallery Shop. Single slides (duplicates and some originals) offered by Slide Library if not available from independent vendors. Only works in the museum's permanent collection are available for sale. New titles added of new acquisitions.

Photography: Slide Library slides shot 80% by staff photographer, the remainder by independent professional photographers. Ektachrome EPY ASA 50 tungsten film used, with tripod and flat field lens.

Production: Slides sold in museum shop are a selection of those produced by Davis Art Slides **(047)** (formerly Rosenthal Art Slides). Slide Library's duplicates made by Spectrum Slides, Buffalo, NY. Color-corrected and contrast-controlled.

Documentation: Free single-page list available from Gallery Shop, showing contents of sets. Artist, title, date, and dimensions given on list. Slides in sets labeled by producer (Rosenthal). No list available from Slide Library, but slides labeled. Orientation marked.

Purchasing: Three sets of twelve slides each offered by the Gallery Shop for $12.50 per set: "Selected Masterpieces of Modern Art," "Selected Masterpieces of Twentieth Century Art," and "French Painting 1782–1906." Slides kept in stock and shipped within two weeks. Minimum order one set from Shop, one slide from Slide Library. Single slides usually priced $2.50 each, postpaid in the United States and Canada. Some slides priced $5.00 each. Prepayment or purchase order not required. Rush orders accepted for a surcharge and filled within one to two days. No returns accepted.

Other Products: Videotapes available of artists interviewed at the Gallery.

Other Sources: The University of Michigan Slide Distribution **(096)** offers sets of painting (260 slides) and sculpture (87 slides). Davis Art Slides **(047)** (formerly Rosenthal Art Slides) offers some of the same slides as singles (258 slides).

Evaluation: Reprinted from 6th ed. Quality, 3 to 4; documentation, 2 to 3; service, 3.

102 American Museum of Natural History

Central Park West at 79th St.
New York, NY 10024-5192
Telephone: (212) 769-5418 or
(212) 769-5420
FAX: (212) 769-5009
Attn: Special Collections
E-mail: speccol@amnh.org
URL: http://nimidi.amnh.org/special.html

Profile: Northwest Coast Native Americans (color and black-and-white artifact photos and black-and-white field photos), AMNH field expeditions (black-and-white), dinosaur and other fossils (black-and-white, some color), Plains Native Americans (black-and-white and color artifacts and black-and-white field photos), gems and minerals (color), book illustrations (color). About 20,000 color slides and transparencies.

Documentation: Catalog forthcoming, will be available on the Web or through the mail for $5.00 per volume (two volumes: "Animals, Vegetables and

Minerals" and "Anthropology"), including more than half a million black-and-white photographs.

Purchasing: $1.50 each (subject to change 1998).

Evaluation: Quality, 4; documentation, 4; service, 4.

103 American Numismatic Association

818 N. Cascade Ave.
Colorado Springs, CO 80903-3279
Telephone: (719) 632-2646
E-mail: ana@money.org
URL: http://www.money.org/index.html

Profile: Slides available for rental only, to ANA members only, "for use as educational programs at club meetings or for educational presentations to schools and civic groups." One hundred sets of various sizes offered in current catalog. Coins of many countries and time periods represented. New sets announced on the website.

Photography: Original photography by ANA staff. Some originals obtained from independent sources.

Production: Slides glass-mounted for circulation.

Documentation: See website. Sets accompanied by lecture notes with description of each slide.

Rental: Resource Center: The ANA Resource Center houses the world's largest numismatic lending library. More than 40,000 items, as well as audiovisual programs, videotapes, and 35mm slide presentations, cover every aspect of the hobby. Members can borrow these items for only the costs of postage and insurance. Exact date of use must be specified on request. Listing of alternate selections recommended. ANA membership number and club name required on all requests and correspondence. Slides shipped via UPS and return via UPS preferred.

104 American Numismatic Society

Broadway at 155th St.
New York, NY 10032
Telephone: (212) 234-3130
Attn: Publications

E-mail: info@amnumsoc.org
URL: http://www.amnumsoc2.org

Profile: Nine slide sets offered of coins: "America's Federal Gold Coinage, 1793–1933" (36 slides, $30); "America's Silver Coinage, 1794–1891" (35 slides, $25); "Coinage of the Americas" (41 slides, $26); "Coinage of El Peri" (36 slides; $30); "Confederate States of America Currency 1861–1865" (30 slides; $20); "Varieties of 1794 Large Cent" (27 slides, $20); "Islamic Coins" (36 slides, $39); "Massachusetts Silver Coinage" (16 slides, $30); and "Money in Early America" (41 slides, $26).

Documentation: Free brochure. Each set accompanied by handbook or audiotape.

Purchasing: Slides sold in sets of 24 to 41 slides, priced as above. Postage added. ANS members receive 10% discount. Prepayment required.

Other Products: Books, medals, *American Journal of Numismatics*, and seven VHS videos: "Making Money in Early Massachusetts," "Brasher-Lima Style Doubloon," "New Yorker in America Token," "Pennsylvania Currency Signers," "Weight Analysis of Abel Buell's Connecticut Coppers," "Unusual Printing Features in Early American Paper Money," and "American Indian Peace Medals of the Colonial Period."

105 Amon Carter Museum

3501 Camp Bowie Blvd.
Fort Worth, TX 76107
Telephone: (817) 738-1933
Attn: Registrar's Office
URL: http://cartermuseum.org

Profile: Approximately 800 color slide titles offered of works in the permanent collection; nineteenth- and twentieth-century paintings and sculpture of the American West. New slides continually added.

Photography: Slides shot by staff photographers.

Production: Mounted in plastic. Slides labeled.

Documentation: 1972 catalog of permanent collection. Free list of available slides. Slides are identified with artist, title, medium, date, and credit line.

Purchasing: Requests must be made in writing to the Registrar's Office. Requests not accepted via electronic mail. Price per slide: $5.00 plus $2.00 service charge. No rush orders accepted.

106   Art Institute of Chicago

Michigan Ave. at Adams St.
Chicago, IL 60603
Telephone: (312) 443-3655
Attn: Image Rights Department

This museum also offers digital products and is listed in the digital section of the directory.

Profile: Color slides available of masterpieces in the permanent collection. New slide titles continually added.

Photography: Slides and large-format transparencies shot by staff photographer in a studio using Ektachrome ASA 100.

Production: Duplicated on Ektachrome #5071. Color-corrected and contrast-controlled. Mounted in cardboard.

Documentation: Comprehensive list available. Slides imprinted on mounts or keyed to list. Orientation marked by asterisk or slide number.

Purchasing: Slides sold singly or in sets. Single slides made to order, $5.00 each from existing transparencies. If new photography required, $25.00 per item charged. Postage charge of $2.50 added to all orders. Prepayment required.

Other Products: CD-ROM available.

Other Sources: Davis Art Slides **(047)** (formerly Rosenthal Art Slides) offers 1,600 duplicate color slides of works in this museum, available singly. Some 280 slides of drawings and prints available from the University of Michigan Slide Distribution **(096)**.

Evaluation: Quality, 3; documentation, 3; service, 3.

107   Asian Art Museum of San Francisco

(including Avery Brundage Collection)
Golden Gate Park
San Francisco, CA 94118
Telephone: (415) 668-8921
FAX: (415) 668-8928
Attn: Hank Forester, Photographic Services
E-mail: hforester@asianart.org
URL: http://www.asianart.org/

Profile: Entire collection of Asian art covered in color slide titles, sold as single duplicates by Photographic Services. Have 10,000 slides of objects of the museum collections. The collection covers art objects from China, Japan, Korea, India, Southeast Asia, and the Middle East. Sets (20 or 30 slides each) offered for sale or rental by Education Department, including five sets on special exhibitions.

Photography: Original photography carried out by staff photographer using 4" x 5" view camera or 35mm camera with 55mm macro lens and studio lighting. Ektachrome ASA 100 plus used for 35mm color slide originals. Larger Ektachrome transparencies and black-and-white negatives also shot.

Production: Duplicated by Kodak. No attempt made to correct color or control contrast. Mounted in plastic.

Documentation: No list or catalog available of single slides. Order by referring to accession numbers (obtainable in published catalogs of the collection). Some slides labeled. Free list of set titles available from Education Department. Sets accompanied by list of identifications.

Purchasing: Free price list available from Photographic Services. Single slides priced $4.00 each. No minimum order. Postage added. Slides kept in stock, and orders shipped within two weeks. Rush orders accepted and filled, if possible, within one week. Returns accepted for exchange only. Special photography carried out within two to three weeks; fees from $100.00 to $150.00, depending on dimensions of the object. Sets from Education Department priced $10.00 each. Postage added ($4.00). Order form attached to list of sets.

Rental: All slide sets may be rented by teachers for a three-week period, including 10 sets not for sale.

Other Products: Black-and-white photographic prints sold by Photographic Services, and color transparencies also available for three-month rental. Two video programs offered for sale or rental by Education Department.

Evaluation: Reprinted from 6th ed. Three-star rating in the fourth edition.

108   Baltimore Museum of Art

Art Museum Dr.
Baltimore, MD 21218
Telephone: (301) 396-7101
Attn: Rights & Reproductions

Profile: Entry reprinted from 6th ed. Duplicate color slides offered of works in the permanent collection, including paintings, prints and drawings, sculpture, American quilts, American furniture, and the art of Africa, the Americas, and the Pacific.

Production: Produced by Sandak (no longer in business).

Purchasing: Slides sold singly, $.75 each. Postage added. Museums and libraries will be invoiced.

109 Bowdoin College Museum of Art

Walker Art Building
Brunswick, ME 04011
Telephone: (207) 725-3000
Attn: Museum Shop

Profile: Entry reprinted from 6th ed. Fifty-one color slide titles offered of works in the permanent collection: 42 of paintings (mostly American, some European) and nine of ancient artifacts.

Photography and Production: Slides shot and duplicated by Dennis Griggs, Tannery Hill Studio. Color-corrected and contrast-controlled.

Documentation: Free list of offerings, periodically revised. Slides labeled. Orientation marked.

Purchasing: Slides sold singly, $2.00 each. No minimum order. Duplicates kept in stock, and orders shipped within one week. Rush orders filled same day. No special photography available. Slides not sent on approval, and returns not accepted.

Evaluation: Two samples sent in 1984: excellent quality.

110 Brooklyn Museum

200 Eastern Pkwy.
Brooklyn, NY 11238
Telephone: (718) 638-5000
Attn: Gift Shop

Profile: Sell about 50 slides in the gift shop for $1.00 each. There is no listing of the slides. Duplicate color slides offered of some works in the permanent collection: African and Oceanic art, Egyptian and Classical art, Oriental art, Western painting and sculpture, decorative arts, and costumes and textiles. New slides continually added.

Photography: Originals shot by staff photographers.

Production: Mounted in cardboard.

Documentation: No list available from either Photo Sales or Shop. Slides labeled. Orientation not marked on museum's own slides.

Purchasing: Buyer must come to the shop in person Wednesdays through Sundays 10 A.M. to 5 P.M.

Evaluation: Quality, 3; documentation, 3; service, 3.

111 Butler Institute of American Art

524 Wick Ave.
Youngstown, OH 44502
Telephone: (216) 743-1711
Attn: Slides

Profile: Approximately 400 duplicate color slides titles offered of the permanent collection. New slides added of new acquisitions.

Photography and Production: Originals shot and duplicated by a local independent professional photographer.

Documentation: Free six-page list. Artist name, title of work, medium, and dimensions given.

Purchasing: Slides sold singly, $2.00 each. Postage added.

Evaluation: Quality, 3; documentation, 1; service, 2. (Evaluation by a single committee member.)

112 Carnegie Museum of Art

4400 Forbes Ave.
Pittsburgh, PA 15213
Telephone: (412) 622-5563
FAX: (412) 622-3112
Attn: Honore Ervin, Coordinator of Photographic Services
E-mail: hervin@ix.netcom.com
URL: http://www.clpgh.or/cma

Profile: Duplicate slides offered of works in the permanent collection, with emphasis on contemporary art. The slides available from the museum are the same subjects as those available (as a set only) from the University of Michigan Slide Distribution (096); a few additional slides may be available. New slides continually added.

Photography: Original slides shot by independent professional photographer.

Production: Duplicated by a local laboratory.

Documentation: No list. Slides labeled with name, dates, nationality of artist; title of work, and date of work. Orientation marked only when necessary.

Purchasing: Slides sold singly, $1.50 each. No minimum order. Slides kept in stock or duplicated to order if necessary. Orders filled within three to four weeks. No rush orders accepted. Postage added. Customers invoiced. Slides not sent on approval. Returns accepted for exchange or refund if valid reason given.

Other Sources: Set offered by University of Michigan Slide Distribution **(096)**.

113   Chicago Architecture Foundation

formerly called ArchiCenter
224 S. Michigan Ave.
Chicago, IL 60604
Telephone: (312) 922-3432
FAX: (312) 922-0481
Attn: Shop
E-mail: shop@architecture.org
URL: http://www.architecture.org/

Profile: One set of 10 slides in a teacher's edition called "Look Up!" costing $15. The set includes the Home Insurance Building, Monadnock Building, Marquette Building, Fisher Building, Carson Pirie Scott & Co., Federal Center, James R. Thompson Center, Harold Washington Library, Sears Tower, and the Chicago Skyline.

114   Chrysler Museum

Olney Rd. and Mowbray Arch
245 W. Olney Rd.
Norfolk, VA 23510-1587
Telephone: (757) 664-6200
FAX: (757) 664-6201
Attn: Slide Library
E-mail: chrysler@norfolk.infi.net
URL: http://sites.communitylink.org/cmhh/

Profile: Some information reprinted from 6th ed. More than 500 duplicate color slide titles offered of the permanent collection, with strength in glass. The list of titles found in the archives is comparable to major works of art on view.

Photography: Originals shot by staff photographer.

Production: Duplicated by a local laboratory.

Documentation: No list. New museum handbook published in 1990. Handbook of glass collection (1989) available from Library. Exhibition catalogs may also be used as reference in ordering. Identifications provided on slide labels.

Purchasing: Slides are priced at $2.50 each. Postage added. Purchase order or prepayment required.

Expansion Plans: Thinking about digital images.

Evaluation: Quality, 4; documentation, 2; service, 3. (Evaluation by a single committee member.)

115   Cincinnati Art Museum

953 Eden Park Dr.
Cincinnati, OH 45202
Telephone: (513) 721-5204, x207
FAX: (513) 721-0129
Attn: Liv Henson
URL: http://www.cincinnatiartmuseum.org

Price Range: $3.50/slide to $75.00/three-month rental of color transparency.

Profile: Slide Library has been around since the 1970s. The CAM offers black-and-white prints, 35mm color slides and 4" x 5" transparencies. The collection contains more than 16,000 slides. There are also at least 5,000 black-and-white negatives and about 300 4" x 5" color transparencies.

Photography: A professional freelance photographer is hired to photograph objects. Only strobe lights are used. Photographic Services technician is present at all times. Works of art may only be moved by art handlers or curator of object being photographed.

Production: When available, originals from the gallery are used. Most often new photography is scheduled as soon as object is accessioned into the collection.

Documentation: Artist names and dates, title of work and dates, medium, credit line, size.

Purchasing: Individual slides are priced at $3.50 for research, $10.00 for publication. For possible slide discounts, contact the museum. Prepayment is required. Orders are completed within two weeks of receipt of payment. Photos are sent via U.S. postal service. A $3.50 shipping and handling charge is added to all orders within the United States. Shipping and handling is $7.00 for international orders.

Rental: 4" x 5" color transparencies, and occasionally 8" x 10" color transparencies. Color transparencies are never purchasable. They are rented for three-month terms.

Expansion Plans: Image inventory is planned, but will probably take several years.

116   Sterling and Francine Clark Art Institute

225 South St.
P.O. Box 8
Williamstown, MA 01267
Telephone: (413) 458-9545
Attn: Museum Shop

Profile: Entry reprinted from 6th ed. with updated information. More than 300 color slide titles offered of the permanent collection, which features nineteenth-century painting, predominantly French. Some Renaissance and Baroque painting and nineteenth-century sculpture included.

Photography: Original slides shot by staff photographer.

Production: Duplicated by World in Color on Ektachrome #5071.

Documentation: Free list; artist and title provided. Slides accompanied by full identifications, except medium and dimensions. Further information supplied on request. Slides sets listed inside back cover of Museum Shop catalog (artist, title only).

Purchasing: Slides sold singly, $1.50 each. Postage added. Sets of 10 slides also offered for $8.00 each. Sales Terms: net 30 days; $5.00 shipping if order is more than $10.00.

Evaluation: Quality, 4; documentation, 2 to 3; service, 4.

117   Cleveland Museum of Art

11150 East Blvd.
Cleveland, OH 44106
Telephone: (216) 421-7340
Attn: Sales Desk or Slide Library

Profile: Reprinted from 6th ed. with some corrections. Some 150 duplicate color slides, produced by Rosenthal Art Slides [now Davis Art Slides **(047)**], sold by Sales Desk. Duplicate color slides also made

to order by Slide Library of objects not available from Sales Desk or other sources. The Slide Library can provide duplicate slides of new museum accessions. Limited edition sets occasionally offered by Slide Library of temporary exhibitions.

Photography: Original photography for Slide Library and Rosenthal slides (35mm slides or larger-format transparencies) carried out by staff photographer in studio using Ektachrome or Kodachrome ASA 64.

Production: Sales Desk slides produced by Davis Art **(047)** (formerly Rosenthal Art Slides). Slides from Slide Library are duplicated from originals onto Ektachrome #5071 by a local professional lab, mounted in cardboard, and shipped in plastic sleeves.

Documentation: Catalog of Rosenthal-produced slides available for $2.00 from Sales Desk or from Davis Art Slides **(047)** (formerly Rosenthal Art Slides); complete identifications provided. Orientation marked on all slides.

Purchasing: Orders should preferably be directed to Davis Art Slides **(047)** (formerly Rosenthal Art Slides) rather than to Sales Desk. Slides ordered from Sales Desk priced $2.00 each; no minimum order. Prepayment required from individuals, purchase order from institutions. Slides sold singly by Slide Library at $2.00 each, plus postage. No minimum order. Order from Slide Library as last resort after checking other sources; use museum handbook to order by accession number. Requests to Slide Library duplicated to order and usually filled within two to four weeks. Rush orders filled within 24 hours for $20.00 surcharge on the order. If the Slide Library cannot supply a desired slide, a request for special photography may be addressed to the curator of the department concerned. All orders to Slide Library must be prepaid. Returned slides accepted for exchange.

Rental: Slides in the collection of the museum's Slide Library loaned locally only, for a service fee.

Exchange: The museum will exchange slides with other museum libraries.

Other Products: The museum is considering production of videotapes.

Other Sources: Davis Art Slides **(047)** (formerly Rosenthal Art Slides) offers 1,100 slides. Eighty-three (duplicates only) from Saskia **(086)**. The museum's Asian collections have been photographed by Asian Art Photographic Documentation **(030)** and the American Committee for South Asian Art **(021)**.

Evaluation: Quality, 3; documentation, 3; service, 3. (Evaluation by a single committee member; reprinted from 6th ed. Duplicates made to order by Slide Library are not always of the highest quality; they are made for the convenience of scholars and teachers who need images that are not otherwise available. Documentation, 3; service, 2 to 3. See also entries for other producers named above.)

118   The Cloisters

Fort Tryon Park
New York, NY 10040
Telephone: (212) 927-3700, x158
Attn: Museum Shop

Profile: Entry reprinted from 6th ed. Approximately 150 duplicate color slides offered of works in the permanent collection (medieval to Renaissance art). These are a selection of the slides available from the Metropolitan Museum of Art's Children's Shop. New titles rarely added. Two sets also available (slide/tape presentations): "A Walk through the Cloisters" and "The Christmas Story."

Production: Slides produced by Rosenthal Art Slides [now Davis Art Slides **(047)**]. A few produced by Visual Media **(097)**.

Documentation: Cloisters slides are included on list available from the Metropolitan Museum of Art **(135)**. Slides labeled and orientation marked.

Purchasing: Slides sold singly, $1.25 each. No minimum order. Postage added. Prepayment required. Shipped within three weeks. Rush orders handled by Metropolitan Museum of Art. Slides not sent on approval, and returns not accepted.

Other Products: Videotapes available.

Other Sources: Single slides offered by Davis Art Slides **(047)** (formerly Rosenthal Art Slides).

Evaluation: For quality and documentation, see Davis Art Slides **(047)** (formerly Rosenthal Art Slides).

119   Colonial Williamsburg Foundation

313 First St.
P.O. Box 1776
Williamsburg, VA 23187-1776
Telephone: (757) 565-8540
FAX: (757) 565-8548

Attn: Marianne Carden, Visual Resources Librarian or Catherine Grosfils, Editorial Librarian
URL: http://www.history.org

Profile: Colonial Williamsburg's Audiovisual Library was established in 1944 as part of the Department of Interpretation. It originally encompassed both a film library and a print and slide library. In 1985, the print and slide library was moved from Photographic Services to the Foundation Library, where it is known as the Visual Resources Section. The Visual Resources Section's primary function is to serve as a photo archive for the Foundation and to provide images to various departments within the Foundation. However, the collection also serves as a resource for outside researchers and publishers looking for images relating to life in the eighteenth century, Williamsburg, colonial architecture, and the decorative arts. The Visual Resources Section is currently adding new color photography to a digital image database and plans to eventually offer CD-ROM products and digital formats to customers. Colonial Williamsburg's AV Distribution Section no longer produces slide sets. However, individual slides can be ordered through the Visual Resources Section as detailed in this entry. The Visual Resources Section cannot handle large-volume orders but can assist with requests for up to 50 slides. Larger orders of more than 15 slides may take longer than two weeks to be processed. Images of some of the objects in the collections of the DeWitt Wallace Gallery and the Abby Aldrich Rockefeller Folk Art Center will eventually be available for examination on the Internet in Academic Press's Image Directory.

Photography: Professional staff photographers photograph museum collection objects and buildings, using a tripod. Stable film is used, and images are color-corrected and contrast-controlled.

Production: Duplicate slides are produced from master slides stored in a cold storage vault. Stable film is used for both duplicates and masters.

Documentation: Individual slides are labeled with the negative number, accession number, title, artist, and date. For architecture, building name and description if view are provided.

Purchasing: Individual slides are priced at $3.00 each plus postage; a $6.00 processing fee is charged for each order. Prepayment by check is required. Orders are filled within two to four weeks, depending on volume. Larger orders of over 15 slides may take longer than two weeks to be processed.

Rental: A sliding scale of fees is available for rental of transparencies for use in publications and exhibits.

Other Products: Videotapes are also available through Colonial Williamsburg's distribution service.

Evaluation: Quality, 4; documentation, 2; service, 1. (Evaluation by a single committee member.)

120   Columbus Museum of Art

480 E. Broad St.
Columbus, OH 43215
Telephone: (614) 221-6801
FAX: (614) 221-8946
Attn: Resource Center
URL: http://www.columbusart.mus.oh.us

Profile: Entry reprinted from 6th ed. More than 2,000 duplicate color slide titles offered of works in the permanent collection: sixteenth- to twentieth-century European paintings, drawings, prints, sculpture, and decorative arts; nineteenth- and twentieth-century American paintings; Chinese and Japanese paintings, ceramics, and sculpture; Pre-Columbian ceramics and other objects; and Inuit art. Many slides available of paintings by George Bellows, who was born in Columbus. Various sets offered based on the permanent collection, among them "Introduction to the Museum," "French Art," "Sculpture," "Face to Face: Portraits in the Columbus Museum of Art," "Far East Treasures," and "George Bellows Paints America." Sets related to temporary exhibitions also available. New slide titles continually added. Digital images to be available in next two to three years.

Photography: Original slides shot on Ektachrome ASA 50 by an independent professional photographer in a professional lighting setup.

Production: Duplicated on Ektachrome #5071 by a local laboratory. Color-corrected and contrast-controlled. Mounted in cardboard or plastic.

Documentation: Free catalog and supplement. Slides labeled with full identifications. Orientation marked when necessary. Sets accompanied by scripts.

Purchasing: Slides sold singly and in sets. Single slides priced $2.00 each. Sets composed of at least 20 slides, priced $25.00. Postage added. Prepayment required on orders of sets. Duplicated to order and shipped within four weeks. Rush orders accepted if possible. Returns accepted if customer is dissatisfied. Special photography carried out on request.

121   Cooper-Hewitt Museum

(Smithsonian Institution)
2 E. 91st St.
New York, NY 10128-9990
Telephone: (212) 849-8405
FAX: (212) 849-8402
Attn: Jill Bloomer

Price Range: Slide, $6.50; slide made from flat art, $20.00.

Profile: Duplicate color slides made of objects in the permanent collection, which includes more than 300,000 objects from 3,000 years of design history: paintings, drawings, prints, textiles, furniture, metalwork, ceramics, glass, woodwork, and wall coverings.

Photography: The Textile and Wall Coverings departments shoot their own record shots. These slides are fine for study purposes only. Professional slides can be done on a request basis.

Production: Slides are duped from slides and 4" x 5" transparencies. Cooper-Hewitt also will make a slide from a black-and-white photograph if that is the only image that exists.

Documentation: All slides are identified with the accession number or call number. Specific caption information can be requested from the appropriate department.

Purchasing: Prepayment required. Approximately two-week turnaround.

Other Products: The Museum Shop (212) 849-8352 carries a large selection of design-related books.

Evaluation: Quality, 3 (based on single committee member; reprinted from 6th ed. Quality, 3; documentation, 3; service, 3).

122   Corcoran Gallery of Art

17th St. and New York Ave., N.W.
Washington, DC 20006
Telephone: (202) 638-3211
Attn: Museum Shop or Registrar's Office

Profile: Entry reprinted from 6th ed. Duplicate color slides offered of works in the permanent collection, which consists mostly of American art and photography. Some nineteenth-century European paintings, drawings, prints, and decorative arts included. New titles continually added to Registrar's collection.

Photography: Slides, negatives, and large-format transparencies shot on Kodak film by an independent professional photographer.

Production: Duplicated on Kodak film. Mounted in cardboard or plastic. Slides sold by gallery shop produced by Sandak (no longer in business).

Documentation: Free list gives artist name, title of work, and date. Slides fully labeled. Orientation not marked.

Purchasing: Slides sold singly. No minimum order. Seventy-eight slides, predominantly American paintings, sold by shop for $1.00 each. Postage added. Duplicates kept in stock by shop and shipped within two weeks. Rush orders filled in one day; surcharge for special shipping. Slides made to order within three to four weeks by Registrar's Office at per-slide cost of $3.50 for a duplicate, $14.00 for new photography. Shipping (by UPS) added. Shipping on foreign orders $3.00. Order form available with list. Prepayment required by both shop and Registrar's Office. Returns accepted by shop for exchange only. Returns accepted by Registrar's Office if customer is dissatisfied.

123   Corning Museum of Glass

One Corning Glass Ctr.
Corning, NY 14830
Telephone: (607) 937-5371
FAX: (607) 937-2252
Attn: Sales Department
E-mail: cmgsales@servtech.com
URL: http://www.pennynet.org/glmuseum/corningm.htm

Profile: More than 1,500 duplicate slides offered of glass objects in the permanent collection: European, English, American, contemporary, Indian, and Far Eastern pieces, as well as glass from ancient times in Egypt, the Near East, the Roman Empire, and the Islamic world. All slides are in color except a few of Steuben glass. New titles continually added.

Photography: Original slides shot by staff photographer using tripod. Fewer than 1% of slides are black-and-white.

Production: Duplicated by World in Color, Scottsville, NY, on Ektachrome #5071. Mounted in cardboard.

Documentation: Photocopied catalog lists contents of sets, some of which correspond to special exhibitions. Slides labeled with complete identifications except nationality of artist. Orientation not marked.

Purchasing: Slides sold singly except for exhibition sets. Priced $1.00 each; $2.50 for special orders. Minimum order two slides. Postage added. 10% discount given on orders of 100 slides or more. Purchase order required. Duplicates kept in stock and shipped within two weeks. Special photography carried out within four weeks. Rush orders accepted for in-stock items only; shipped within one week. Slides not sent on approval, and no returns accepted.

Other Products: Videotape available: "The Techniques of Glassmaking."

Evaluation: Reprinted from 6th ed. Quality, 3 to 4; documentation, 3; service, 3 to 4.

124   Dallas Museum of Art

1717 N. Harwood St.
Dallas, TX 75201
Telephone: (214) 922-0220, x232
Attn: Museum Shop

Profile: Entry reprinted from 6th ed. Two hundred seventy-five duplicate color slide titles offered of works in the permanent collection, including the Wendy and Emery Reves Collection of Impressionist and Post-Impressionist paintings. Duplicate slides of works not on list are available by special request from the museum's slide librarian.

Photography: Original slides shot by staff photographer.

Production: Duplicated by Superior Graphics, Dallas, TX. Mounted in plastic. Shipped in vinyl sleeves in bubble-lined envelope.

Documentation: Free list available; full information given for each slide except dimensions. Slides labeled with full identification. Orientation not marked.

Purchasing: Slides sold singly, priced $2.00 each. Postage added. No minimum order. Duplicates kept in stock, and orders filled promptly upon receipt. Rush orders accepted. Prepayment required from individuals, purchase order from institutions. Slides not sent on approval, and returns not accepted, but mistakes will be corrected.

Evaluation: Quality, 4; documentation, 3; service, 3.

125 Delaware Art Museum

2301 Kentmere Pkwy.
Wilmington, DE 19806
Telephone: (302) 571-9590
Attn: Museum Store

Profile: Entry reprinted from 6th ed. One hundred twelve color slide titles offered of the permanent collection, chiefly Pre-Raphaelite art and American illustration. No expansion of slide holdings planned.

Photography: Transparencies (35mm or larger) shot by staff photographer on Ektachrome ASA 50.

Production: Duplicated on Kodak slide duplicating film (probably Ektachrome #5071) by Chan Davies Photo Lab, Wilmington, DE. Contrast-controlled, but color not corrected.

Documentation: Free list, to which slides are keyed for identification.

Purchasing: Slides sold singly, $1.00 each plus $.25 postage. Prepayment required on foreign orders. Slides kept in stock and shipped within two weeks. No rush orders accepted. No minimum order. Returns accepted for refund or exchange. No special photography carried out.

Evaluation: Reprinted from 6th ed. Quality, 2 to 3, based on several samples sent in 1984.

126 Denver Art Museum

100 W. 14th Ave. Pkwy.
Denver, CO 80204
Telephone: (303) 576-2793
Attn: Sales Desk

Profile: Entry reprinted from 6th ed. Limited selection of slides (approximately 50) offered of the permanent collection, featuring European paintings, Pre-Columbian art, Spanish Colonial art, and Native American art.

Photography: Original slides shot by staff photographer in studio.

Production: Duplicated on Ektachrome by a commercial laboratory.

Documentation: Free list. Orientation marked.

Purchasing: Slides sold singly, $.50 each. Prepayment required on first order. No returns accepted.

Other Sources: Single slides offered by Saskia (086).

127 Detroit Institute of Arts

5200 Woodward Ave.
Detroit, MI 48202
Telephone: (313) 833-7913
Attn: Photo Service Department

Profile: Entry reprinted from 6th ed. More than 10,000 duplicate color slide titles offered of the permanent collection. Most accessioned pieces have been thoroughly photographed, a notable exception being textiles. New slides continually added.

Photography: Slides shot by staff photographers in studio on Ektachrome.

Production: Duplicated in-house on Ektachrome #5071; color-corrected in batches. Mounted in cardboard.

Documentation: Mailing list kept. Catalog (1986) priced $4.50. Identification consists of period/nationality, slide number, artist, title, artist's dates, and museum accession number. No information provided about specific media (e.g., type of print), dimensions, or date of work. Slides currently keyed to catalog, but museum is investigating systems for imprinting mounts. New catalog may possibly be issued in the near future, but no date for this is confirmed. Orientation not marked.

Purchasing: Order form inserted in catalog. Slides sold singly, $1.50 each. No minimum order. Discounts no longer given. Postage added. Prepayment required on foreign and personal orders. Duplicates kept in stock, or made to order only if stock depleted. Shipped within four to six weeks. No returns accepted. Slide sets (on rather old film stock) available from Education Department. New photography, if needed, is priced at $25.00 per item and will be carried out within one to three months.

Rental: This service has been discontinued.

Other Products: Black-and-white photographic prints sold and large-format color transparencies rented for reproduction.

Other Sources: As of mid-1989, the museum's policy is to maintain control over the distribution of images of its objects. No vendors are authorized to sell slides of its holdings.

Evaluation: Quality, 3 to 4; documentation, 2 to 3; service, 2 to 3.

128 Dumbarton Oaks

(Harvard University)
1703 32nd St., N.W.
Washington, DC 20007
Telephone: (202) 342-3246
FAX: (202) 342-3207
Attn: Curator, Byzantine Visual
Resources, Rachel Podol
Gift Shop: Diana McLeish (Part-Time)

Profile: Entry reprinted from 6th ed. with some updated information. Six nine-slide sets of duplicate slides offered of objects in the Dumbarton Oaks Byzantine Collection. Single slides sold for scholarly use only from an archive of 25,000 images documenting Byzantine art and architecture worldwide. Less than 10% of the slides are black-and-white. New slides continually added of new acquisitions.

Photography: Originals (slides, negatives, and large-format transparencies) shot by staff photographer or traveling scholars, or derived from sponsored fieldwork.

Production: Stable duplicates made from originals by Colorfax Labs, Washington, DC. Color-corrected and contrast-controlled. Mounted in cardboard. Shipped in boxes or between cardboards.

Documentation: *Handbook of the Byzantine Collection* (1967) available for $6.00 plus $2.50 postage. Slides keyed to lists provided with sets. Identifications complete except dimensions of objects not always given. Orientation not marked.

Purchasing: Photo price lists available on request; fees for nonscholarly uses are higher. For scholars and educational institutions, sets priced $12.50 each, singles $3.00. If more than 10 singles are ordered, the price is discounted to $2.00 each. Postage added. No minimum order. Pro forma invoice will be sent upon receipt of order; goods shipped after payment is received. Sets kept in stock and shipped within three weeks of receipt of payment. Single slides duplicated to order. No rush orders accepted. Slides not sent on approval, and returns not accepted. Original photography carried out by special request; curatorial fee charged.

Other Sources: Each department of Dumbarton Oaks has its own slide program. Orders should be addressed accordingly. Slides are available from the Dumbarton Oaks House Collection, from Studies in Landscape Architecture, and from Pre-Columbian Studies **(129).**

Evaluation: Quality, 3 to 4; documentation, 2 to 3; service, 2 to 3.

**129 Dumbarton Oaks—
Pre-Columbian Collection**

(Harvard University)
1703 32nd St.
Washington, DC 20007
Telephone: (202) 342-3265
FAX: (202) 625-0284
Attn: Pre-Columbian Collection
E-mail: churchw@doaks.org
URL: http://www.doaks.org

Profile: Images (slides, black-and-white photographs and 4" x 5" transparencies) for approximately 600 Pre-Columbian objects from the Robert Woods Bliss Collection.

Pre-Columbian cultures include Aztec, Mixtec, Teotihuacan, Olmec, Maya, Veracruz, Cocle, Veraguas, Tairona, Sinu', Inca, Huari, Chimu, Nazca, Moche, and Chavin.

Purchasing: Sets of nine slides are priced at $17.00 per set (10 different sets). Individual slides are priced at $5.00 each for scholarly/personal use, and at $10.00 each for commercial use.

Other Products: Black-and-white photographs; transparencies rented at $60 for scholarly publication and $100 for commercial publication ($200 for nonexclusive world rights). Dumbarton Oaks is examining the possibility of offering digital images.

**130 Eiteljorg Museum of
American Indians and
Western Art**

3000 N. Meridian St.
Indianapolis, IN 46206
Telephone: (317) 636-9378
Attn: Bob Tucker, Curator of Collections
URL: http://www.a1.com/QandA/eiteljorg/

Profile: Sells slides. Be sure to direct inquiries to Bob Tucker.

**131 Field Museum of
Natural History**

Roosevelt Rd. at Lake Shore Dr.
Chicago, IL 60605-2496
Telephone: (312) 922-9410, x248
Attn: Photography Department

Profile: Entry reprinted from 6th ed. Duplicate color slides offered of artifacts in the museum's anthropology collection. Holdings listed in order of strengths: North America, South Pacific, Africa, China, Tibet, South America, Egypt. Slides of plant models, dinosaurs, mammals, minerals, and museum dioramas are also available. Approximately 20,000 color slides in the archives.

Photography: All original transparencies produced by three staff photographers using 35mm, 120mm, and 4" x 5" formats and Kodak and Fuji films.

Production: Duplicated in-house, processed at an outside laboratory.

Documentation: No list available. Captions not routinely provided on slide mounts but may be requested. Orientation not marked.

Purchasing: Mail order preferred by Photography Department; telephone orders for information are accepted but must be confirmed in writing. Requests should be specific, including when possible a photocopy from a published source of the desired image, with complete reference citation. Duplicate slides from the Photography Department priced $10 each, plus postage. Prepayment required. Small orders (fewer than 10 slides) are shipped within two to three weeks of receipt of payment. Special photography undertaken upon request; orders filled within four to six weeks. All original negatives and transparencies retained by museum. Returns accepted for exchange or refund if image damaged in transit. Several sets available from Museum Store.

Other Sources: Five hundred eighty-five duplicate color slides offered by Davis Art Slides **(047)** (formerly Rosenthal Art Slides).

Evaluation: Quality, 3; documentation, 2; service, 2. (Evaluation by a single committee member.)

132 Freer Gallery of Art

(Smithsonian Institution)
1050 Independence Ave.
Washington, DC 20560
Telephone: (202) 357-4880, x237
FAX: (202) 633-9770
Attn: Scott A. Thompson
E-mail: thompsc@asia.sivm.edu

This museum also offers digital products and is listed in the digital section of the directory.

Profile: The Freer Gallery of Art and the Arthur M. Sackler Gallery together comprise the Smithsonian National Museums of Asian Art. The Freer Gallery was established with a bequest from Charles Long Freer and includes Chinese art, Japanese art, Korean art, Indian art, Islamic art, Egyptian art, early Christian and Byzantine art, art of the ancient Near East, and nineteenth-century American painting (especially Whistler). The Freer Gallery provides photographs, slides, and transparencies of objects in the collection, and grants permission to publish images in scholarly and commercial publications.

Photography: Objects are photographed by professional photographers in our studios. Large-format 4" x 5" Ektachrome transparencies and 4" x 5" black-and-white negatives are produced in-house.

Production: Duplicate 4" x 5" transparencies and 35mm slides are made from the originals.

Documentation: A mailing list is maintained. Any basic object information available upon request. Slide labels contain title, artist, date, and medium.

Purchasing: Individual slides are priced at $5.00 each. Prepayment is generally required, but university purchase orders are accepted. Stock slides shipped immediately after payment. Special order slides require two to three weeks minimum. Minimum U.S. surface shipping $4.50, or rush shipping via Federal Express for $15.00. Fee structure not yet determined for digital images. Contact museum for information. Prepayment is required for digital products, but University purchase orders are welcomed. Orders are usually filled within two to three weeks.

Rental: No rental or borrowing of slides. Rental of 4" x 5" transparencies for publication.

Digital Products: CD-ROMs in both Windows and MAC formats are available and are produced using a Leaf 4" x 5" film scanner or a Umax flatbed scanner. Original 4" x 5" transparencies, slides or 4" x 5" black-and-white negatives can be scanned at any resolution, but normally 400 dpi or less is used. Photoshop 4.0 is used for manipulation, including color-correction and cropping. Entire views and details can be provided. Any detail, format, resolution, and size can be special ordered. Museum will custom scan film when needed. Any format and any image viewing software can be used. CD-ROMs are provided for one-time or multiuser applications, but not for networked use.

Other Products: Black-and-white 8" x 10" prints sold and 4" x 5" color transparencies rented for publication.

Evaluation: Quality, 3; documentation, 3; service, 3. (Evaluation by a single committee member.)

133 Frick Collection

1 E. 70th St.
New York, NY 10021
Telephone: (212) 288-0700
FAX: (212) 628-4417
Attn: Sales and Information Department
URL: http://www.frick.org

This museum also offers digital products and is listed in the digital section of the directory.

Price Range: $1.00 to $5.00 for slides and $49.99 for PhotoCD.

Profile: Approximately 100 color slides offered of works in the museum's permanent collection: primarily paintings, with details; also, room views, sculpture, and porcelain. New titles occasionally added.

Photography: Original slides shot by staff photographer on Ektachrome ASA 160 using Nikon camera in studio.

Production: Duplicated by a local laboratory on Ektachrome #5071. Color-corrected and contrast-controlled. Mounted in plastic.

Documentation: Free list. Slides labeled. Identifications include name of artist, title of work, and collection.

Purchasing: Individual slides are priced at $1.00 and $5.00. Purchase orders accepted; premade slides sent within the week; custom orders approximately one month.

Digital Products: PhotoCD available in both Windows and MAC formats.

Other Sources: No vendor is authorized by the museum to sell slides of its holdings.

Evaluation: Quality, 2 to 4; documentation, 1 to 2; service, 1 to 4.

134 Galleries

New York, NY

Profile: Vendors offering slides of works shown in New York galleries include Art in America **(027)**, Educational Resource **(053)**, Larry Qualls **(082)**, and Universal Color Slide Co. **(095)**.

135 Isabella Stewart Gardner Museum

2 Palace Rd.
Boston, MA 02115
Telephone: (617) 566-1401
Attn: Museum Shop

Profile: Entry reprinted from 6th ed. Duplicate color slides offered of works in the permanent collection.

Photography: Original transparencies (mostly 4" x 5", some 8" x 10") shot by staff photographer.

Production: Single slides now duplicated in California. Sets produced by Scala/Art Resource. Stock of GAF Panavue slides will not be replenished when exhausted.

Documentation: Slides listed in Museum Shop catalog. Artist and title given.

Purchasing: Slides sold singly ($1.00) or in sets of six ($6.95). Order form included in Museum Shop catalog. Postage added. Duplicate slides of works not listed in the catalog may be obtained for $3.00 each. Prepayment in U.S. funds required. Orders filled within four to six weeks. Customers may specify "no GAF slides."

Other Products: Posters and postcards offered.

Evaluation: Quality, 4; documentation, 4; service, 3. (Evaluation by a single committee member.)

136 J. Paul Getty Museum

P.O. Box 2112
Santa Monica, CA 90406
Telephone: (213) 459-7611

Profile: Entry reprinted from 6th ed. Seventeen slide sets offered for sale, one (12 slides) of views of the museum building and 16 (six slides each) of works in the permanent collection. Paintings, decorative arts, Greek vases, and manuscript illuminations featured. New sets occasionally added.

Photography: Original large-format transparencies shot by staff photographers.

Production: At present, produced from originals by Frank Holmes Laboratory, Los Angeles, on Kodak film #5072. Color-corrected and contrast-controlled. Mounted in cardboard and protected by plastic sleeves.

Documentation: Free list. Contents of sets described: artist name and dates, title of work. Orientation marked on slides, and slides labeled.

Purchasing: Slides sold in sets only. Small sets priced $5.95 or $6.95. Large set $10.95. Minimum order one set. Purchase order required from institutions, prepayment from individuals. No discounts. Slides kept in stock and shipped within one week. Rush orders filled for a surcharge of $14.00. Slides not sent on approval, but returns accepted for exchange. Slides not available in sets may be purchased singly from Registrar.

Evaluation: Quality, 3 to 4; documentation, 3 to 4; service, 3 to 4.

137   Harvard University Art Museums

32 Quincy St.
Cambridge, MA 02138
Telephone: (617) 495-2389
Attn: Photographic Services

Profile: Entry reprinted from 6th ed. Duplicate color slides offered of selected objects in the Fogg Art Museum (Western art), the Arthur M. Sackler Museum (Ancient, Oriental, and Islamic art), and the Busch-Reisinger Museum (twentieth-century Germanic art). New slides continually added. Many slides available by request that are not on list.

Photography: Original slides shot by staff photographers on Ektachrome EPY ASA 50, using tripod or copystand and filters as appropriate.

Production: Duplicated on Ektachrome #5071 and processed by Boris Master Color, Boston. Color-corrected and contrast-controlled. Mounted in cardboard. Small orders put in sleeves, larger orders packed in boxes.

Documentation: Free list, under revision in 1989. Slides labeled with complete information, space permitting. Orientation marked by accession number, which is on top or along left side.

Purchasing: Slides sold singly. No minimum order. Slides kept in stock priced $2.00; duplicates made to order from available masters priced $4.00. Postage added. Shipped within one to two weeks. Rush orders filled with 50% surcharge. Original photography priced $20.00 to $25.00. Prepayment required. Slides not sent on approval, and returns not accepted.

Other Products: Black-and-white photographic prints sold, and color transparencies rented for reproduction.

Evaluation: Quality, 4; documentation, 4; service, 4. (Evaluation by a single committee member.)

138   High Museum of Art

1280 Peachtree St., N.E.
Atlanta, GA 30309
Telephone: (404) 892-3600, x382
Attn: Customer Service Manager

Profile: Entry reprinted from 6th ed. Sixty-seven duplicate color slides offered of works in the permanent collection, predominantly paintings.

Photography: Originals shot by independent professional photographer.

Documentation: Free list (artist and title only).

Purchasing: Slides sold singly, $2.00 each. No minimum order. Shipped within one to two weeks. Rush orders shipped out next day air.

Other Sources: University of Michigan Slide Distribution **(096)** offers a set of 1,150 slides.

139   Hirshhorn Museum and Sculpture Garden

c/o Smithsonian Institution Museum Shops
Distribution Center Facility, 3301 75th Ave.
Landover, MD 20785
Telephone: (301) 341-5400
Attn: Office Management

Profile: Entry reprinted from 6th ed. Duplicate color slide titles offered of works in the permanent collection.

Production: Davis Art Slides **(047)** (formerly Rosenthal Art Slides).

Documentation: Free list (contact Davis Art Slides for Rosenthal printout—168 items).

Purchasing: Slides sold singly, $1.25 each. Postage added at 15%.

Other Sources: Also available from Davis Art Slides **(047)** (formerly Rosenthal Art Slides).

Evaluation: See Davis Art Slides **(047)** (formerly Rosenthal Art Slides).

140 Hispanic Society of America Museum

613 W. 155th St.
New York, NY 10032
Telephone: (212) 926-2234
Attn: Publications Department

Profile: Entry reprinted from 6th ed. A recently produced set of 12 slides, "Sorolla," available for $17.50, postpaid. A few single slides produced in 1988/1989. Miscellaneous other single slides still offered (old stock). A very old set, "A Visit to the Hispanic Society," a record with 62 accompanying slides, can still be obtained.

Production: Sorolla set produced by Scala/Art Resource, Inc. See Davis Art Slides **(047)** (Scala Distributor for U.S. as of 1998).

Documentation: Free brochure describes Sorolla set, which is accompanied by text in English and Spanish. One page list of single slides available (recent productions).

Purchasing: Single slides priced $1.00 each. Postage added. Please inquire as to availability. Pro forma invoice will be sent.

Evaluation: Quality, 3; documentation, 3; service, 3. (Evaluation by a single committee member.)

141 Huntington Library and Art Gallery

1151 Oxford Rd.
San Marino, CA 91108
Telephone: (818) 405-2100
Attn: Bookstore or Photo Services

Profile: Entry reprinted from 6th ed. Duplicate color slides of selected works in the collections offered: eighteenth- and nineteenth-century British art and American art from 1750 to 1930. A set of 12 botanical garden slides available for $6.95. If new titles are added, they will be of the gardens.

Photography: Slides shot by staff photographers on Ektachrome ASA 100 daylight film. Garden slides shot by freelance photographer.

Production: Art slides produced by Rosenthal (*see* Davis Art Slides) **(047)**. Some remaining old stock may have been duplicated by Frank Holmes Laboratories, San Fernando, CA, which continues to produce the garden slides. Rosenthal stock mounted in plastic, others in cardboard.

Documentation: Single-page list of titles available free. Minimal information given on list. Slides labeled and keyed to Rosenthal catalog. Orientation marked on Rosenthal slides, not on others.

Purchasing: Duplicates kept in stock and shipped within four to six weeks. No rush orders accepted. Slides sold singly, $1.75 each. No minimum order. Prepayment required from individuals. No credit cards accepted by mail or phone. Purchase orders accepted from institutions. If desired images are not offered by Bookstore, they can be requested from Photo Services. Special orders filled within two to three weeks at cost of $5.00 per slide or $7.00 each if from bound volumes.

Other Products: Black-and-white photographic prints sold by Photo Services, and 4" x 5" color transparencies rented for reproduction.

Other Sources: One hundred five slides available directly from Davis Art Slides **(047)** (formerly Rosenthal Art Slides). Museum prefers that orders be sent to Davis Art Slides, as the staff available to fill mail orders is limited.

Evaluation: Quality, 4; documentation, 4; service, 3. (Evaluation by a single committee member.)

142 Indianapolis Museum of Art

1200 W. 38th St.
Indianapolis, IN 46208-4196
Telephone: (317) 923-1331, x171
FAX: (317) 931-1978
Attn: Ruth V. Roberts, Photography/Rights & Reproduction
E-mail: ima@indy.net
URL: http://www.ima-art.org/

Profile: We are planning CD-ROMs by collection type, i.e. Asian Art. Also the museum plans to include imaging for the collection management system, part of which will be accessible by the public. 4" x 5" transparencies will be scanned for digital images. Duplicate color slides sold singly.

Photography: Original works are photographed by a staff photographer in studio using Kodachrome EPN (ASA 100) for 4" x 5" transparencies and 35mm originals.

Production: SE slide duplicating film is used for duplicating slides. Some duplicating is done in-house, and large orders are sent to an outside lab.

Purchasing: Individual slides are priced at $5.00 per slide. Discounts are occasionally negotiated on large orders. Invoice is sent with order. Order is usually filled within one to two weeks.

Rental: Patrons pull their own slides. May borrow for up to one week for a nominal fee.

Other Products: Sell teacher packets that accompany temporary exhibitions that typically contain slides and a suggested curriculum. Color transparencies and black-and-white prints also sold.

Expansion Plans: Planning slide sets by collection type.

143   International Museum of Photography

George Eastman House
900 East Ave.
Rochester, NY 14620
Telephone: (716) 271-3361, x319
FAX: (716) 271-3970
Attn: Janice Madhu
E-mail: jkm@geh.org

Price Range: Black-and-white, $7.50; color, $10.00.

Profile: Photography collection includes nearly 400,000 photographs and negatives dating from invention of photography to the present day. More than 8,000 photographers are represented in the collection, including virtually all the major figures in the history of the medium. The collection includes original vintage works produced by nearly every process and printing medium employed. Major collections include vintage prints of Alvin Langdon Coburn and Nickolas Muray, nineteenth-century photographs of the American West, early French photography, and the largest collection of daguerreotypes in the world.

Photography: Original slides shot by staff photographers on Ektachrome, sometimes on Kodachrome ASA 40.

Production: Duplicated in-house on Ektachrome and sent out for processing.

Documentation: No catalog or list available. Printed works may serve as a reference.

Purchasing: Individual slides are priced at $10 per slide. Orders are not processed until payment is received. Make checks payable to George Eastman House. Fees are not refundable. Delivery time varies with size and complexity of the order. Allow three weeks for most orders after payment has been received. When ordering, provide as complete an identification of each image as possible, keeping in mind that photographs are usually cataloged by photographer, not by subject matter.

Other Products: Black-and-white photographs, 4" x 5" transparencies.

144   Joslyn Art Museum

2200 Dodge St.
Omaha, NE 68102
Telephone: (402) 342-3300
Attn: Museum Shop

Profile: Entry reprinted from 6th ed. Offers 134 color slide titles of painting, sculpture, and decorative arts in the permanent collection. In addition, seven slides available of the museum architecture. Of special interest are 48 tableaux and 33 vignettes by Karl Bodmer (aquatints from *Travels in the Interior of North America in the Years 1832–34*). New slides infrequently added.

Photography: Slides shot by an independent photographer on Kodak film, using tripod.

Production: Duplicated by Midwest Photo on Kodak film. Color-corrected and contrast-controlled. Mounted in plastic.

Documentation: Free brochure. Artist's name and nationality given, with title and date of work. Slides labeled. Orientation marked.

Purchasing: Slides sold singly, $1.00 each. No minimum order. Postage added. Prepayment required from individuals, purchase orders from institutions. Duplicates kept in stock and shipped within one to three weeks. Rush orders accepted; no surcharge. Slides not sent on approval, and returns not accepted. No special photography offered.

Other Products: Videotapes available.

145   Kimbell Art Museum

3333 Camp Bowie Blvd.
Fort Worth, TX 76107-2744
Telephone: (817) 332-8451
Attn: Bookstore or Slide Curator

Profile: Entry reprinted from 6th ed. Duplicate color slides offered of the museum building by Louis Kahn, the permanent collection, and exhibitions initiated by the museum. Included in the permanent collection, in addition to European art, are objects from Africa, Asia, Mesoamerica, and ancient cultures.

Photography: Slides shot by museum photographer on Ektachrome ASA 100 or Agfachrome ASA 100, usually in studio, occasionally in galleries. 4" x 5" photography also carried out.

Production: Duplicated by Color Place, Dallas, TX. Color-corrected by film lot. Contrast-controlled. Mounted in plastic or cardboard.

Documentation: Free list. Slides labeled and keyed to list, which provides accession number, artist, title, and date. Orientation marked only when necessary.

Purchasing: Slides sold in sets on site, singly by mail order. No minimum order. Slides ordered from bookstore priced $1.25 each plus postage. Prepayment required. Slides kept in stock and shipped within several weeks. Special orders for slides not stocked by the bookstore are handled by the Slide Curator. Slide Curator also has responsibility for limited-issue exhibition sets. Slides not sent on approval, but bookstore makes exchanges for flawed slides.

Exchange: Slide Curator is interested in exchanging slides with other institutions.

Other Sources: A set of 200 slides offered by University of Michigan Slide Distribution **(096)**.

Evaluation: Quality, 4; documentation, 3 to 4; service, 3.

146   Laumeier Sculpture Park
12580 Rott Rd.
St. Louis, MO 63127
Telephone: (314) 821-1209
Attn: Education Department

Profile: Entry reprinted from 6th ed. General set, "Sculptures at Laumeier," composed of 20 duplicate color slides. Five six-slide packets also offered: "Figurative Sculpture" and four monographs on individual artists.

Photography: Original slides shot by staff photographer and independent professionals.

Production: Stable duplicates made from originals at a local laboratory. Packaged in plastic sleeves.

Documentation: No list. Slides labeled and keyed to lists accompanying sets. Complete identifications given. Orientation marked only when necessary.

Purchasing: Slides kept in stock. Sets not sent on approval. No rush orders accepted.

Rental: Slides also available for rental.

Evaluation: Reprinted from 6th ed. Rated by Nancy DeLaurier, based on a 1982 order: quality, 3 to 4; documentation, 3.

147   Los Angeles County Museum of Art
5905 Wilshire Blvd.
Los Angeles, CA 90036
Telephone: (213) 857-6116
FAX: (213) 936-5755
Attn: Naomi Weiss
E-mail: nweiss@art.lacma.org
URL: http://www.lacma.org

Profile: The Museum/Museum Slide Library has no formal slide sales program although some sporadic slide sales have been offered. By specific request anything from the museum's permanent collection may be ordered, but requester must provide complete information, including museum's accession number. Slide librarian will order duplicate either from existing slide or 4" x 5" transparency from museum's photographic services department. Digital images not yet available to the public, but the museum is digitizing these images, with the hope that it will be possible in the future. Call for information.

Photography: Original works are photographed using 4" x 5" film by in-house Photo Services department in studio or galleries. Professional lighting and equipment used.

Production: We duplicate slides either from 4" x 5" original or best 35mm dupe available. Fuji Provia 4" x 5" and 35mm for originals. Ektachrome dupe film 35mm.

Documentation: Usually tombstone information.

Purchasing: Cost ranges from $5.00-$10.00 per slide depending on original format ($10.00 per slide for special orders.) Prepayment is generally not required because it usually needs to be determined whether or not a photograph exists. Shipping cost varies from $3.00 to $15.00, sometimes waived if just one slide in normal envelope. Orders can take up to eight weeks. No rush orders. Federal Express only if recipient has Federal Express account number.

Rental: Visual Resource Center rents slides, both of the museum's permanent collection, and several others.

Digital Products: Although not yet available to the public, images are being scanned using a flatbed scanner into Macintosh or PC workstation for editing. Original 4" x 5" transparencies; 8" x 10" prints, and 35mm slides are scanned at resolutions of 72-300 dpi and manipulated with Photoshop for color-correction and cropping. Both entire and detail views are being stored.

Other Products: Some videotapes.

Expansion Plans: Sell sets of slides: curatorial selections from the permanent collection that have popular or scholarly value. Pilot sets of European Painting & Sculpture and Pre-Columbian are in the works now. Continuation of this program will depend on sales volume.

Evaluation: Quality, 4; documentation, 3; service, 3. (Evaluation by a single committee member.)

148   Meadows Museum and Gallery

Owen Fine Arts Center
Southern Methodist University
Dallas, TX 75275
Telephone: (214) 692-2516
Attn: Registrar

Profile: Entry reprinted from 6th ed. Ninety-eight color slide titles offered of the permanent collection of Spanish art (fifteenth to twentieth century), as well as slides of the sculpture court (twentieth-century international works). New slides added only of new acquisitions.

Photography: Original 4" x 5" transparencies shot by independent professional photographers, using view camera and Ektachrome #6118.

Production: Duplicated by BWC Photolabs, Dallas, TX, on Ektachrome #5071. Contrast-controlled. Color-corrected on request. Mounted in plastic. Packaged in plastic covers.

Documentation: Free list; information complete. Slides keyed to list. Orientation marked by number placement.

Purchasing: Slides sold singly, $.75 each, plus postage. Order form attached to list. No minimum order. Prepayment required, payable to Meadows Museum-SMU. Duplicates kept in stock and shipped within one week. Rush orders filled within one to two days; surcharge for express mail. Returns not accepted. Special photography undertaken only with approval of director; fee variable.

Evaluation: Quality, 3; documentation, 3; service, 3.

149   Memorial Art Gallery

University of Rochester
500 University Ave.
Rochester, NY 14607-1415
Telephone: (716) 473-7720
FAX: (716) 473-6266
Attn: Curatorial Department
E-mail: maginfo@mag.rochester.edu
URL: http://www.rochester.edu/MAG/

Profile: Entry reprinted from 6th ed. Approximately 1,000 duplicate color slide titles offered of objects in the permanent collection, which features European art from the Middle Ages through the seventeenth century; nineteenth- and early twentieth-century French painting; Native American art and American folk art; and contemporary prints. New titles continually added.

Photography: Slides shot on Ektachrome by an independent professional photographer (formerly by a staff photographer).

Production: Duplicated on Ektachrome #5071 by New Image, Rochester, NY. Color-corrected and contrast-controlled. Mounted in plastic or cardboard.

Documentation: No list available. Slides labeled. Orientation marked.

Purchasing: Slides sold singly, $4.00 each, postpaid. No minimum order and no discounts. Slides in stock shipped within 10 days; if duplicated to order, within four weeks. No rush orders accepted. No returns accepted. Special photography carried out on request.

Expansion Plans: Collection is being put on computer.

150   Metropolitan Museum of Art

Fifth Ave. at 82nd St.
New York, NY 10028
Telephone: (212) 879-5500
FAX: (212) 570-3879
Attn: Children's Bookshop

Profile: Entry reprinted from 6th ed. No response to 1984 or 1989 questionnaire. Entry based on recent list, former entry, and response to the 1989 questionnaire by The Cloisters. Duplicate color slides offered of selected works in the permanent collection. Slide sets sometimes offered of current exhibitions.

Production: Five hundred slides produced by Rosenthal Art Slides (*see* Davis Art Slides) **(047)**. A few still produced by Visual Media **(80)**.

Documentation: Free list. Artist, title, accession number given. Slides labeled by producers.

Purchasing: Slides sold singly, $1.25 each. Order form attached to list. Postage added. Shipping charge on all foreign orders, $7.95. Rush orders filled overnight for extra $10.00 to cover express shipping. Prepayment required in U.S. funds, drawn on a U.S. bank.

Rental: Slide Library loans slides, in person only, for a fee, to educators.

Other Sources: See also The Cloisters entry **(118)**. Slides may be ordered directly from Davis Art Slides **(047)** (formerly Rosenthal Art Slides). Sets available from Asian Art Photographic Distribution **(30)** include "Buddhist Sculpture," "Ancient China: Weber Galleries," and "Chinese Painting." The John M. Crawford, Jr., Collection of Chinese Painting and Calligraphy, recently acquired by the museum through bequest, has also been photographed by AAPD.

Evaluation: Quality, 4; documentation, 3; service, 3.

151 Milwaukee Art Museum

750 N. Lincoln Memorial Dr.
Milwaukee, WI 53202
Telephone: (414) 224-3200
Museum Shop: (414) 224-3210
FAX: (414) 271-7588
Attn: Slide Library
E-mail: mccann@mam.org
URL: http://www.mam.org/

Profile: Profile updated; rest of entry reprinted from 6th ed. Museum's permanent collection includes nearly 20,000 works. Much of the collection is available in slide format. Included are works from the Bradley Collection (nineteenth-century American), the Flagg Tanning Corporation Collection (Haitian), the von Schleinitz Collection (nineteenth-century German), the Frank Lloyd Wright and Prairie School Collection of Drawings, the Landfall Press Archive of contemporary editioned prints, Folk and Outside Art of works in all media from the nineteenth century, and the Brooks Stevens Archive: models, drawings, photos. New titles continually added. Slides available of decorative arts even though not listed in catalog.

Photography: Original slides shot on Ektachrome ASA 50 by staff photographer.

Production: Duplicated by Kolor Krome on Ektachrome #5071. Color-corrected and contrast-controlled. Mounted in cardboard.

Documentation: Catalog $9.00. Identification consists of artist's name and dates, title and date of work, and sometimes medium. Slides labeled and orientation marked. Materials and dimensions not given.

Purchasing: Slides sold singly and in sets. Single slides priced $1.75 each, postpaid. Set prices vary. No minimum order. Discount sometimes given on large orders. Prepayment required. Duplicated to order and shipped within two to three weeks. Slides not sent on approval, but returns accepted for exchange or refund.

Rental: Slide sets available for rental; no singles.

Evaluation: Quality, 4; documentation, 4; service, 4. (Evaluation by a single committee member.)

152 Minneapolis Institute of Arts

2400 Third Ave. S.
Minneapolis, MN 55404
Telephone: (612) 870-3196
FAX: (612) 870-3004
Attn: Heidi S. Raatz, Slide Librarian
(Only for slides)
E-mail: hraatz@artsmia.org
URL: http://www.artsmia.org

This museum also offers digital products and is listed in the digital section of the directory.

Profile: Slides available of works in the permanent collection, which features paintings, sculpture, drawings, prints, decorative arts, textiles, photography, antiquities, and the arts of Oceania, Africa, the Americas, and Asia. Items not available through Rosenthal Art Slides [now Davis Art Slides **(047)**] can be requested; a duplicate will be supplied provided an original master slide is available.

Photography: Originals are photographed by professional staff photographers, who use Kodak E100S film with electronic flash in the studio; Ektachrome T64 film in galleries with existing tungsten lighting.

Production: Slides from slide library duplicated on Ektachrome #5071 by ProColor, Minneapolis, MN. Color-corrected and contrast-controlled if necessary. Mounted in plastic.

Documentation: All slides produced by Slide Library labeled with full identifications. No catalog or brochure from Slide Library. Brochure available from Davis Art Slides **(047)** (formerly Rosenthal Art Slides) of 265 slides produced by them. Full identifications sent with permission/licensing information for digital images.

Purchasing: Individual slides are priced at $5.00 each; additional charges may apply if new photography is required. Invoice sent with slides (small orders). Larger orders and orders from institutions should include a purchase order. Orders usually filled within two weeks (longer time frame if new photography is required). Slides sent via U.S. mail; sleeved and packed in padded mailers. Postage and handling charges added. Slides not sent on approval.

Rental: Rental sets, slides with accompanying curriculum materials, available.

Digital Products: CD-ROMs in both Windows and MAC formats are produced using PhotoCD and a flatbed scanner. Transparencies, minimum size 2¼", are scanned at resolutions ranging from 150 dpi to 1000 dpi and manipulated with Photoshop for color-correction and cropping. Entire views are offered in .JPG format for viewing with Photoshop. CD-ROMs are licensed for one-at-a-time use but not for networked use. Please contact Permissions & Licensing Department (612) 870-3191 for more information.

Other Products: Please contact Curriculum Materials Department. Two CD-ROMs are available from the Museum Shop: "A Prairie School Gem: The Purcell-Cutts House" and "Prints and Processes." Contact Museum Shop (612) 870-3100.

Evaluation: Quality, 3 to 4; documentation, 3 to 4; service, 3.

153 Morse Gallery of Art

151 E. Wellbourne Ave.
Winter Park, FL 32789
Telephone: (407) 644-3686
Attn: Museum Shop

Profile: Entry reprinted from 6th ed. Sixty-six duplicate color slide titles offered of the Tiffany exhibit— glass, lamps, windows, jewelry, and paintings.

Photography: Originals shot by staff photographer.

Production: Duplicated by World in Color.

Documentation: Free list. Titles of works provided.

Purchasing: Slides sold singly, $1.00 each. Postage added.

Evaluation: Reprinted from 6th ed. Review in the fall 1986 issue of *Stained Glass* stated that the slides were "not of uniformly good quality."

154 Munson-Williams-Proctor Institute

310 Genesee St.
Utica, NY 13502
Telephone: (315) 797-0000, x2135
FAX: (315) 797-5608
Attn: Museum Registrar
E-mail: dwinderl@MWP1.edu

Profile: Approximately 500 duplicate color slide titles offered of works in the permanent collection, plus several hundred slides of Fountain Elms architecture and furnishings. Collection includes some nineteenth-century European paintings, drawings, and prints and nineteenth- and twentieth-century architecture, sculpture, paintings, drawings, prints, and decorative arts from the United States.

Photography: Original slides shot by independent professional photographer.

Production: Stable duplicates produced from originals by commercial laboratories (Kodak?). Mounted in plastic.

Documentation: No list available. Slides labeled with full identifications. Orientation marked.

Purchasing: Slides sold singly, $5.00 each. No minimum order. Quantity discount offered. Postage added. Prepayment required in U.S. funds. Duplicates kept in stock (or made to order if necessary) and shipped within one to two weeks. Rush orders accommodated if possible. All requests must be in writing. Phone orders not taken.

Rental: Color transparencies. Contact museum for details.

Other Products: Black-and-white photographic prints also sold, $15 each.

155 Museum of American Textile History

800 Massachusetts Ave.
North Andover, MA 01845
Telephone: (508) 686-0191
Attn: Photographic Services

Profile: Entry reprinted from 6th ed. Formerly Merrimack Valley Textile Museum. Fifteen thousand color slide titles offered from the curatorial library collections, including images of textiles. Other holdings documented include prints and photographs of textile technology, mills, labor, and industrial and preindustrial machinery. New titles added infrequently.

Photography: Slides shot by independent professional photographers (50%), staff members (25%), and scholars (25%), on various films. Approximately 10% of the images are black-and-white.

Production: Duplicated by local firm from originals or duplicates. Color-corrected and contrast-controlled.

Documentation: Catalog available on premises only. Slides labeled. "Twenty-five dollars per hour research time (per staff member) may be charged in situations where staff time is extensively utilized."

Purchasing: Slides sold in sets and singly. Duplicates, $3.00 each. New slides (minimum 10), $8.00 each. Slides duplicated to order and shipped within three weeks. No rush orders accepted. Slides not sent on approval, and returns not accepted.

Rental: Slide programs rented on subjects related to the history of the textile industry. Five slide/tape presentations available for rental fee of $10 each: "Daily Work," "Bleak Prospects," "Machine Shop Village," "Merrimack Valley," and "The Industrial Revolution."

156 Museum of Contemporary Art, Chicago

220 E. Chicago Ave.
Chicago, IL 60611-2604
Telephone: (312) 397-3896
FAX: (312) 397-4099
E-mail: sgengo@mca.chicago
URL: http://www.mcachicago.org/

Price Range: $5.00 per slide.

Profile: Inventory of about 200 slides taken from Chicago's newest major museum and one of the nation's largest facilities devoted to the art of our time. The Museum of Contemporary Art (MCA) offers exhibitions of the most thought-provoking art created since 1945. The MCA documents contemporary visual culture through painting, sculpture, photography, video and film, and performance. Among the artists whom the MCA has collected in depth are Alexander Calder, Donald Judd, Sol LeWitt, Bruce Nauman, and Robert Smithson. The collection also includes key works by Francis Bacon, Ann Hamilton, Alfredo Jaar, Jasper Johns, Jeff Koons, René Magritte, Ed Paschke, Richard Serra, Cindy Sherman, Loran Simpson, and Andy Warhol.

157 Museum of Contemporary Art, Los Angeles

250 S. Grand Ave. at California Plaza
Los Angeles, CA 90012
Telephone: (213) 621-2766
FAX: (213) 620-8674
Attn: Kim Cooper, Librarian
E-mail: mocakc@earthlink.net
URL: http://www.moca-la.org/

Profile: Entry reprinted from 6th ed. About 14,000 works from permanent collection plus an additional several thousand installation views from temporary exhibitions, installations, events, and the museum buildings. New slides continually added. Sandak slides sold by shop.

Photography: Original slides shot on Ektachrome ASA 64 by independent professional photographers, using tripod.

Production: Duplicates on Ektachrome #6121 made from originals at A & I Lab, Los Angeles. Color-correction and contrast-control not attempted. Mounted in cardboard. Placed in archival sleeves for shipment.

Documentation: Free list available from Photographic Services, updated annually. Slides labeled with complete identifications, except nationality and dates of artist. Orientation marked. No list available from shop, but telephone inquiries welcomed.

Purchasing: Slides sold singly, $2.50 each. 20% discount on orders of 50 slides or more. Postage added. Duplicates kept in stock, and orders shipped within three days to two weeks. Rush orders filled within three days. Payment must be in U.S. funds, but no prepayment is necessary. Slides sent on approval, and returns accepted for exchange or refund. Sandak-produced slides available from Museum Store in small sets; Sandak's coverage expanded in March 1990. (Contact museum about Sandak slides as Sandak ceased business in 1997.)

Rental: Single slides loaned for two weeks for a fee, plus a small charge for postage and handling. Up to 10 slides may be borrowed for $5.00, from 10 to 49 for $10.00, or 50 for $15.00.

*158   Museum of Fine Arts, Boston

465 Huntington Ave.
Boston, MA 02115
Telephone: (617) 369-3724
FAX: (617) 267-9773
Attn: Photographic Sales/Slides MFA
Enterprise
E-mail: nluongo@mfa.org (for
Photographic Sales)
nfujiwara@mfa.org (for MFA Enterprise)
URL: http://www.mfa.org

This museum offers licensing of digital images and is listed in the digital section of the directory.

Profile: Slides had been sold in the Slide Library until August 1996. Slide sales were transferred to the retail division, MFA Enterprise, at that time. Catalog has been discontinued, but slides are available by mail/fax/E-mail. Some 8,000 images of MFA objects currently in stock for purchase. Special orders are accommodated for other items for which no master slides exist. The 8,000 images, currently part of the sales inventory, are intended to be online in the early part of 1998. These will be for reference and ordering use.

Photography: Images are photographed in-house by MFA photographers from original object. Items are shot in the Photo Studio with appropriate lighting. Images are shot in large format and slides are reduced.

Production: Duplicates of Ektachrome reductions are what customers receive.

Documentation: Slides are accompanied by printed information sheets.

Purchasing: Both individual slides and sets are available. Individual slides are priced at $3.00/slide. No discounts except 10% for MFA members. Sets are priced at approximately $2.00/slide (preselected);

sets include from 5 to 250 slides. Prepayment is required: check, VISA, MasterCard, American Express, purchase orders. Orders are filled upon receipt when in stock. Special orders take up to two weeks. Rush orders are twice the total cost and guaranteed within a week. Postage and handling varies for U.S./Canada/Europe and on slide quantities.

Rental: Slide rental is allowed for local educators only. Public hours: Monday 10 A.M. to 1 P.M., Wednesday 1 P.M. to 7 P.M. Call for an appointment.

Digital Products: Contact MFA Enterprises, Rights and Licensing to negotiate use of digital images.

Other Products: Black-and-white photos and transparency rentals for reproduction are available through MFA Enterprises, Rights and Licensing.

Evaluation: Quality, 2 to 4; documentation, 3 to 4; service, 3 to 4. (All but one evaluator rated 3 to 4 for quality.)

159   Museum of Fine Arts, Houston

1001 Bissonnet
P.O. Box 6826
Houston, TX 77005-6826
Telephone: (713) 526-1361
FAX: (713) 526-4973
Attn: Slide Librarian, Hirsch Library

Profile: Entry reprinted from 6th ed. Orders by mail handled by Slide Library rather than museum's Gift Shop, which stocks a small selection of Rosenthal [now Davis **(047)**] slides and an 18-slide set of Impressionist and Post-Impressionist paintings for sale on site. Subjects represented in approximately 4,000 original color slides are antiquities; art of the Near East, the Far East, and Africa; Pre-Columbian art; and European and American painting, sculpture, photography, decorative arts, prints, and drawings. Bayou Bend Collection of American furniture, paintings, and silver included. New titles continually added.

Photography: Original slides shot by independent professional photographer on Ektachrome ASA 50, using tripod.

Production: Original slides duplicated on Ektachrome #5071 at National Photographic Laboratories, Houston, TX. No color-correction or contrast-control attempted. Nearly 500 slides produced by Rosenthal Art Slides (now Davis Art Slides). Set of Impressionist and Post-Impressionist paintings produced by Scala/Art Resource.

Documentation: No comprehensive list available of Slide Library holdings. The slide librarian is willing to supply a custom list in response to a specific inquiry. *Guide to the Collection* (1981) may be used as a reference in ordering and identifying; it is available by mail order from the Gift Shop. The 1975 catalog of the Bayou Bend Collection is out of print, but may be accessible in libraries. Slides not labeled but keyed to identification list supplied with order. Full information provided, but artists' dates and nationalities sometimes omitted. Orientation marked on all slides.

Purchasing: Slide Library duplicates made to order, mounted in cardboard, and packed in padded mailing envelopes (boxes for large orders). Orders usually filled within two weeks. Rush orders accepted; extra charge for two-day orders 100%, for four-day orders 10%. Prepayment preferred, but purchase orders accepted from institutions. Orders of fewer than five slides discouraged. Slides priced $1.50 each. Postage charged on overseas orders. Payment accepted in U.S. funds only. Returns accepted for exchange or refund if customer is dissatisfied. Art Resource set (18 slides) may be ordered from Slide Library for $15.00 plus postage.

Other Sources: Some 475 duplicate color slides available from Davis Art Slides, and more to be added in the near future; orders for these should be addressed to Davis Art Slides **(047)** (formerly Rosenthal Art Slides) rather than the museum. Sandak slides are being evaluated for quality, and the museum is providing new originals as needed. (Contact museum for availability as Sandak ceased business in 1997.)

Evaluation: Quality, 3; documentation, 3; service, 3.

160　Museum of Modern Art

11 W. 53rd St.
New York, NY 10019-5486
Telephone: (212) 708-9702
Attn: Museum Store
URL: http://www.moma.org

Profile: See Davis Arts Slides **(047)** to order. Previously, approximately 750 duplicate color slide titles offered of works in the permanent collection: paintings, sculptures, drawings, prints, and photographs. Exhibitions of the 1960s, 1970s, and 1980s documented in sets by Sandak (Sandak ceased business in 1997).

Purchasing: Contact Davis Art Slides **(047)**.

161　Museum of Modern Art of Latin America

Organization of American States
1889 F St., N.W.
Washington, DC 20006
Telephone: (202) 458-6016
Attn: Audio-Visual Unit

Profile: Entry reprinted from 6th ed. More than 3,000 color slide titles offered in 312 sets. Series titles are "Culture in Latin America," "Scenery in Latin American Countries," "Pre-Columbian Art," and "Art in Latin America." New titles continually added. The museum's own permanent collection represented, as well as special exhibitions of Latin American artists there and elsewhere, including the Museum of Modern Art, New York. Other museum collections documented include:

> Museo Nacional de Antropologia, Mexico City, Mexico
>
> Museo del Oro, Bogota, Colombia
>
> Museo Nacional de Antropologia y Arqueologia, Lima, Peru

Photography: Slides shot by staff photographers on Ektachrome professional film ASA 160 using Nikon equipment.

Production: Printed by Consolidated Visual Center on Eastmancolor #5384. Color-corrected and contrast-controlled. Mounted in cardboard. Packaged in plastic sleeves.

Documentation: Mailing list kept. Free catalog, in English, lists set titles. Each set accompanied by a "descriptive pamphlet" in English (a few also available in Spanish). *The Museum of Modern Art of Latin America, Selections from the Permanent Collection*, an illustrated catalog, priced $12. Orientation marked by number placement.

Purchasing: Slides sold in sets of 10, $10, postpaid. Minimum order one set. 40% discount given on purchase of a complete series (56 to 113 sets). All 3,120 slides priced $1,700. Prepayment required. Make checks payable to OAS Audio-Visual Program. Overseas postage and insurance added. Orders usually filled within four weeks. Returns accepted ("rarely") "if the slides do not meet curriculum needs or are defective."

Other Products: Filmstrips, 16mm films, and videocassettes offered.

Evaluation: Quality, 2 to 3; documentation, 1 to 2; service, 2.

162   National Academy of Design

1083 Fifth Ave.
New York, NY 10128
Telephone: (212) 369-4880

Profile: Entry reprinted from 6th ed. Slides, 4" x 5" color transparencies, and black-and-white photographs offered for rental, covering the academy's collection of nineteenth- and twentieth-century American art. Four hundred black-and-white and 100 color images available.

Photography: Independent photographer hired on freelance basis.

Production: Originals usually lent, but duplicates occasionally made. No attempt made to correct color or control contrast.

Documentation: No list. Images labeled with artist, title, and collection. Orientation not marked.

Rental: Images offered individually; no minimum order. Prices based on actual costs for each job. Time to fill order varies, depending on photographer's current work load.

163   National Gallery of Art

Constitution Ave. at 6th St., N.W.
Washington, DC 20565
Telephone: (202) 842-6462

Profile: Slide orders are referred to Davis Art Slides (formerly Rosenthal) **(047)**. All previous slide productions have been discontinued. Davis Art Slides will also market the old Sandak stock of National Gallery of Art objects (Gregory P. J. Most, Chief Slide Librarian, 10/97).

Purchasing: Address orders to Davis Art Slides **(047)**.

Other Products: Postcards, color reproductions, and videocassettes available for purchase.

Other Sources: Other sources of slides of National Gallery of Art objects include Academic Challenge **(019)**, Dick Blick Co. **(050)**, Slides for Education **(088)**, and Universal Color Slide Co. **(095)**.

Evaluation: Quality, 3 to 4; documentation, 3 to 4; service, 3 to 4.

164   National Museum of African Art

(Smithsonian Institution)
950 Independence Ave., S.W.
Washington, DC 20560
Telephone: (202) 357-4654
Attn: Eliot Elisofon Photographic Archives
E-mail: NMAfAweb@NMAfA.si.edu
(webmaster)
URL: http://www.si.edu/organiza/museums/
africart/start.htm

Profile: Entry reprinted from 6th edition with updated information from Photo Archivist Paul Wood. More than 35,000 color slide titles included in archives holdings: objects in the museum's collection, field photographs, and donated collections. Several thousand new slides added annually.

Photography: Various photographers, professional and amateur, represented in holdings. Most museum objects shot on Kodachrome. Archive of Eliot Elisofon, *Life Magazine* photographer, featured among many others.

Production: Duplicated on Ektachrome #5071 by a local laboratory. Color-corrected and contrast-controlled, if necessary. Mounted in plastic.

Documentation: Free general guide to the collection and price list. Identification computer-imprinted on mounts. In accepting donations to the archives, scholarly documentation of images is highly valued by the staff.

Purchasing: Slides sold singly, $6.00, postpaid. Price does not include rights for reproduction. Contact museum for information on reproduction. No minimum order. Prepayment or purchase order required. Slides usually duplicated to order and shipped within six weeks. Rush orders accepted; surcharge of 100%. No rush orders for more than 50 slides accepted. No special photography offered. Slides not sent on approval, and returns accepted for exchange only when damaged.

Rental: Forty slides and explanatory text loaned for three weeks.

Other Products: Videotapes available for three-week loans. Please allow two weeks for delivery and limit request to two items. The requester will be responsible for return postage. 180,000 transparencies; 80,000 black-and-white images.

Evaluation: Quality, 4; documentation, 4; service, 4.

165 National Museum of American Art

c/o Smithsonian Institution Museum Shops
Distribution Center Facility, 3301 75th Ave.
Landover, MD 20785
Telephone: (301) 341-5400
Attn: Office Management

Profile: Entry reprinted from 6th ed. No response to 1989 questionnaire. Entry repeated from fifth edition, with revisions. Offers 353 color slide titles of works in the permanent collection of American art, colonial era to the present. New slides continually added. Sets of slides documenting exhibitions sometimes available.

Photography: 4" x 5" transparencies shot on Ektachrome #6118 by staff photographers using a view camera and professional lighting techniques in a studio. Paintings and graphic works usually photographed unframed.

Production: Single slides produced by Rosenthal Art Slides [now Davis Art Slides **(047)**] on Ektachrome #5071. Mounted in plastic or cardboard. Sets from exhibitions produced by the Office of Printing and Photographic Services, Smithsonian Institution.

Documentation: Mailing list kept. Free slide list, revised biennially, gives full information. Slides labeled and keyed to list. Orientation marked. Listed also in Davis Art Slides catalog. Sets accompanied by checklist giving full identifications.

Purchasing: Slides sold singly, $1.25 each. No minimum order. Postage added at 15%. Discount of 10% for Smithsonian Associates. Slides kept in stock and shipped within three weeks. Rush orders filled within three days; no surcharge. Slides not sent on approval. Returns accepted for exchange or refund if damaged. Prices on exhibitions sets vary, but all are based on per-slide cost of less than $1.00. Original photography carried out within two to three months for $50.00 fee. For the latter, address inquiries directly to the museum at Eighth and G Streets, N.W., Washington, DC 20560.

Exchange: "We are happy to exchange slides with other museums, generally those with American collections. This is usually negotiated on a slide-for-slide, or even exchange, basis."

Other Sources: Slides may be ordered directly from Davis Art Slides **(047)** (formerly Rosenthal Art Slides).

Evaluation: Quality, 3; documentation, 3; service, 3. (Evaluation by a single committee member.)

166 National Museum of the American Indian

Smithsonian Institution, George Gustav
Heye Center
One Bowling Green
New York, NY 10004
Telephone: (212) 514-3700
Attn: Photo Archive and Photo Services
Dept.

Executive Offices:
470 L'Enfant Plaza, S.W.
Suite 7102
Washington, DC 20560
Telephone: (202) 357-2700
URL: http://www.si.edu/cgi-bin/nav.cgi

Price Range: $1.00 to $12.00.

Profile: The Photo Archive at the National Museum of the American Indian constitutes a collection of approximately 100,000 images and depicts many aspects of Native American life in the Western Hemisphere. The chronological span of the collection ranges from early daguerreotypes to contemporary prints. Images are available by written request for research or publication purposes. Database reports on specific topics (e.g., tribe subject) are available at no charge. Established in 1989, the museum will be located in three facilities: the Heye Center in the Alexander Hamilton U.S. Custom House in New York City, now open; a Cultural Resources Center in Suitland, Maryland, scheduled to open in 1998; and a museum to open in Washington, DC, in 2002.

Photography: Concern for the safety and handling of objects in the museum's collection is a prime factor in determining whether original photography may be performed. The decision to permit photography of any object rests with the Curatorial and Conservation Departments.

Documentation: Slide catalog is available at a cost of $3.00.

Purchasing: Individual slides from catalog are priced at $1.00 each. The cost for custom dupes is $10.00 for noncommercial use and $12.00 for commercial use. Advance payment is required before an order is processed. Checks or money orders should be payable in U.S. dollars to: National Museum of the American Indian. Orders for duplicate slides and transparencies or slides from the Slide Catalog are generally shipped two to three weeks from date of payment.

Other Products: 4" x 5" Transparencies; 5" x 7", 8" x 10", 11" x 14" black-and-white prints; 5" x 7", 8" x 10" color prints; books; recordings.

167   National Museum of Women in the Arts

1250 New York Ave., N.W.
Washington, DC 20005-3920
Telephone: (202) 783-5000
Attn: Museum Shop

Profile: Entry reprinted from 6th ed. Two sets of 12 slides each offered of works in the permanent collection. One set features historical artists, the other twentieth-century artists. More sets may be added in the future.

Production: Slides made by Sandak (Sandak ceased business in 1997).

Documentation: Free list gives complete identifications. Slides labeled. Orientation marked.

Purchasing: Each set priced $13.95.

Evaluation: Quality, 4; documentation, 2; service, 4. (Evaluation by a single committee member.)

168   National Portrait Gallery

(Smithsonian Institution)
F Street at Eighth, N.W.
Washington, DC 20560
Telephone: (202) 357-2791
Attn: Office of Rights & Reproductions

Profile: Entry reprinted from 6th ed. Color slides offered of most of the permanent collection, some of the study collection, and a few items from the Graphics File. New slides continually added.

Photography: Originals (slides and larger-format transparencies) shot by staff photographer in studio. Frames of paintings removed.

Production: Stable duplicates made from originals. Mounted in cardboard and sleeved. Shipped in cardboard mailers.

Documentation: Illustrated catalog (Checklist of Permanent Collection, 1987) available from Museum Shop, $24.95 plus 15% shipping. Updated every three to five years. List arranged by sitters' names. Other information supplied includes artist's name and dates, dates of sitter, date of work, medium,

size, accession number, and donor. Indexed by artist. Some information also provided on slide labels (artist, title, sitter, date). Orientation not marked.

Purchasing: Originals supplied when available; otherwise, duplicates made. Stock on hand is approximately 50% originals. Slides sold singly, $8.00. Free single-page price sheet available on request. No rush or telephone orders accepted. Pro forma invoice will be sent. Orders shipped after receipt of payment, within four to eight weeks. No returns accepted. Special photography fee, if necessary, $50.00.

Other Products: Black-and-white photographic prints also sold, and color transparencies rented for reproduction.

169   Nelson-Atkins Museum of Art

4525 Oak St.
Kansas City, MO 64111-1873
Telephone: (816) 751-1214
FAX: (816) 561-7154 (Museum FAX)
Attn: Sales Desk or Slide Library

Profile: Approximately 1,000 duplicate color slides offered of objects in the permanent collection. Many slides of Asian art included. Western art, ancient through twentieth century, also represented. New titles continually added. The museum plans to digitize images from the permanent collection and make them available for a variety of uses.

Photography: Slides are photographed by staff photographer from artworks directly on Ektachrome in the photography studio with modern photographic equipment and lighting.

Production: Slides are duplicated by a local photo lab on Ektachrome #5071 from original slides taken by staff photographer.

Documentation: No printed slide/image catalog; slide lists in major areas of the collection, free upon request. Slide information includes country/culture, artist, title of work, date, medium, dimensions, location/owner with accession number.

Purchasing: Individual slides are priced at $3.00 each in all cases. University purchase orders accepted; slides delivered within two to four weeks; large orders may take longer. Shipping and handling is $3.00 to $10.00 for U.S. orders and $7.00 to $14.00 for all other countries.

Expansion Plans: Digital version of images from collection.

Evaluation: Quality, 3 to 4; documentation, 2 to 4; service, 3.

170 New Britain Museum of American Art

56 Lexington St.
New Britain, CT 06052
Telephone: (203) 229-0257

Profile: Entry reprinted from 6th ed. Original color slides offered of items in the collection of American art, 1740 to the present.

Photography: Shot by a professional museum photographer on Kodak film.

Production: Original slides mounted in plastic.

Documentation: No list.

Purchasing: Slides sold singly, $1.75 each. No minimum order. Slides kept in stock. No returns accepted.

171 North Carolina Museum of Art

2110 Blue Ridge Rd.
Raleigh, NC 27607-6494
Telephone: (919) 839-6262
FAX: (919) 733-8034
Attn: Museum Shop
URL: http://www2.ncsu.edu/ncma

This museum also offers digital products and is listed in the digital section of the directory.

Profile: Art Museum owned by the state of North Carolina. Collections include: Ancient Classical, Pre-Columbian, African, Judaica, European, American, 20th Century. Sells slides and one CD-ROM.

Documentation: Captions on each slide.

Purchasing: Individual slides are priced at $2.25 each. Purchase orders and charge cards are accepted.

Other Products: Posters, prints, notecards, postcards.

172 Norton Simon Museum

411 W. Colorado Blvd.
Pasadena, CA 91105
Telephone: (626) 449-6840
FAX: (626) 796-4978
Attn: Louise Milline, Assistant to Bookshop Manager (for orders)
URL: http://www.nortonsimon.org/

Profile: Fine Art Museum including European works for the Renaissance to mid-twentieth century. Sculptures by Rodin, Maillol, and Moore, a unique set of Degas' original master bronzes, as well as Indian and Southeast Asian Sculpture. Approximately 140 duplicate color slide titles offered of works in the permanent collection, with emphasis on European paintings.

Photography: 4" x 5" color transparencies shot by an independent professional photographer.

Production: Produced by Frank Holmes Laboratories, San Fernando, CA or by Spectra American, Sun Valley, CA. Color-corrected and contrast-controlled. Mounted in cardboard.

Documentation: Free list, updated annually. Identifications consist of artist, title, date. Slides labeled. Orientation marked.

Purchasing: Individual slides are priced at $2.00 each. Postage added. Purchase orders accepted; prepayment from individuals and overseas orders. Orders filled in one to two weeks. UPS or USPS. Slides not sent on approval; no returns accepted. No special photography available.

Rental: Color transparencies (three months' rental).

Other Products: Small prints: 10" x 12" full-color prints with brief descriptions on reverse, $2.00 each.

Evaluation: Reprinted from 6th ed. Quality, 3; documentation, 3; service, 3.

173 Oriental Institute Museum

University of Chicago
1155 E. 58th St.
Chicago, IL 60637
Telephone: (312) 702-9520
Attn: Archaeological Archives Photographic Service or Gift Shop

Profile: One hundred slide titles available from Gift Shop. Approximately 10,000 color slide titles offered by the Archaeological Archives Photographic Service; field photographs included as well as museum objects. Art and archaeology of the Ancient Near East, Egypt, and Islamic countries featured. New slide titles continually added.

Photography: Slides shot by staff and excavation photographers.

Production: Duplicated by Kodak and local laboratories.

Documentation: Free list of museum objects only available from Gift Shop; full information provided. No list of holdings of the Archaeological Archives. Identifications for slides from the latter source supplied on invoice or separate sheet, keyed to slides.

Purchasing: Single slides priced $.50 from Shop, $2.00 from Archaeological Archives. Prepayment required. Returns accepted for exchange. Special photography undertaken on request.

Other Sources: Seventy-one duplicate color slides offered by Davis Art Slides **(047)** (formerly Rosenthal Art Slides).

Evaluation: Quality, 4; documentation, 3; service, 3. (Evaluation by a single committee member. 6th edition ratings: quality, 2 to 3; documentation, 2; service, 2 to 3.)

174   Pennsylvania Academy of the Fine Arts

Broad and Cherry Streets
Philadelphia, PA 19102
Telephone: (215) 972-7620
Attn: Museum Shop

Profile: Offers 130 color slide titles of the permanent collection of American art.

Photography: Original 4" x 5" transparencies shot by an independent professional photographer.

Production: Duplicates made from original transparencies.

Documentation: Free list. Artist, title, and date provided. Slides labeled.

Purchasing: Slides sold singly, $1.00 each. Postage added. No minimum order. Prepayment required. Rush orders accepted. Returns accepted for exchange. No special photography undertaken.

Evaluation: Quality, 3; documentation, 2; service, 3.

175   Phoenix Art Museum

1625 N. Central Ave.
Phoenix, AZ 85004-1685
Telephone: (602) 257-1880
Attn: Photographic Services

Profile: Approximately 200 duplicate color slide titles offered of works in the permanent collection: European art, fifteenth to twentieth century; American art, eighteenth to twentieth century; Asian art (Japanese, Chinese, Indian); Mexican, colonial to present; costumes; and miniatures (Thorne Rooms). New slides continually added. Small sets of duplicate color slides sold in museum shop.

Photography: Originals shot by independent professional photographer on various tungsten films: Fuji ASA 64, Kodak ASA 64 #4108, Kodak EPY Ektachrome ASA 50, and Kodak ASA 160. Professional equipment used, including color-correction filters and polarizers.

Production: Duplicated from original transparencies by local laboratories, Image Craft or Photo Concepts. Color-corrected and contrast-controlled. Mounted in plastic or cardboard. Shipped in sleeves with cardboard support.

Documentation: No list. Slides labeled with full identifications. Orientation marked with arrow if necessary.

Purchasing: Slides sold singly, $6.00 each. Additional copies of same slide, $1.50. Postage added. Prepayment required in U.S. funds, drawn on a U.S. bank. Duplicates made to order and shipped within three to four weeks. Rush orders filled; 100% surcharge. Returns accepted for exchange.

Other Products: Photographic prints available in black-and-white or color, 5" x 7" or 8" x 10".

Other Sources: One hundred twenty-six slides available from Davis Art Slides **(047)** (formerly Rosenthal Art Slides) as a set, or singly.

176   Pierpont Morgan Library

29 E. 36th St.
New York, NY 10016
Telephone: (212) 685-0008
FAX: (212) 685-7913
Attn: Photography & Rights Department
Marilyn Palmeri, Manager and Debbie
Coutavas, Associate

Profile: Photography department has been established since 1940s to provide photographic materials of the library's collections for study, scholarly publication, lectures, commercial publications, TV and video, World Wide Web, and CD-ROM use.

Photography: Professional photographer in a professional photo studio. Film type varies according to materials. Fuji, Kodachrome slides, EPY, EPN, EPP, 4" x 5" and 8" x 10" color films, various black-and-white films. All new photography must be approved by Curators and Conservation staff.

Production: All originals are photographed on formats requested by client. If client requests 35mm, a 35mm original is produced and duplicates are made from this original using Fuji or Kodachrome film.

Documentation: Accession numbers, page numbers, artist/author/composer/title, imprint information, date, if known, type of Book, Gospels, Book of Hours, Bible, etc.

Purchasing: After placement, order is researched, then approved by Curator and Conservation. Invoice is generated. Once paid, order is processed. Duplicates: one week to four weeks from date of payment. New originals: six weeks from date of payment. Contact Davis Art Slides **(047)** (formerly Rosenthal Art Slides) for duplicate color slides.

Rental: Slides are sold; 8" x 10" , 4" x 5" rental for three months; black-and-white are sold.

Other Products: Black-and-white photos, color 4" x 5", and 8" x 10" transparencies.

Evaluation: Quality, 4; documentation, 4; service, 3 to 4.

177　Pilgrim Society

Pilgrim Hall Museum
75 Court St.
Plymouth, MA 02360-3891
Telephone: (508) 746-1620

Profile: Approximately 1,500 slide titles offered of objects associated with the Pilgrims at Plymouth: paintings, monuments, furniture, scenes, and other items of historical interest. New slides continually added.

Photography: Originals (slides and large-format transparencies) shot by staff photographer on various films.

Production: Duplicated at a local laboratory (Plymouth Camera or Ayotte's Photography, both of

Plymouth, MA). Color-corrected and contrast-controlled.

Documentation: Free brochure. Many slides available that are not listed. Identifications provided include name of artist or architect, dates of artist or architect, title of work or name of building, date of work, materials, dimensions, and location for architecture. Orientation not marked.

Purchasing: Slides sold singly or in sets. No minimum order. Originals and duplicates kept in stock; duplicates made to order only when necessary. Orders usually filled within five days of receipt. Rush orders completed in two days; surcharge of approximately $10.00. Single slides priced $2.50 each; sets of five slides also $2.50. Postage added. Slides not sent on approval.

Other Products: Videotapes available. 4" x 5" color transparencies may be rented for $20 each if in stock, or made to order for $125 each.

178　Portland Art Museum

Oregon Art Institute
1219 S.W. Park Ave.
Portland, OR 97205
Telephone: (503) 226-2811
Attn: Slide Library
E-mail: paminfo@pam.org
URL: http://www.pam.org

Profile: Entry updated from website with some information reprinted from 6th ed. The Portland Art Museum houses a diverse "permanent" collection of more than 32,000 works of art. Collections can be divided into two camps: one of Eurocentric origins that also incorporates art from regions of the Pacific Rim, including Northwest Coast Native American art; and the other made up of works from three major Asian cultures. Selected slides are available from the museum's collections. Duplicate color slides offered, partially representing the permanent collection. Through a recent grant, all works by Japanese artists were photographed, including 829 ukiyo-e prints, 722 prints from the twentieth century, and 212 objects (paintings, sculpture, ceramics, and decorative arts). Other subjects available in slides include Northwest Coast Indian art and the Gebauer Collection of Cameroon art.

Photography: Originals (mostly slides, some 4" x 5" transparencies) shot by slide librarian, using a Leica camera on copystand or a studio setup centered around the Leica with tripod and Broncolor lighting system. Films used in-house are Ektachrome EPY ASA 50 and Kodachrome PKM ASA 25. Most photography of three-dimensional objects, and of very large flatwork, is done by independent professionals. Documentation project on Japanese art entirely photographed by an independent professional.

Production: Duplicates always made from camera originals except by special request when no original is available. Duplicating film is Ektachrome #5071. Duplicates made by Photocraft, Portland, OR. Color-corrected. Lab tries to get an exact match to the original but will adjust either lights or darks if asked. Mounted in plastic and sleeved. Large quantities packed in boxes. Shipped in padded envelopes.

Documentation: No list. Slides labeled with artist name, title of work, date, media, dimensions, and accession number. More information provided on request. Orientation marked.

Purchasing: Slides sold singly, $2.00 each. No minimum order. Postage added. Prepayment in U.S. funds is requested. Purchase orders not necessary. Duplicates kept in stock and shipped within one to two weeks. No rush orders accepted. Slides not sent on approval, and returns not accepted.

Exchange: Requests for exchange of slides welcomed.

Evaluation: Reprinted from 6th ed. Quality, based on one sample, 3; documentation, 2 to 3.

179 Preservation Society of Newport County

The Breakers
Ochre Point Ave.
Newport, RI 02840
Telephone: (401) 847-6543
Attn: Museum Store

Profile: Entry reprinted from 6th ed. Sixty-five duplicate color slide titles offered of seven Newport mansions (the Breakers, the Elms, Marble House, Chateau-sur-Mer, Rosecliff, Kingscote, and Hunter House) and of the topiary gardens at Green Animals. New titles occasionally added.

Photography: 4" x 5" transparencies shot by an independent professional photographer on Kodak film.

Production: Duplicated on Ektachrome #5071 by World in Color, Elmira, NY.

Documentation: Free order sheet provides brief description of views for each house. No information given about architect, dates of construction, or furnishings. Slides labeled. Orientation marked.

Purchasing: Slides sold in sets of five, $2.50 per set. Postage added. Prepayment or purchase order required. Slides kept in stock and shipped within one to two weeks. Rush orders accepted. Slides not sent on approval, and no returns accepted.

Evaluation: Quality, 2; documentation, 1; service, 2. (Evaluation by a single committee member. Reprinted from 6th ed.: Slides intended for tourist market rather than scholarly use.)

180 Princeton University Art Museum

Princeton, NJ 08544
Telephone: (609) 452-3788
FAX: (609) 258-6877
Attn: Photo Services
E-mail: krichter@princeton.edu
URL: http://webware.Princeton.edu/artmus/

Profile: Between 200 and 300 duplicate color slides offered of objects in the permanent collection. New slides continually added.

Profile, New Technology: Looking into the issues.

Photography: Slides shot from originals and some from transparencies.

Production: Duplicates from original slides by Kodak onto Ektachrome #5071. Mounted in cardboard.

Documentation: Catalog $3.00, postpaid. Slides labeled. Complete identifications given except dimensions. Orientation marked with arrows only when needed.

Purchasing: $5.00 each plus postage and handling. No minimum order. Prepayment required. Request that orders be in writing; E-mail or fax fulfill this request. Duplicates usually made to order and shipped within eight to ten weeks. If slides are in stock, order can be filled in about a week. Slides not sent on approval, and no returns accepted.

181 Rhode Island School of Design Museum of Art

224 Benefit St.
Providence, RI 02903
Telephone: (401) 454-6535

FAX: (401) 454-6556
Attn: Melody Ennis, Photographic Services
E-mail: meenis@risd.edu
URL: http://www.risd.edu

Profile: Rhode Island School of Design has over 1,500 slides of objects in the Museum's collection. New slides are continuously added.

Photography: All slides are taken by the museum photographer. Objects are filmed in studio unless object cannot be moved, then done in situ.

Documentation: A catalog is available. Slides are labeled with name of artist, nationality and dates, title, date of work, medium, and museum accession number.

Purchasing: Individual slides are priced at $5.00 each. The following discounts apply: orders of 50-100 slides, 25% discount; orders of 101+ slides, 33% discount. Prepayment in U.S. dollars required; purchase orders accepted. Postage additional. Orders are filled within two to three weeks. Shipped in U.S. mail.

Rental: Available from the Educational Department for two weeks' rental. Please call Education at (401) 454-6534.

Evaluation: Quality, 3 to 4; documentation, 3 to 4; service, 3.

182   John and Mable Ringling Museum of Art

(State Art Museum of Florida)
5401 Bayshore Rd.
P.O. Box 1838
Sarasota, FL 33578
Telephone: (813) 355-5101
Attn: Gallery Shop

Profile: Entry reprinted from 6th ed. Approximately 100 duplicate color slide titles offered of paintings and drawings in the permanent collection. Slides of the buildings and grounds also available.

Photography: Negatives shot by staff photographer.

Production: Most of the art slides produced by Sandak, which ceased to exist in 1997. Although a few slides produced by GAF remain, they will not be restocked. Sandak slides mounted in cardboard.

Documentation: Free list; GAF titles separated from Sandak's. Sandak slides labeled with full identifications and orientation marked.

Purchasing: Slides sold singly, $1.00 each. No minimum order. No discounts. Postage added. Prepayment required only from customers who have not paid for previous orders. Purchase orders accepted from institutions. Slides kept in stock and shipped within several days. Returns accepted only for exchange.

Other Products: Black-and-white photographic prints available from Registrar.

Evaluation: Quality, 3; documentation, 3; service, 3. (Evaluation by a single committee member.)

183   Saint Louis Art Museum

Forest Park
St. Louis, MO 63110-1380
Telephone: (314) 721-0067, x266
Attn: Resource Center, Department of Education

Profile: Entry reprinted from 6th ed. Approximately 4,000 to 5,000 duplicate color slide titles offered of objects in the permanent collection: European art, Oriental art, African art, Pre-Columbian art, Native American art, ancient art, and contemporary art. Special exhibitions documented in sets only. New slides continually added.

Photography: Original slides shot by independent professional photographers (75%) and staff photographer, on Ektachrome ASA 100 or Kodachrome ASA 64. Tripod used.

Production: Duplicates made on Ektachrome #5071 by local laboratories, usually from originals. Color-correction not attempted, but only good originals are selected for duplication. Mounted in cardboard. Shipped in plastic sleeves or boxes.

Documentation: No list currently available; out-of-print slide catalog (1978) may be available in libraries. Free brochure describes services of Resource Center. In-house files of holdings maintained. Slides labeled with name of artist, title of work, date of work, city and collection, and materials. Slide kits accompanied by information sheets for each object depicted; bibliography and introductory text also provided. Additional information supplied on request. Orientation not marked.

Purchasing: Slides sold singly and in sets. Some images in sets not available singly. Single slides priced $1.00 each, postpaid. Sets of 20 slides priced $20.00 (with audiotape, $30.00), discounted 20% to educators. Payment in U.S. funds required, check or cash. No minimum order. Duplicates kept in stock and shipped within one to two weeks. Rush orders will be filled as quickly as possible. Slides not sent on approval, and returns not accepted.

Rental: Single slides and slide kits loaned free of charge to Missouri educators, students, and individual researchers. Refundable deposit equal to purchase price required. Loan period is two weeks. Slides may be picked up in person or ordered by mail. Order form provided in brochure. Videotapes also available for free loan. There are four satellite resource centers located in Missouri, one in Illinois. The Resource Center is a regional loan center for slide programs, videotapes, and 16mm films from the National Gallery of Art.

Other Products: Videotapes produced by the museum sold for $50. The museum's Public Information Department sells black-and-white photographic prints and lends large-format color transparencies for reproduction.

Other Sources: Two sets offered by University of Michigan Slide Distribution **(096)**: American painting (130 slides) and European painting (170 slides).

Evaluation: Reprinted from 6th ed. Take care to specify in your request whether you wish to purchase or borrow slides. Quality, 2 to 4; documentation, 3 to 4; service, 3 to 4.

184   Shelburne Museum

Route 7
Shelburne, VT 05482
Telephone: (802) 985-3346
Attn: Photographic Services

Profile: Entry reprinted from 6th ed. Duplicate color slides offered of objects in the permanent collection. American fine art, decorative art, folk art, and utilitarian objects featured. Some slides of architecture available. European fine and decorative arts also represented. New titles continually added.

Photography: Slides and 4" x 5" transparencies shot by staff photographer on Ektachrome or sometimes on Kodachrome in a studio.

Production: Duplicated on Kodak slide duplicating film by Lightworks, Burlington, VT. Color-corrected and contrast-controlled. Mounted in cardboard, plastic, or glass.

Documentation: No list available. Information provided with slides as requested.

Purchasing: Slides sold singly, $3.00 each when sold to nonprofit organizations, $4.00 each to others. Postage added ($2.00). No minimum order.

Prepayment or purchase order required unless credit has been established. Some slides kept in stock, others duplicated to order. Orders filled within three weeks. Rush orders accepted with 50% surcharge; sent within one to two weeks. Slides sometimes sent on approval by special arrangement. Original photography carried out at $40.00 per slide for nonprofit organizations; price for others $70.00. Minimum of three weeks required to fill special orders.

185   David and Alfred Smart Museum of Art

5550 S. Greenwood
Chicago, IL 60637
Telephone: (773) 702-0200
FAX: (773) 702-0312
Attn: Mcsharma
E-mail: smart-museum@midway.uchic
URL: http://smartmuseum.uchicago.edu/

Profile: Smart Museum founded in 1974 by David and Alfred Smart, creators of *Esquire Magazine*. It is located on the University of Chicago campus and houses the Fine Arts Collection of the University as well as featuring groundbreaking temporary exhibitions.

The photo/imaging service provides color transparencies, slides, and black-and-white prints of work in the permanent collection, mostly for use in academic or scholarly publications.

Photography: Professional photographer's work is on site. He specializes in fine art photography and provides necessary backdrops and lighting. 4" x 5" transparencies are given by photographer after each shoot. Duplicates are kept on file. Original slide are kept for duplication as well.

Production: All dupes are made by Gamma Photo Labs, Chicago, using Kodak film.

Documentation: Images are sold for purpose of reproduction. A contact-invoice is sent that details the conditions under which the images can be reproduced. If the image is a straight sale for personal use, an information letter is enclosed.

Purchasing: Individual slides are priced at $3.00 each. Payment must be received before images sent. Orders placed are processed within one day. Usually the images are mailed out the day payment is received.

Rental: Rentals of images are made on a case-by-case basis. Cost is $40, and the image is rented for a three-month period.

Other Products: Color transparencies $40; black-and-white prints $10.

186 Smith College Museum of Art

Elm St. at Bedford Terrace
Northampton, MA 01063
Telephone: (413) 585-2770
FAX: (413) 585-2782
Attn: Michael Goodison
E-mail: mgoodison@ais.smith.edu

Profile: Color slides of its holdings sold directly by the museum on a limited basis as a service to scholars and students. All but serious inquiries are discouraged because the museum's policy is not to promote its slide sales as a business. It may be possible to obtain certain slides from exhibitions by special arrangement.

Photography: Original slides shot by independent professional photographer.

Production: Mounted in plastic.

Documentation: Slides labeled.

Purchasing: Slides sold singly. No minimum order. Discount of 25% given to students. If slides are in stock, orders filled within days; if made to order, within several weeks.

Evaluation: Quality, 3; documentation, 3. (Evaluation by a single committee member. Reprinted from 6th ed.: Rated by one member of Evaluation Committee: quality, 4; documentation, 3. "Service depends on whether slide is in stock. If it isn't, one must wait.")

187 Taft Museum

316 Pike St.
Cincinnati, OH 45202
Telephone: (513) 241-0343
FAX: (513) 241-7762
E-mail: taftmuse@fuse.net
URL: http://www.taftmuseum.org/

Price Range: Sets of six slides each $4.95.

Profile: The permanent collections include European and American master paintings, such as works by Rembrandt, Hals, Gainsborough, Sargent, Ruisdael, Turner, and Corot; Chinese ceramics, primarily porcelains of the Kangxi reign; and European decorative arts, featuring an extensive collection of French Renaissance Limoges enamels and seventeenth-

through eighteenth-century watches. The museum shop sells seven sets of slides: "The Baum Taft House," "17th-Century Dutch Paintings," "18th- and 19th-Century English Paintings," "Barbizon Paintings," "American Paintings and Taft Family," "Chinese Porcelains," and "Decorative Arts."

Evaluation: Quality, 3; documentation, 4; service, 3. (Based on a single committee member.)

188 Terra Museum of American Art

664 N. Michigan Ave.
Chicago, IL 69611
Telephone: (312) 664-3939
Attn: Shelly Roman, Rights and Reproductions, x1226
Bookstore, x1211

Price Range: $3.00 per slide.

Profile: The Terra Museum of American Art, founded by Daniel Terra, was originally located in Evanston but moved to its current location in 1987. The museum includes works by Whistler, Sargent, Winslow Homer, Cassat, Stuart Davis, Hartley, Marsh, O'Keeffe, Marin, and Dove and prints by Hopper. Slides are sold individually. The bookstore keeps about 60-100 titles in stock. If the slide is not in stock, requests should be made to the Curatorial Department, which will arrange to have it produced for the same $3.00 cost. Inquiries about the holdings of the museum are welcome.

189 Toledo Museum of Art

Monroe St. at Scottwood Ave.
P.O. Box 1013
Toledo, OH 43697
Telephone: (419) 255-8000
Attn: Slide Library

Profile: Entry reprinted from 6th ed. Approximately 3,000 color slide titles (mostly originals, duplicates if supply of originals is exhausted) offered of the permanent collection, with emphasis on Ancient Greek vases. New titles continually added (50 in 1988).

Photography: Slides shot by staff photographer on Ektachrome ASA 160. Items photographed in the gallery, using tripod, with existing light (skylight and spotlights) or in studio with Totalite system.

Production: Duplicated by Kodak, Findlay, OH. Color-corrected and contrast-controlled. Mounted in Gepe mounts with anti-newton ring glass.

Documentation: No general list available. Consult published catalogs of the museum's collections of American paintings, European paintings, and glass. List and addenda offered of slides of Greek, Etruscan, and Roman art. No information provided about subjects depicted on vases, but museum accession number given. Also, no dimensions provided on list. Slides labeled. Orientation marked.

Purchasing: Slides sold singly. No minimum order. Purchase order required from institutions. Payment must be in U.S. funds. Slides priced $3.00 postpaid, $3.50 to customers outside the continental United States. Slides kept in stock and shipped within 10 days. Rush orders filled within three days; no surcharge. Slides not sent on approval. Returns accepted for exchange or refund if slides are damaged or customer is dissatisfied. Special photography carried out to order within two weeks, $13.00 per slide.

Other Sources: Davis Art Slides (formerly Rosenthal Art Slides) **(047)** offers 276 slides of painting, sculpture, and decorative arts. Although the museum shop sells Rosenthal slides, orders are best sent directly to Davis Art Slides **(047)** (formerly Rosenthal Art Slides). Set of 200 slides, including many details, available from the University of Michigan Slide Distribution **(096)**. Sandak slides formerly available have been discontinued.

Evaluation: Reprinted from 6th ed. Quality, documentation, and service all rated 2 by one advisor in 5th ed. "We believe we are much improved" (Carolyn Papsidera Putney, Slide Curator, Toledo Museum of Art).

190 Uncommon Objects

(Museum Store for Allen Memorial
Art Museum)
Oberlin College
39 S. Main St.
Oberlin, OH 44074
Telephone: (216) 775-2086
Attn: Shirley Hull
E-mail: jenny_wilker@qmgate.cc.
oberlin.edu
URL: http://www.oberlin.edu/allenart/

This image provider also offers digital products and is listed in the digital section of the directory.

Price Range: Slides sold singly, $5.00 each plus shipping.

Profile: Offers 300 color slide titles of works in the permanent collection: paintings, sculpture, works on paper, and decorative arts. Slides of the Frank Lloyd Wright House also are available. A few new titles occasionally added.

Photography: Slides shot on Kodak film by an independent professional photographer using Nikon equipment. Objects lit by quartz lamps.

Production: Duplicated on Ektachrome by an independent professional laboratory. Color-corrected and contrast-controlled. Mounted in cardboard.

Documentation: Free list, revised more or less annually. Artist, title, medium, and dimensions given. Slides labeled on mounts. Orientation marked by label placement.

Purchasing: Single slides priced $2.00 each. No discounts. No minimum order. Postage added. Duplicates kept in stock, and orders usually shipped within five days after receipt of payment. Rush orders filled same day if items are in stock, with no surcharge. Slides shot to order within one to three weeks of works not previously photographed; fee of $15.00 per slide charged. Prepayment required on all orders. Returns accepted for exchange or refund if slides are of unacceptable quality.

Digital Products: *The Museum CD-ROM, Masterworks for Learning: A College Collection Catalogue,* does include full-screen images of 171 important works in the collection. These copyrighted images are not downloadable and cannot be used for other purposes. The CD-ROM includes scholarly entries about these 171 works and a complete collection database. It sells for $29.95, plus $5.00 shipping.

Evaluation: Reprinted from 6th ed. Quality, 3; documentation, 3 to 4; service, 3 to 4.

191 University of California, Berkeley Art Museum

2625 Durant Ave.
Berkeley, CA 94720-2250
Telephone: (510) 643-8584
FAX: (510) 642-4889
Attn: Stephanie Cannzo, Curatorial Assistant
E-mail: lcalden@uclink2.berkeley.edu
URL: http://www.bampfa.berkeley.edu

Profile: Inventory of approximately 200 works; request will often require new photography. No list is available because the museum does not market slides.

Photography: Originals (slides, negatives, and large-format transparencies) shot by staff photographer.

Production: Duplicates made from originals. Color-corrected. Slides mounted in plastic.

Documentation: No list. Slides labeled with name of artist, title of work, date of work, materials, dimensions, and city and collection. Orientation marked.

Purchasing: Cost for duplicating an existing image is $15 for commercial and $10 for nonprofit. Reproduction fees for publication are additional.

192　University of Iowa Museum of Art

Riverside Dr.
Iowa City, IA 52242
Telephone: (319) 335-1727
Attn: Curator of Collections

Profile: Entry reprinted from 6th ed. Two large sets of slides offered: "101 Masterworks [from the permanent collection]" (160 slides) and "Art and Life in Africa" (200 slides). The latter represents highlights of the collection of Mr. and Mrs. C. Maxwell Stanley (most of which has been given to the museum).

Production: Duplicates made to order from master sets.

Documentation: List for each set gives full identifications, including dates and nationalities of artists. (No dates provided for African objects.) Catalogs corresponding to each set are also available.

Purchasing: "Masterworks," $160; "Art and Life in Africa," $125.

Evaluation: Quality, 4; documentation, 4; service, 3.

193　University Museum of Anthropology and Archaeology

University of Pennsylvania
33rd and Spruce Streets
Philadelphia, PA 19104
Telephone: (215) 898-4040 (Shop)
(215) 898-6720 (Photographic Archives)

Profile: Entry reprinted from 6th ed. Contact museum for availability. Seventeen slide sets, totaling about 500 images, offered by Shop, representing objects in the permanent collection. Non-Western art featured. Sets include art and artifacts from China, South America, Mesoamerica, the Mediterranean, Africa, Polynesia, the Near East, and Alaska. Slide holdings are not being increased.

Photography: Original slides shot by staff photographer many years ago.

Production: Duplicated from duplicates. Mounted in cardboard.

Documentation: Free catalog. Slides keyed to catalog. Descriptive text supplied with each set.

Purchasing: Slides sold only in sets. Minimum order one set. Price list available on request. Per-slide cost in most sets less than $1.00. Prices include shipping charges. Discounts offered to museum members. Prepayment required of all but established accounts, in U.S. dollars, checks drawn on U.S. banks only. Sets kept in stock, and orders filled within two to four weeks. Rush orders sent within two days via UPS or Federal Express. Slides not sent on approval, but returns accepted if damaged. Special photography handled by Photographic Archives.

Evaluation: Reprinted from 6th ed. Quality, 3; documentation, 2 to 3; service, 3.

194　Wadsworth Atheneum

600 Main St.
Hartford, CT 06103
Telephone: (203) 278-2670
Attn: Slides

Profile: Entry reprinted from 6th ed. Seventy-two color slide titles offered of works in the permanent collection. Most are duplicates, but occasionally originals are available. American and European paintings and decorative arts featured. New titles occasionally added. Duplicates from original 35mm slides available by special order of most objects in the collection, including several dozen major paintings that are not on the list.

Photography: 4" x 5" transparencies shot with Linhof camera on Ektachrome #6118 by an independent professional photographer.

Production: Duplicated on Ektachrome #5071 by Century Color Laboratories, East Hartford, CT. Color-corrected and contrast-controlled. Some duplicates made by Kodak's Fair Lawn, NJ, laboratory. Mounted in cardboard.

Documentation: Mailing list kept. Free brochure. Slides keyed to list in brochure. Identifications consist of artist's name, dates, and nationality; title of work; city and collection; date of work; and materials. Orientation not marked.

Purchasing: Slides sold singly, $2.00 each. No minimum order. Postage added. 10% discount given to educational institutions, museums, and libraries, applicable only to slides listed in brochure. Prepayment required by check or money order drawn on a U.S. bank. Some duplicates kept in stock; copies made to order when necessary. Orders filled within two weeks if in stock, or within eight weeks if made to order. Special order slides $7.00. New originals made on request for $20.00 to $25.00. No returns accepted.

Evaluation: Quality, 3 to 4; documentation, 2 to 3; service, 2 to 4.

195   Walker Art Center
Vineland Pl.
Minneapolis, MN 55403
Telephone: (612) 375-7600
Attn: Book Shop

Profile: Entry reprinted from 6th ed. Through 1989, slide sales administered by Slide Library. Color slides offered of works in the permanent collection: twentieth-century art, primarily American. Slides of the Minneapolis Sculpture Garden also available. Special requests accepted for duplicate slides of any work in the collection that has been photographed.

Photography: Originals (slides and large-format transparencies) shot by staff photographers on Ektachrome films (EPY ASA 50, EPT ASA 160, EPP ASA 100, and EPR ASA 200). "Appropriate professional methods always employed to satisfy specific problems and needs."

Production: Duplicates made from originals on Ektachrome by ProColor, Minneapolis. Color-corrected and contrast-controlled. Mounted in plastic. Shipped in sleeves and insulated packing envelopes.

Documentation: Slides labeled with name of artist, title, city and collection, date of work, and sometimes dimensions and materials. Orientation marked.

Purchasing: [Practice described here may change when slide sales are taken over by the Book Shop.] Original slides occasionally available. Slides sold singly, $2.00 each from catalog, $4.00 each for special orders. No minimum order. Postage added.

Prepayment preferred, but will invoice. Payment must be in U.S. dollars. Slides kept in stock, and orders filled within two weeks. Rush orders filled with no extra charge.

Rental: Slide packets, in carousels, accompanied by script, loaned by Education Department for $3.00 each plus UPS shipping cost.

Evaluation: Reprinted from 6th ed. Three samples sent: quality, 3; documentation, 2 to 3.

196   Walters Art Gallery
600 N. Charles St.
Baltimore, MD 21201
Telephone: (301) 547-9000, x254
Attn: Photograph Services

Profile: Entry reprinted from 6th ed. Some 3,000 color slides (originals or duplicates) offered of the permanent collection: sculpture, painting, manuscripts, and decorative arts from the Ancient Near East through the nineteenth century, including Oriental art. New slides continually added.

Photography: Slides shot by staff photographer in the galleries with tripod, or in a studio, using Ektachrome ASA 160 EPT #5037.

Production: Duplicated by a local laboratory (Blakeslee Lane, Baltimore) on Ektachrome #5071. Color-corrected and contrast-controlled. Mounted in cardboard or plastic and packed carefully for shipment.

Documentation: Not all items kept in stock. Slides labeled with accession number. Further information available on request.

Purchasing: Slides sold singly at $4.00 each. No discounts. Postage added for orders of more than 10 slides ($2.00 U.S., $3.00 foreign). Prepayment in U.S. funds required on all orders. Orders filled within two to three weeks unless special photography is required. Rush orders filled with 50% surcharge; if duplicate must be made to order, four to five days required.

Other Products: Black-and-white photographs and microfilms sold. Color transparencies rented.

Other Sources: Davis Art Slides (formerly Rosenthal Art Slides) (047) offers 675 duplicate color slides, including 192 slides of 175 watercolors executed by Alfred Jacob Miller in the American West in 1837. More slides may be offered by Davis Art Slides (047) (formerly Rosenthal Art Slides). Rosenthal slides are not sold by the museum, although slides of the same objects can be obtained from Photograph Services. Direct order from Davis Art Slides recommended when desired images are available, for faster service, lower price, and predictable quality and documentation.

Evaluation: Reprinted from 6th ed. Four-star rating in the fourth edition. Quality of originals varies, however, with older holdings not always meeting the standards set for new photography.

197 Winterthur Museum

Route 52
Winterthur, DE 19735
Telephone: (302) 888-4840
FAX: (302) 888-4950
Attn: Jennifer Menson, Photographic Services, Registrar's Office

Profile: Entry reprinted from 6th edition with updated prices. Slides no longer distributed by Slide Library. Photographic services for the museum collection now handled by the Registrar's Office. Approximately 40,000 color slide titles offered of the permanent collection: American fine arts and decorative arts 1640–1850. Exterior views, changing exhibitions and room installations documented as well. New slide titles continually added.

Photography: Original slides shot by staff photographers on Ektachrome (70%), Kodachrome (25%), and Fujichrome (5%).

Production: Duplicates made from originals by several local laboratories on various films. Color-correction not attempted. Mounted in plastic. Shipped in sleeves and cardboard mailers, or in boxes for large orders.

Documentation: Partial list available for cost of photocopying. (List of lists available free.) Most slides keyed to list. Some labeled. Identifications include name of artist, title of work, date of work, and materials. For architecture, architect, building name, and date provided. Orientation not marked.

Purchasing: Both originals and duplicates available. Slides sold singly, $3.50 each (to nonprofit institutions). Postage added. No minimum order. Orders must be submitted in writing. Slides kept in stock and usually shipped within two to three weeks. Duplicates made to order only if necessary. Payment in U.S. funds requested. Slides not sent on approval, and returns not accepted. Rush orders filled for an additional fee.

Other Products: Black-and-white photographic prints and 4" x 5" color transparencies available.

Evaluation: Reprinted from 6th ed. Quality, 2 to 4; documentation, 3; service, 3.

198 Worcester Art Museum

55 Salisbury St.
Worcester, MA 01609-3196
Telephone: (508) 799-4406, x233
Attn: Coordinator of Photographic Services

Profile: One hundred fifteen duplicate color slide titles offered of masterpieces of the permanent collection. Other slides available by special request. (Most of the permanent collection has been photographed.) Small limited-edition sets sometimes offered in conjunction with temporary exhibitions. Set of 12 slides of the Asiatic Collection available for $12.00. New slide titles continually added (about 10 in 1989).

Photography: Originals shot by staff photographer using Kodachrome #5070 ASA 40 for 35mm work, Ektachrome #6118 professional tungsten film for 4" x 5" transparencies. View camera, tripod, quartz lights, and color-correction filters employed; lights and lens are polarized.

Production: Stocked slides produced from 4" x 5" transparencies. Production carried out by Industrial Color Lab, Framingham, MA, on Ektachrome #5071. Color-corrected. Contrast-controlled if necessary. Special-order duplicates made from 35mm original slides at a Kodak laboratory. Mounted in plastic (stocked slides) or cardboard (special orders). Shipped in plastic sleeves and cardboard.

Documentation: Mailing list kept. Free list, frequently revised, giving artist's name, dates, and nationality; title of work; date; materials; dimensions; and accession number. Slides labeled with full information. Orientation marked only when necessary.

Purchasing: Slides sold singly and in small sets. Price for single slides $2.25 each. No discounts. Postage added. Per-slide cost in sets is less. Prepayment preferred. Slides not sent on approval. Returns accepted only if slide is defective. Orders usually filled within two to four weeks, but an effort will be made to meet specified deadlines. Within five days considered rush; 100% surcharge. Original slides available by special order, $18.00 each; allow two to four weeks for delivery.

Rental: Slide Library holdings loaned, in person only.

Other Sources: The museum has no authorized distributors.

Evaluation: Quality, 3 to 4; documentation, 3 to 4; service, 3 to 4.

199   Frank Lloyd Wright House & Studio Foundation

951 Chicago Ave.
Oak Park, IL 60302
Telephone: (708) 848-1606 (bookshop)
(708) 848-9518 (catalogue order department)
URL: http://www.wrightplus.org/

This image provider also offers digital products and is listed in the digital section of the directory.

Profile: The Home and Studio served as the private residence and architectural office of Wright during the first 20 years of his professional career, 1889–1909. There are seven $5.50 slide sets (five slides each) of Unity Temple exteriors and Unity Temple interiors, three sets of houses in Oak Park, Wright House (one exterior, four interiors) and Wright Studio (one exterior, four interiors). A boxed set of 20 slides of Falling Water is $15.00.

Digital Products: The following CDs are sold in the bookshop: the Luna CD of the *Houses of Frank Lloyd Wright* ($199), an interactive disc of *Falling Water* ($50) and the *Frank Lloyd Wright Companion* ($60).

200   Yale Center for British Art

1080 Chapel St.
P.O. Box 2120 Yale Station
New Haven, CT 06520
Telephone: (203) 432-2800
Attn: Museum Shop

Profile: Entry reprinted from 6th ed. Approximately 100 color slide titles offered of the permanent collection: British art from the Elizabethan period onward. Also, six slides available of the museum building by Louis Kahn.

Photography: 4" x 5" transparencies shot by staff photographer in studio.

Production: Produced by Sandak (Sandak ceased business in 1997). Mounted in cardboard.

Documentation: Free list. Artist's name and title of work provided. Slides labeled with full information. Orientation marked.

Purchasing: Slides sold singly. Postage added. No minimum order. Prepayment required from overseas and from individuals, in U.S. funds. Slides kept in stock and shipped within two weeks. Rush orders filled within two days if slides are in stock. Express mail charges added to customer's cost. Slides not sent on approval. Returns accepted only if damaged in shipment. Special photography (originals or duplicates) carried out by Registrar; cost varies.

Evaluation: Quality, 3; documentation, 3; service, 2 to 3.

201   Yale University Art Gallery

1111 Chapel St.
P.O. Box 2006 Yale Station
New Haven, CT 06520
Telephone: (203) 432-0602
Attn: Sales Desk

Profile: Entry reprinted from 6th ed. Approximately 100 color slide titles offered of selected items (paintings, drawings, sculpture, decorative arts) from the permanent collection. New slide titles occasionally added.

Photography: 4" x 5" photography (transparencies or negatives) carried out mostly by staff photographer, sometimes by Sandak staff (Sandak ceased operations in 1997). Objects photographed in studio, usually on Ektachrome.

Production: Produced by Sandak. Mounted in cardboard.

Documentation: Free list; artist and title given. Slides labeled with full information. Orientation marked.

Purchasing: Slides sold singly, $1.50 each. Discounts offered to educational institutions, from 10% to 20% depending upon quantity ordered. Postage added. No minimum order. Prepayment required from new customers. Purchase orders accepted from institutions. Slides kept in stock and shipped within one week. Rush orders can be filled within 24 hours. Slides not sent on approval, and no returns accepted. Special photography handled by Rights and Reproductions Department.

Evaluation: Quality, 3; documentation, 3; service, 2. (Evaluation by a single committee member.)

PART III

ASIA, AUSTRALIA, BRITAIN, EUROPE, and IRELAND

AUSTRALIA

202 Contemporary Art Resource

P.O. Box 815, Newtown
Sydney, New South Wales 2042
Australia
Telephone: 02 9718 9576
Attn: Sandra Ristway

Profile: Duplicate color slide titles offered of contemporary art (Sydney and Venice biennials, for instance), primarily exhibitions of contemporary art with large installation vistas in gallery spaces plus close-ups of many examples. Sometimes there are no detailed shots of some works.

Photography: Original slides shot by an independent professional and traveling scholars. No current information on film and equipment used.

Production: Duplicated from originals by a local laboratory on Ektachrome #5071. Mounted in plastic and stored in plastic sleeves. Presented in plastic folders for each set, which can be used for storage if preferred.

Documentation: Mailing list kept. Free list, updated yearly. Sets generally accompanied by an exhibition catalog and/or a review or critical essay that may also be purchased with sets. Slides labeled with name of artist and keyed to list. Identifications on list consist of artist, title of work, and date of work. No nationality or life dates supplied, but supplemented by reference to biographies (with nationality and life dates) available in the more detailed accompanying texts/catalogs.

Purchasing: Slides sold in sets only. Prices vary according to set. Subscription program available. Postage added.

Evaluation: One slide librarian familiar with the company rated image quality good to excellent, depending on the photograph. Lighting varies. Rates the vendor as a very valuable supplier for slides and accompanying catalogs and publications relating to Australian biennials and triennials.

Museums

203 Art Gallery of Western Australia

Perth Cultural Centre, James Street Mall
P.O. Box 8363
Perth 6000 Western Australia
Telephone: 08 9492 6600
FAX: 08 9492 6655
Attn: Administration Centre
E-mail: admin@artgallery.wa.gov.au
URL: http://www.artgallery.wa.gov.au/

Profile: Fifth edition entry repeated. More than 300 color slide titles offered of items in the permanent collection. New titles continually added. Australian art and crafts featured. A few sets of British and European art available, including two sets of Art Nouveau. Eleven sets available that are derived from the exhibition "The Colonial Eye," representing the life and landscape of Western Australia from 1798 to 1914.

Photography: Slides shot by staff photographer.

Production: Printed on Eastmancolor #5381 by Custom Colour. No attempt made to correct color or control contrast.

Documentation: Free list, updated annually. Artist, title, and date provided. Slides keyed to list. Three comprehensive illustrated catalogs accompany "The Colonial Eye" set. Orientation not marked.

Purchasing: Slides sold only in sets of eight. Minimum order one set. Price per set $6.50 retail or $5.00 tax exempt (Australian dollars). "The Colonial Eye" exhibition set (88 slides) priced $50.00. Postage added. Prepayment required from overseas. Slides kept in stock and shipped within one week. Rush orders filled in one day; no surcharge. Slides not sent on approval, and no returns accepted. No special photography undertaken.

204   National Gallery of Victoria

180 St. Kilda Rd.
Melbourne, Victoria 3004 Australia
Telephone: 03 9208 0244
FAX: 03 9208 0241
Attn: Jennie Moloney, Photography &
Copyright Coordinator
E-mail: jennie.moloney@ngv.vic.gov.au
URL: http://www.ngv.vic.gov.au/

Price Range: Slides are still sold individually at $5.00 (Australian) per image (1998).

Profile: Entry reprinted from 6th ed. Approximately 15,000 duplicate color slides offered of works in the permanent collection, which includes paintings (Australian and International), works on paper, sculpture, photographs, antiquities (including Greek vases), Asian art (bronzes, ceramics, painting etc), ceramics, glass, Pre-Columbian art, metalwork, costumes and textiles, furniture, and Aboriginal art. Systematic photographic campaign carried out since 1975. New titles continually added (200 in 1989). Some 1,000 items available that are not listed in catalog.

Photography: Original slides shot by staff photographer on Ektachrome ASA 100. Professional equipment used in studio, including tripod and perspective-correcting lens.

Production: Duplicates made from originals on Ektachrome ASA 100 by a local laboratory. Color-corrected and contrast-controlled. Mounted in plastic.

Documentation: Mailing list kept. Two slide catalogs are now available. Both published in 1993.

One features painting, sculpture, photography and P&D. The other features decorative arts, Aboriginal art, and Asian art. Both are available free upon request. Identifications consist of accession number, artist, title, medium, and nationality. Slides labeled with artist, title, and catalog number. Orientation marked by number placement.

Purchasing: Slides sold singly, $5.00 each (Australian dollars). No minimum order. Postage added. Purchase order or prepayment required in Australian dollars. Slides kept in stock; duplicated to order if necessary. Usually shipped within one week. Rush orders accepted at no surcharge. No returns accepted. The slides are sold on the condition that they are not reproduced in any way.

AUSTRIA

205   Ars Nova Medienverlag

A-1160 Vienna
Panikengasse 41/11-15 Austria
Telephone: 01143-1-4923726
FAX: 01143-1-4923726
Attn: Helmut Weihsmann

Price Range: $40 to $150 per set.

Profile: Since its founding in 1980 Ars Nova has published an interesting body of work and displayed many facets of contemporary architecture and design on slide material. The collection of Weihsman's work features the vernacular and academic fields of architecture, street art of murals, graffiti, supergraphics, buildings, and environments not bounded by conventions yet underrated and documented by the media. The slide topics are designed with a philosophy of the tomorrow—and their content and context express dissatisfaction with the present and their contemporaries as a form of protest. Ars Nova has provided slide sets to major institutions and university or museum libraries, including: Columbia University (NYC), Yale University-School of Architecture (New Haven); Musee d'Orsay (Paris); Metropolitan Museum of Art (NYC); Cooper-Hewitt Museum (NYC); University of Amsterdam; Ecole du Architecture (Geneva); Victoria and Albert Museum (London); TU-Berlin; Universitaria Veneziana di Architettura, Tokyo Book Center for Global Architecture (Tokyo); Centre Georges Pompidou-CCI (Paris); NGBK-Berlin;

Institute of Fine Arts (NYC); and several hundred university libraries in the United States, Europe, Australia, and Asia.

Photography: Originals photographed on Kodak film by architectural photographers and staff professionals. Kodachrome ASA 64, 200 and Kodak #5071 lab process film (stable color proof guarantee).

Documentation: Catalog available. Mailing list kept although regular mailings stopped in 1989 for fiscal reasons. Printed booklets, in German and English, for larger sets of 150-200. Slide-by-slide information in key data (architect, year, address of building, artist, muralist, and museum).

Purchasing: Slides available only in sets, priced $40 to $150 with 70% discounts for orders over $500 and free shipping. Prepayment requested. Airmail or priority mail shipment.

Other Products: Publishes textbooks and other books by Helmut Weihsmann.

206   Kunstverlag Hofstetter

A-4910 Ried im Innkreis
Oberachgasse 4a Austria
Telephone: (43) 07752 2425
Attn: Ina (Hofstetter) Ehrenstorfer

Profile: Reprinted from 6th ed. Several thousand color slide titles offered of art and architecture in Austria, excluding the Tyrol. Permanent collections of several Austrian museums documented, among them:

Diözesanmuseum Wien

Landesmuseum Joanneum Graz

Salzburger Museum Carolino Augusteum

Salzburger Residenzgalerie

Stadtmuseum Linz

New titles continually added (about 100 in 1989).

Photography: Originals (slides and larger-format transparencies) shot by an independent professional photographer.

Production: Formerly, slides produced on unstable print film (Eastmancolor #5381) from internegatives, in "super-slide" format. New production is 35mm on Kodak duplicating film or Fuji film (stable). Production is carried out in a West German laboratory, Herrmann & Kraemer, Garmisch-

Partenkirchen. Color-corrected and contrast-controlled. Mounted in plastic and sleeved individually for shipment in boxes.

Documentation: Free list in German; supplements issued when necessary. Slides labeled in German with full identifications except for nationality of artist. Dates of artist sometimes provided. Orientation marked (number is at top of a vertical slide).

Purchasing: Slides sold in sets of six slides at a per-slide cost of approximately $1.00. Singles also offered. Minimum order 50 slides. Postage added. Payment in Austrian schillings requested. Slides kept in stock or made to order if necessary. If in stock, slides shipped within one week. Slides sent on approval, and returns accepted for exchange or refund.

Other Products: Overhead sheets (for projection) also available, and color transparencies rented for reproduction.

Evaluation: In the 6th edition, a problem with older, unstable film was noted. It also noted that original photography was good and that new production should be high quality.

Museums

207   Landesmuseum Joanneum, Alte Galerie

A-8010 Graz
Neutorgasse 45 Austria
Telephone: 43-316-8017-4770
FAX: 43-316-8017-4847
Attn: Dr. Christine Rabensteiner
E-mail: post@emj-ag.sturk.gv.at

Profile: Approximately 50 duplicate color slide titles offered of the permanent collection: painting, sculpture, and stained glass from medieval to baroque. Special collection of late baroque oil sketches.

Photography and Production: Kunstverlag Hofstetter **(206)**.

Documentation: Brief identifications in German on mounts.

Purchasing: Slides sold in small sets. Slides kept in stock and shipped within one week. Returns accepted for exchange.

Evaluation: Reprinted from 6th ed. Two samples sent: "super slide" format, acceptable color and sharpness. See Hofstetter entry above.

208   Kunsthistorisches Museum

A-1010 Vienna I
Burgring 5 Austria
Attn: Dr. Georg Kugler

Profile: Reprinted from 6th ed. Slides produced by Meyer no longer sold.

209   Österreichishe Galerie

A-1037 Vienna
Postfach 134 Austria
Telephone: (0222) 78 41 14 or 78 41 21
Attn: Museum Bookshop

Profile: Entry repeated from 5th ed. One hundred duplicate color slide titles offered of Austrian art from the Middle Ages to the present. Seventeen slides of the Schloss Belvedere included.

Photography: Slides shot by an independent professional photographer.

Production: Duplicated to order from originals. No attempt made to correct color or control contrast. Mounted in plastic.

Documentation: Free list in German. Artist and title of work provided. Slides labeled in German. Orientation marked.

Purchasing: Slides sold singly or in sets. No minimum order. Single slide 12.00 Austrian schillings. One six-slide set offered of paintings by Klimt, another of paintings by Schiele, 60.00 Austrian schillings per set.

Other Sources: Slides of nineteenth-century Austrian paintings and some baroque paintings available from Saskia **(086)**.

Evaluation: Reprinted from 6th ed. Based on sample order, quality of slides of paintings rated 4; slides of architecture rated 3; soft definition noted on the latter. Documentation, 2; service, 3.

BRITAIN

The following British phone numbers are listed with the U.K. international code, i.e. 44, followed by a (0). The zero is used only in the U.K. and, then, instead of the 44. This is followed by a 1 and a three-digit local exchange or area code and then fi-

nally a six-digit local number. Some of the numbers listed were received with spaces in the local number resembling U.S. codes. These numbers were listed as given. The reader is reminded that this is being written in 1998 and, as elsewhere in the world, the codes are likely to change due to the need for new numbers.

210   Austin, James/Fine Art Photography

Wysing Arts, Fox Rd.
Bourn, Cambridgeshire CB3 7TX
United Kingdom
Telephone: 44 (0) 1 954 718871
FAX: 44 (0) 1 954 718500

Profile: Entry reprinted from 6th ed. More than 1,000 duplicate color slide titles offered of French, English, and Italian architecture of various time periods. Medieval architecture featured, including stained glass windows. New titles continually added (about 100 in 1989).

Photography: All originals, mostly 35mm slides, shot by James Austin on Fujichrome ASA 50 and ASA 100 (75%) and Kodachrome ASA 25 (25%). Nikon camera, tripod, perspective-correcting lens, and flash lighting used as appropriate.

Production: Duplicated in-house from originals onto Kodachrome ASA 25, processed by Kodak. Color-corrected and contrast-controlled. Mounted in plastic and shipped in slide boxes or plastic sleeves.

Documentation: Mailing list kept. Free catalog. Revisions or supplements issued annually. Full identification given for architecture except dates of architect(s). For art, artist, title, city and collection, and date provided. Slides not labeled but keyed to catalog. Orientation marked only when necessary.

Purchasing: Slides sold singly or in sets. Minimum order 12 slides. Fixed price per slide; no discounts. Postage added. Purchase orders accepted from institutions. Prepayment required from individuals. Payment in pounds sterling requested, or in U.S. dollars plus bank charges. Duplicated to order and shipped within two to three weeks. Rush orders filled within one week at no surcharge. No returns accepted, although damaged or defective slides will be replaced if sent back promptly.

Evaluation: Quality, 4; documentation, 4; service, 3 to 4.

211 AVP (Audio-Visual Productions) *See under Digital Section*

212 Barry Capper - Art Historical Slides

52, Hanney Rd.
Steventon, near Abingdon
Oxfordshire OX13 6AL United Kingdom
Telephone: 44 (0) 1 235 831383
FAX: 44 (0) 1 235 831383

Profile: Capper is a graduate in History of Art (University of London) and undertook a course in photography at Leicester Polytechnic. He began forming a slide collection for his teaching of pre-University students in 1978. The collection of slides, now about 15,000, covers British architecture, sculpture, stained glass, gardens, and fine arts and a core collection of French and Italian architecture, sculpture, and paintings. He also provides black-and-white prints and color prints for publishers (e.g., Yale University Press, Oxford University Press, Cambridge University Press).

Photography: Originals photographed by Capper using natural light if possible, with tripod. Kodachrome 25 or 64 professional film. Nikon cameras and lenses and some Leica equipment.

Production: 35mm duplicates are provided by Capper on Ektachrome duplicating film 50-366 and processed by Oxford Color Ltd.

Documentation: Catalog sent to mailing list from previous orders. Slide documentation includes artist, title, date, view information, and location.

Purchasing: Single slides are offered at $3.60 each with a discount of 10% on orders of 100 slides or more. Payment after receipt of order. Mr. Capper states that he tries to ensure that orders are completed reasonably quickly. Postage and bank charges, where applicable, are additional.

Other Products: Black-and-white prints and commissions for slides.

Expansion Plans: Travel to Italy and Spain to add to existing portfolio.

Evaluation: Quality, 3 to 4; documentation, 1 to 3. (Evaluation of samples; most evaluators rated the documentation at 3.)

213 Bodleian Library

Broad St.
Oxford OXI 3BG United Kingdom
Telephone: 44 (0) 1 865 277214
FAX: 44 (0) 1 865 277187
Attn: Mrs.Rigmor Batsvik/
Dr. Bruce Barker-Benfield
E-mail: western.manuscripts@bodley
URL: http://www.bodley.ox.ac.uk/welcome.html

This library also offers digital products and is listed in the digital section of the directory.

Price Range: £1.00 to £36.00 (and VAT where applicable).

Profile: Built up since the late 1950s to provide immediate sales from stock of color images from medieval manuscripts, in conjunction with an iconographic card index and other in-house search tools. Medieval manuscripts of the Bodleian Library, Oxford, with others from Oxford College Libraries, and minor coverage of other holdings of the Bodleian Library (printed books and ephemera). See our Internet site for current free-access imaging projects. The library hopes to develop a color digitizing service on demand, when funding allows.

Photography: Originals shot by staff photographers. Manuscript and other materials photographed flat or on cradle under vertical Nikon camera, lit previously by photo Pearl lights and now by Bowens flash.

Production: The older stock of master negatives (filmstrips and individual slides) was mostly filmed from the originals in the library's own photographic studio on Eastmancolor negative film #5247, from which copies for sale are now printed on Fuji #3518 film. New slides are now both filmed from the originals in the studio and copied from the resulting masters on Kodak Ektachrome professional film ASA 100.

Documentation: Filmstrips and slide sets accompanied by identification lists.

Purchasing: Individual slides are available for £1.00 plus postage and packing (and VAT where applicable). Sets as unmounted filmstrips: six levels £6.00-£36.00 + P&P (and VAT). Prepayment required. Stock slides and filmstrips supplied within one week of receipt of payment (pro forma invoice sent if required). Overseas orders sent by airmail post at standard charge of £6.00 (P&P). Less for internal U.K. orders.

Other Products: The library's photographic studio supplies nonstandard 35mm images and other types of photographs (large-format color transparencies, black-and-white bromide prints, microfilms) to order, with a waiting period of two to three months.

Evaluation: Quality, 4; documentation, 2 to 3; service, 3 to 4. (Evaluation by a single committee member.)

214   Bridgeman Art Library (London and New York)
See under Digital Section

215   British Architectural Library Drawings Collection and Heinz Gallery

(Royal Institute of British Architects—RIBA)
21 Portman Square
London WIH 9HF United Kingdom
Telephone: 44 (0) 171 307 3628
FAX: 44 (0) 171 486 3797
Attn: Philippa Martin
E-mail: dwgs@inst.riba.org
URL: http://www.riba.org/

Profile: The Institute of British Architects (later Royal I.B.A.) was founded in 1834. The collection was first formed when a number of architects donated examples of their work. This practice still continues today. The earliest drawing dates from c.1520. The largest collection of British Architectural drawings in the world, numbering more than 500,000 items, includes British architects from the Renaissance to the present day and also drawings by foreign architects, including 300 designs and sketches by Andrea Palladio.

Photography: Original drawings are photographed in a photography room on site where professional photographers are employed to photograph works using Ilford Ortho plus for black-and-white prints (also Kodak plus ex-pan for black-and-white prints), and Kodacolor Ektachrome 64T for slide and color transparencies.

Purchasing: Slides are priced at £8.50 per slide with discounts of 5% for orders of more than 50 items. The fee is invoiced by the photographers

when the order is dispatched. All overseas orders must be paid in pounds sterling. Postage and packing (and VAT for U.K. orders) are extra. There is a minimum charges of £10.00 excluding P&P and VAT. Photography is usually ready for dispatch within 14 days from receipt of order. An express delivery is available at a surcharge of 100%.

Rental: Color transparencies can be rented for a month at a charge of £45.

Other Products: Photographic prints of all drawings, books and exhibition catalogs, color facsimiles, postcards, and exhibition posters.

216   British Library Reproductions

British Library
96 Euston Rd., St. Pancras
London NW1 2DB United Kingdom
Telephone: 44 (0) 171 412 7614
FAX: 44 (0) 171 412 7771
Attn: Reproduction Enquiries
E-mail: bl-repro@bl.uk
URL: http://www.bl.uk

This museum also offers digital products and is listed in the digital section of the directory.

Profile: The British Library has operated a photographic service for many years. Text copies (photocopies), microfilm, and photographs are offered for commercial reproduction. The world-renowned collections include 17 million books and 250,000 unique historical manuscripts. This is a unique source of visual inspiration to scholars, publishers, and advertisers. The library hopes to announce a CD-ROM catalog to permit remote browse.

Photography: Slides, negatives, and large-format transparencies shot by staff photographers. Nikon equipment and Ektachrome ASA 64 are used for 35mm slides with lighting by electronic flash.

Production: Duplicates are made in-house on Ektachrome #5071 film.

Purchasing: Prices vary. Individual slides are available. At the time of writing (November 1997) the price for the first slide is £10.21, and thereafter slides are priced at £8.17 each. Prices are reviewed in April each year. The pictures themselves are prepaid. Reproduction rights fees are paid on publication of the picture.

Rental: Large transparencies are hired for three months, and 35mm slides as well.

Digital Products: CD-ROMs are being prepared using MAC equipment with large-format transparencies scanned and then manipulated with Adobe Photoshop software.

Other Products: Large-format transparencies, black-and-white prints, microfilm, paper copies.

217　Central Saint Martins College of Art & Design

Southampton Row
London WC1B 4AP United Kingdom
Telephone: 44 (0) 171 514 7015
FAX: 44 (0) 171 514 7016
Attn: Dali Salivadori
E-mail: shortcourse@cstm.co.uk
URL: http://www.csm.linst.ac.uk/

Price Range: £35 to £400.

Profile: Central Saint Martins is the U.K.'s largest college of art and design. It is part of the London Institute and has 2,800 students studying in the heart of London. There are two subscription services available to other educational institutions: the Contemporary Art Slide Scheme (CASS) and the Contemporary Design Slide Scheme (CDSS). The archive also is licensed through the Bridgeman Art Library.

Photography: CASS images photographed by professional photographer from actual art works in galleries. CDSS images supplied by originating designers. Archive images photographed from originals.

Documentation: Announcements are sent to mailing list annually. Slides include artist name, title, materials, size, and date.

Purchasing: Slide sets are available by subscription at £425 per year for subscription; back issues are available. Payment accepted in U.K. by purchase order, from non-U.K. buyers by pounds sterling payment in advance by check or credit card. Subscription includes shipping and handling.

Other Products: Other slide sets available for purchase: "Joyce Clissold and Footprints," "Nineteenth Century Japanese Actor Prints," "Rietveld Furniture," and "Schroeder House." Contact college for details.

Evaluation: Quality, 2 to 4; documentation, 2 to 4; service, 4. (Evaluation by a single committee member.)

218　Centre for the Study of Cartoons and Caricature

The Library, University of Kent
Canterbury, Kent CT2 7NU United Kingdom
Telephone: 44 (0) 1 227 764000, x3127 or x3128

Profile: Entry reprinted from 6th ed. Eleven 30-slide sets offered of British twentieth-century political cartoons from the archive at the University of Kent. New sets infrequently added. All slides are black-and-white.

Photography: Original slides shot by staff photographer on 35mm microfilm.

Production: Produced by the university's photographic unit on Kodalith 3. Mounted in Gepe anti-newton ring glass mounts.

Documentation: Mailing list kept. Free list. Slides keyed to list. Identifications provide artist, title, date of work, and city/collection. Orientation marked.

Purchasing: Slides sold in sets only, priced from £25 to £30. Minimum order one set. Postage added. No discounts. Purchase order required from institutions. Payment in pounds sterling requested. Sets kept in stock and shipped within two weeks. No rush orders accepted. Sets sent on approval for four weeks. Damaged goods billed at cost.

Evaluation: Reprinted from 6th ed. "Perfectly adequate in quality" (*International Bulletin*, 1982, no. 3).

219　Commonwealth Association of Architects (CAA)

66 Portland Pl.
London WIN 4AD United Kingdom
Telephone: 44 (0) 171 636 8276
FAX: 44 (0) 171 636 5472
Attn: CAA Projects Limited
URL: http://www.tcol.co.uk/comorg/caa.htm

Profile: Entry reprinted from 6th ed. Only second page of questionnaire filled out. Entry based also on 1987/1988 catalog. Slide programs, accompanied by audiocassettes, offered for the training of architects on subjects such as environmental design, landscape architecture, vernacular architecture, building conservation, and building techniques. New sets occasionally added.

Documentation: Mailing list kept. Free catalog, updated biannually. Script of audiotape included in each set; some also accompanied by manuals. Additional copies of manuals sold. Airmail postage added to overseas orders.

Purchasing: Slide programs consist of 24 slides plus documentation, unless otherwise noted in the catalog. Prepayment in pounds sterling required from pro forma invoice; UNESCO coupons accepted. Rush orders discouraged. Returns accepted "only if faulty."

Other Products: Videos and 16 mm films available for rent or purchase outside the United Kingdom only.

220   Drake Educational Productions, Ltd.

St. Fagans Rd.
Fairwater, Cardiff CF5 3AE Wales,
United Kingdom
Attn: R. G. Drake, Managing Director

Profile: Filmstrips, slides, and wall charts offered on a wide range of general subjects. Listed under "Creative Arts" in catalog are two slide sets of contemporary artists at work (including one of Henry Moore), three sets of nineteenth- to twentieth-century painting, seven sets of modern design, and two sets of prints by Old Masters. Double-frame filmstrips, which can be mounted as slides, also available on techniques of painting, history of art, ceramics, and architecture.

Documentation: Free catalog with price list. Titles of set listed but not contents. Sets usually accompanied by teacher's notes. Audiocassette included in "Contemporary Artists at Work" sets.

Purchasing: Sold as double-frame filmstrips or mounted in plastic. Sets of 12 slides including "Contemporary Artists at Work" sets. Surcharge of 20% added to overseas orders. Postage added. Pro forma invoices issued, and slides shipped within five days of receipt of payment. Slides not sent on approval.

221   Focal Point Audiovisual, Ltd.

251, Copnor Rd.
Portsmouth, Hants. PO3 5EE
United Kingdom
Telephone: 44 (0) 1 705 665249
FAX: 44 (0) 1 705 695723
Attn: D. J. Ellis, General Manager

Profile: Duplicate color slides offered in sets of painting, drawing, architecture, sculpture, decorative arts, ceramics, and photography. Many subjects other than art covered as well. Works in the collections of the British Museum and the Victoria and Albert Museum represented.

Photography: Original slides shot on Kodachrome ASA 64 by staff photographer, other professional photographers, and traveling scholars. Natural light used when possible; otherwise, floodlights or double flash with reflectors. Tripod employed.

Production: Produced by Filmstrip Services, Ltd., on Kodak Eastman film #6011. Contrast-controlled. Mounted in plastic and sleeved in plastic viewing wallets or plastic boxes.

Documentation: Free catalog, updated annually, briefly describes sets. "Most programmes in our list are supplied with teaching notes." For art, artist's name, dates, and nationality are given, with title of work. (Sample documentation for University of Sussex set on "Abstraction" supplied a list of identifications with full information in addition to text and bibliography.) For architecture, location, name of building, dates of construction, and description of views provided. Orientation marked by number placement (top right corner).

Purchasing: Slides sold in sets only. Minimum order one set. Current price list inserted in catalog. In 1997, University of Sussex series (20-slide sets) priced £14.75 each. Educational discount of 15% given. Shipping cost added. Purchase order required. Payment requested in pounds sterling. Sets kept in stock and usually shipped by return mail. Orders sent on three-week approval within the United Kingdom.

Other Products: Videos and filmstrips also offered.

Evaluation: Reprinted from 6th ed. Sample set from University of Sussex series sent in 1984 (20 slides): quality, 2 to 3; documentation, 4. Color muted, resolution slightly soft, dust and scratches on masters duplicated on copies.

*222   Icarus

158 Boundaries Rd.
London SW12 8HG United Kingdom
Telephone: 44 (0) 1 81-682-0900
FAX: 44 (0) 1 81-682-0900
Attn: Patrick Doorly

Price Range: U.S. $.79 to $3.00.

Profile: Icarus was launched in 1985 to make and distribute slides of British Museum prints. In 1990 it published computer generated plans and cross-sections of Italian architecture, and in 1993 published slides of the architecture of Expo '92 in Seattle. The collection of images includes 35mm slides of master prints from the British Museum and microfiches; 35mm slides of plans and elevations of Italian architecture AD300-1500; and 35mm slides of the architecture of Expo '92 in Seattle. The slides are being posted on the World Wide Web by Image Directory at www.imagedir.com.

Photography: 1) Photographed with macro 35mm camera in the British Museum directly from the finest impressions of the master prints using Kodak technical pan film, and 2) computer-generated architectural photographs and drawings imaged by a professional image recorder and printed on Eastman #4384 archive-quality color film.

Production: The negatives are contact printed on to the positive film. Black-and-white mask prints photographed on Kodak technical pan negative-Agfa positives. Color originals on Kodacolor to Eastman #5384 archive-positive film. A centimeter scale against one side of the print allows the size of the original work of art to be judged from the projected images.

Purchasing: Master Prints are priced at $.79 per slide or in sets at $.69 per slide for the complete set; Italian Architecture singles are priced at $3.90 each or in sets at $3.50 per slide for the complete set; Expo '92 singles are priced at $3.00 per slide or in sets at $1.80 per slide for the complete set. Payment from institutions due within 30 days of order date. Private orders must be prepaid.

Other Products: Microfiches of the slides of British Museum prints.

Evaluation: Quality, 3 to 4; documentation, 2 to 4; service, 3 to 4.

223　Lambton Visual Aids

5 & 9, Side (rear)
Newcastle-on-Tyne NEI 3JE United Kingdom
Telephone: 44 (0) 1 91 232 2000

Profile: Entry reprinted from 6th ed. More than 7,000 color slide titles offered of painting and sculpture, illustration, caricatures and cartoons, tattoos, advertising, photography, graphic design, industrial design, fashion, architecture, interior design, and garden design. Approximately 2% of holdings are black-and-white. Company began as a fundraising

project of Amber Films, founded 1968. Originally intended to provide visual aids to one art college, but gradually accepted commissions from others.

Photography: Original slides shot by staff photographer on Kodachrome, Ektachrome, and Agfachrome, using Nikon camera. Many slides are of book plates, in which case the book citation is noted in the catalog and in information accompanying slides. Most of the books used as sources are old, rare, or unusual.

Production: Duplicated from originals onto Ektachrome #5071 using equipment developed by the members of Amber. Color-corrected and contrast-controlled. Mounted in glass (plastic frame). Sleeved on request.

Documentation: Mailing list kept. Free catalog (1981) lists set titles only. Larger catalog of other Amber activities, including Lambton Visual Aids, also available. Slides not labeled but keyed to list with minimal identifications. References to sources provided in notes. Orientation not marked.

Purchasing: Slides sold in sets of 24 (unless otherwise stated), priced £20 per set. Minimum order one set. No discounts. Postage added. Purchase orders accepted. Orders invoiced. Payment in pounds sterling requested; make checks payable to Amber/Side. Duplicated to order and shipped within four to six weeks. No rush orders accepted. Slides not sent on approval, and no returns accepted.

Other Products: Films and videos available.

Evaluation: Reprinted from 6th ed. One member of Evaluation Committee gave this vendor the highest rating on quality, documentation, and service.

224　Manchester Metropolitan University

Department of History of Art & Design
Cavendish St.
Manchester M15 6BG United Kingdom
Telephone: 44 (0) 161 247 1929/2930
FAX: 44 (0) 161 247 6393
Attn: Dr. Elizabeth Coatsworth, Slide Librarian
E-mail: E.Coatsworth@mmu.ac.uk

Price Range: Price of sets range from £15 to £120 (+ VAT in United Kingdom) plus postage applicable.

Profile: This service, to produce sets of slides for educational use, was set up in 1985 and quickly expanded to serve all Higher and Further Education Institutions and the school sector in Great Britain.

Over the last four years the scheme has expanded into the international market. In 1995 the Design Council Slides Collection was acquired, and sets are now being produced that draw on images from this important archive of manly twentieth-century British design. The Archive currently comprises more than 100 sets of slides on design, fine art, architecture, non-Western crafts, popular media, and aspects of cultural history of interest to academics. About 12 new slide sets are added to the catalog each year.

Photography: By professional photographer, using E6 compatible film (e.g., Ektachrome, Fujichrome) shot in studio or on location as appropriate.

Production: 35mm slide duplicated from original master slides that range from 35mm to 4" x 5". The original images are the property of the university (see above) or acquired directly from the museum, gallery, artist, or author. Original produced in Ektachrome, Fujichrome and copies on E6-compatible Ektachrome slide duplicating film.

Documentation: Mailing list kept; mailings twice a year. Slides are accompanied generally by a commissioned text or a related publication such as an exhibition catalog; a few slide sets are accompanied by a single listing only.

Purchasing: E-mail orders are accepted. Slide discounts negotiable. Some discounts for multiple sets are included in the catalog. Slides can be obtained by sending a purchase order, E-mail, or written request. Orders are filled and dispatched within two weeks of receipt and sent out with a confirmation of delivery note. Invoices to follow. Postage is charged on all packages, and varies according to weight. VAT is charged on all U.K. purchases. Usual options for payment available.

Rental: The Design Council collection only has a postal/personal loan scheme available for use within the U.K. only. For terms, contact J.Davis@mmu.ac.uk.

Other Products: Books and videos published by the Manchester Metropolitan University Department of History of Art and Design are also marketed by the Slide Library and are in the catalog.

Expansion Plans: Plans for selling individual slides (as soon as it is practical) and digitized images are in process of development in response to requests from customers. A World Wide Web site also is being planned for the full catalog and images.

*225 Miniature Gallery

2 Birds Hill
Oxshott, Surrey KT22 OSW United Kingdom
Telephone: 44 (0) 1 372 842448
Attn: Derek Carver

This image provider declined to participate because of dissatisfaction with the 6th edition evaluation process.

Profile: Entry reprinted from 6th ed. Company in business 30 years. Exhibitions in Great Britain and Europe covered selectively. The Peggy Guggenheim, Woodner, and Thyssen-Bornemisza collections documented in recent years. Sets of duplicate color slides are limited issues and eventually go "out of print" except in occasional cases where demand is sufficient to justify a reissue. New titles continually added. Slides to which Miniature Gallery holds copyright may be published for scholarly purposes at no charge if permission is first requested in writing.

Photography: Original photography carried out by Derek Carver in the exhibition galleries.

Production: Current production is on Ektachrome reversal film with E6 processing, carefully supervised by Derek Carver. Color-corrected and contrast-controlled. Film in plastic mounts; packed in plastic boxes.

Documentation: No catalog. Mailing list kept, and *Art-Slide News* issued irregularly (several times annually) to announce new offerings. Past productions that are still available are listed in each issue of *Art-Slide News*. Slides keyed to identification lists by number. Printed self-adhesive labels supplied. Artist name and dates, title of work, date of work, dimensions, and collection given on lists and labels. City locations not consistently provided for collections. Nationality of artists not given. Media given only if other than oil on canvas. Errors in identifications corrected in subsequent issues of *Art-Slide News* or accompanying memoranda.

Purchasing: Slides sold in sets only. Prices vary, but in general the slides are inexpensive (approximately $1.50 each). Payment accepted in pounds sterling or U.S. dollars at the current exchange rate. Institutions invoiced. Postage added to invoices for orders outside the U.K. To prepay, add 8% to cover second-class airmail shipment. U.K. orders subject to VAT. Returns accepted if sent back within seven days of receipt, accompanied by a letter of explanation.

Evaluation: Quality, 3 to 4; documentation, 3 to 4; service, 3 to 4.

226 Oxford University Press (London, USA, and Canada) *See under Digital Section*

227 University Colour Slide Scheme (UCSS)

Courtauld Institute of Art
Somerset House, Strand
London WC2 ORN United Kingdom
Telephone: 44 (0) 171 873 2508
FAX: 44 (0) 171 873 2772
E-mail: catherine.jefferis@courtauld.ac.uk
Attn: Mrs. Catherine Jefferis

Profile: The UCSS was set up in 1966 to answer the needs of the Courtauld Institute, the Courtauld slide library, and other universities and colleges wishing to build their own slide collections. UCSS is a nonprofit organization producing 35mm color slides for teaching and research purposes only. Temporary exhibitions in London and elsewhere in the United Kingdom are photographed to make sets of slides with details as well as reproduction of whole works of art. It is a condition of membership not to reproduce UCSS slides in any way. This restriction is to honor contracts with private owners' collections and museums who gave us permission to photograph their works.

Photography: Original works of art are photographed in situ normally within the context of a temporary exhibition. Shot by professional staff photographer on Agfa RSX50 film and processed in Agfa lab. Some originals provided by museums may be on different films.

Production: Originals are duplicated in-house on same Agfa RSX 50 films.

Documentation: Identification lists (artist's name and dates, title of work, date, size, media, and location) sent with each set. Four circulars a year sent to all subscribers, covering each yearly output.

Purchasing: Purchase is by yearly subscription offering sets of slides. The yearly subscription is paid at beginning of the year. Three levels. Category A: 540 slides for £465; Category B: 300 slides for £285; and Category C: 60 slides for £175. Slides are sent within four to six weeks of returning date of order. Shipped surface mail unless airmail surcharge is paid with subscription.

Evaluation: Quality, 2 to 4; documentation, 2 to 4; service, 3.

228 Visual Publications

The Green, Northleach
Cheltenham GL54 3EX United Kingdom
Telephone: 44 (0) 1 451 860519
FAX: 44 (0) 1 451 860215
Attn: Peter Loveday

Profile: Audiovisual publisher since 1948. Company supplies slide books to schools, colleges, and universities. Subjects include art & design and history. Each title, set, or book contains an average of 36 slides chosen by experts, accompanied by documentation for each slide. Company plans to offer CD-ROMs over the next five years as quality improves.

Photography: Originals are photography by professional or author photographers on Kodachrome or Ektachrome; otherwise from loaned originals from institutions. Originals are photographed using Kodachrome or Ektachrome film.

Production: Slides are duplicated using Fuji #3518.

Documentation: A catalog is sent to mailing list annually. Slide books of approximately 36 images with individual and linking texts and booklets. Each slide preprinted and number keyed with text.

Purchasing: If ordering from the United States or Canada, contact Dupuy Art Images **(052)**. Dupuy is the sole agent for Visual Publications in the United States and Canada. From other countries, contact Visual Publications for pricing, discounts, and purchasing instructions.

Expansion Plans: Art since 1945; interior decoration.

Evaluation: Quality, 3; documentation, 3 to 4. (Evaluation of samples.)

229 Whitaker, Jeremy

Land of Nod
Headley Downs, Bordon, Hampshire
GU35 8SJ United Kingdom
Telephone: 44 (0) 1 428 713609
FAX: 44 (0) 1 428-717698

Profile: Major Jeremy Whitaker is a man of many tastes. He served 15 years in the Coldstream Guards and retired in 1967 to become an architectural photographer. In this capacity, Mr. Whitaker photographed the historic houses of Great Britain. His work has appeared in books and magazine articles. Now he has opened a bed and breakfast, the Land of Nod, in Hampshire with a website at http://www.s-h-systems.co.uk/hotels/landofn.html. The best way to reach Mr. Whitaker is by fax.

Production: Slides are made on demand from transparencies. A list may be obtained by faxing Mr. Whitaker.

230   World Microfilms Publications, Ltd.

23 N. Wharf Rd.
London W2 1LA United Kingdom
Telephone: 44 (0) 171 262 2178
FAX: 44 (0) 171 262 1708
Attn: S. C. Albert
E-mail: microworld@ndirect.co.uk
URL: http://www.microworld.ndirect.co.uk/wmcats.htm

This vendor also offers digital products and is listed in the digital section of the directory.

Profile: Slide sets available in addition to more numerous microform titles. Thousands of duplicate color slide titles offered in sets in the following series: "Pidgeon Audio Visual Library of Tape/Slide Talks," "RIBA Exhibitions," "Masters of Architecture," "Historic Houses," "The Indian World," and "Artists Talking." Exhibitions documented at the Royal College of Art's Henry Moore Gallery and at the Heinz Gallery of the Royal Institute of British Architects. Slides available of manuscripts in the Lambeth Palace Library, London, and of the Winchester Bible. New sets continually added. The company is gradually entering CD-ROM market, mainly with illuminated manuscripts.

Photography: Originals shot in various formats on various films by various photographers, including staff and independent professionals. In recent correspondence with a slide curator in the United States, Mr. Albert stated that the company could not afford to hire professional photographers to shoot originals of architectural monuments, and therefore often relied upon the work of the architects themselves or architectural historians and lecturers. In quite a lot of cases, photographs (even if they are quite old) of buildings at the time of completion have been used, to depict the work as the architect intended. Film used in approximately 50% of original work is Kodak #5247.

Production: Slides produced on Fuji positive film or Kodak's Eastmancolor #5384 print film by Filmstrip Services, Ltd., London. Some slides of historic houses produced by Trans-Globe, a separate company that formerly used unstable film; presumably these are now printed on the low-fade Eastmancolor. Color-corrected and contrast-controlled. Mounted in "Geimuplast" mounts and shipped in boxes.

Documentation: Mailing list kept. Free brochures sent monthly announcing new sets. Contents lists available on request. Imprinted on mounts, keyed to contents list accompanying each set. Orientation marked only when necessary. Audiotapes included in the tape/slide talks.

Purchasing: The North American distributor for slides and CD-ROMs is Films for the Humanities [(056) in Digital Section]. Slides sold in sets only. Minimum order one set. Prices listed in brochures. Discount given on prepaid orders. Prepayment required from individuals, purchase orders from institutions. Shipping and insurance costs added. Payment accepted in pounds sterling or U.S. dollars. Sets kept in stock and usually shipped within seven to ten days. Rush orders sent by return post if goods in stock; no surcharge. Slides not sent on approval, but defective slides will be replaced.

Digital Products: CD-ROMs, Windows format with tech support. Minimal equipment needed for viewing: 8MB RAM/486/SVGA. Images are scanned from color microfilm in 256 colors and color-corrected with Alchemy software used for manipulation. The Alchemy software offers the purchaser the opportunity to enlarge the image *ad infinitum*, thus allowing the finest detail to be seen as clearly as possible. CD-ROMs are sold for multiuse, networked applications with Alchemy viewing software included in CD-ROM. As for slides, the North American distributor for CD-ROMs is Films for the Humanities.

Other Products: Microforms, CD-ROMs, videotapes, computer programs, audiotapes.

Expansion Plans: Continuing publication of slides, tape/slides, microforms, videotapes, and audiotapes.

Evaluation: Quality, 1 to 3; documentation, 1 to 3; service, 1 to 4.

Museums

231 Atkinson Art Gallery

Lord Street, Southport
Merseyside PR8 IDH United Kingdom
Telephone: 44 (0) 1704 533133, x2110
FAX: 44 (0) 151 934 2107

Profile: Entry repeated from 5th ed. Approximately 1,800 color slide titles offered, covering the entire permanent collection of eighteenth- and nineteenth-century watercolors, Victorian genre painting, and British painting 1900–1940.

Photography: Original slides shot by gallery technician on various films.

Production: Duplicated in-house on various films. Mounted in cardboard.

Documentation: No list available. Orientation marked.

Purchasing: Slides sold singly, priced 75 pence each. Postage added. Payment requested in pounds sterling. Slides duplicated to order. Some originals sold. Orders filled within three weeks. Rush orders shipped within 10 days. Slides sent on approval. Returns accepted for exchange or refund "if quality is genuinely inadequate."

232 Birmingham Museum and Art Gallery

Chamberlain Square
Birmingham B3 3DH United Kingdom
Telephone: 44 (0) 121 303 2834
FAX: 44 (0) 121 236 6227
Attn: Publications Unit

Profile: Entry repeated from 5th ed. Approximately 90 color slide titles offered of fine art and archaeological artifacts from the permanent collection. New titles infrequently added.

Photography: Large-format transparencies shot by an independent professional photographer.

Production: Duplicated from originals. Unstable Eastmancolor film no longer used. Color-corrected and contrast-controlled.

Documentation: Free list. Slides labeled.

Purchasing: Slides sold singly, 30 pence each. Postage added. Minimum order 20 slides. Prepayment required in pounds sterling. Slides shipped within two weeks. Rush orders filled within one

week. No special photography undertaken. Slides not sent on approval, and no returns accepted.

Evaluation: Reprinted from 6th ed. Numerous samples sent in 1984: quality variable, documentation variable. Some slides on unstable film, already pink. Some others (new production?) good to excellent quality and labeled with full information. One member of the committee gave this vendor 3 to 4 ratings on quality, documentation, and service. Perhaps old stock has been phased out.

233 British Museum Publications, Ltd.

46 Bloomsbury St.
London WCLB 3QQ United Kingdom
Telephone: 44 (0) 181 323 1234
Attn: Publishing Manager

Profile: Entry reprinted from 6th ed. Five slide booklets (12 slides) and five slide sets (six slides) offered of masterpieces in the British Museum collection. Ancient Egyptian, Assyrian, Greek, and Roman art featured. One set available of medieval treasures. Two single slides offered of the Rosetta Stone and the rock crystal skull. According to the response to the questionnaire, these are "the only slides sets and booklets we now produce." (In 1984, approximately 900 slides were available.)

Photography: Original slides shot by staff photographers of the British Museum, in studio when possible.

Production: Produced by a German laboratory, presumably on low-fade Eastmancolor film. Mounted in plastic and packaged in plastic sleeves.

Documentation: Free single-page list of sets and booklets. Booklets accompanied by commentaries written by British Museum experts: introductory text plus notes on each slide. All slides imprinted on mounts with basic identification. Orientation marked.

Purchasing: Prices given on list; VAT included in United Kingdom prices. Postage added. Pro forma invoice issued; payment required before goods are shipped. Slides kept in stock and shipped within six to eight weeks. No rush orders accepted. Slides not sent on approval, and no returns accepted.

Other Sources: More than 2,000 slides of prints are available from Icarus (**222**). Slides not available from British Museum Publications may be ordered from the British Museum's Photographic Department (Great Russell Street). Each department of the museum will send, on request, a list of slides from which duplicates can be ordered.

Evaluation: Quality, 4; documentation, 4; service, 2. (Evaluation by a single committee member.)

234 Christ Church Picture Gallery

Christ Church
Oxford OX I 1 DP United Kingdom
Telephone: 44 (0) 1 865-276172
FAX: 44 (0) 1 865 202429
Attn: Dennis Harrington
E-mail: dennis.harrington@christ-chur
URL: http://www.chch.ox.ac.uk

Profile: Duplicate color slides offered of selected works from the permanent collection of European paintings and drawings of the fourteenth through eighteenth centuries.

Photography: Original photography by professional photographers undertaken at studio at Ashmolean Museum, Oxford, England.

Production: Duplicated on Agfachrome by Ashmolean Museum Photographic Department. Color-corrected and contrast-controlled. Mounted in plastic or in Gepe mounts with anti-newton ring glass.

Purchasing: Individual slides are priced at 75 pence each with a discounted price of £4.00 for six slides. Prepayment required in pounds sterling. Pro forma invoice sent, slides dispatched upon receipt of payment. Special photography normally requires two to three weeks.

Evaluation: Reprinted from 6th ed. Quality, 3; documentation, 2 to 3; service, 2.

235 Courtauld Institute Galleries

Somerset House, Strand
London WC2R 2LS United Kingdom
Telephone: 44 (0) 181 872 0220

Profile: Entry based upon information from the 4th edition (1980). One hundred eleven slides offered of European painting, Renaissance through modern, with emphasis on nineteenth-century French.

Documentation: Free list. Artist and title provided.

Purchasing: Original slides sold singly.

Evaluation: Reprinted from 6th ed. Quality, 3 to 4; documentation, 3; service, 3. Limited selection.

236 Dulwich Picture Gallery

College Rd.
London SE21 7BG United Kingdom
Telephone: 44 (0) 181 693 5254
FAX: 44 (0) 181-693-0923
URL: http://www.dulwich.co.uk/gallery.htm/

Profile: Entry reprinted from 6th ed. Seventy duplicate color slides offered of works in the permanent collection (Old Masters, seventeenth and eighteenth centuries), and six of the museum's architecture. A few new titles added from time to time.

Photography: Originals (slides or large-format transparencies) shot by an independent professional photographer.

Production: Produced by Woodmansterne (Woodmansterne no longer sells slides as of 1997). Mounted in plastic and sealed in glassine envelopes.

Documentation: Free list. Artist's surname and title of work provided. Slides labeled with artist, artist's dates, title of work, city, and collection. Architecture slides labeled with architect and building name. Orientation marked.

Purchasing: Slides sold singly. No minimum order. Postage added. Orders sent on receipt of payment in pounds sterling. Rush orders accepted at no surcharge. Returns accepted for exchange. Special photography undertaken by freelance photographer.

Evaluation: Reprinted from 6th ed. Two samples sent: quality, 3 to 4; documentation, 2 to 3; service, 3.

237 Fitzwilliam Museum

Trumpington St.
Cambridge CB1 1RD United Kingdom
Telephone: 44 (0) 1 223 332900
Attn: Shop Manager, Fitzwilliam Museum Enterprises, Ltd.
URL: http://www.fitzwilliam.cam.ac.uk

Profile: Entry reprinted from 6th ed. List sent in response to questionnaire. Fifth edition entry used to fill in gaps in information. Ninety-seven slides offered of works in the permanent collection: fine arts, decorative arts, antiquities, manuscripts, coins, and medals. Sets of six slides each available of Cambridge architecture, Cambridge Colleges, and the Backs. New slides occasionally added.

Photography: Slides shot by the museum's photographer.

Production: Produced by Woodmansterne (Woodmansterne no longer sells slides as of 1997).

Documentation: Free single-page list and single-page addendum dated 1986. Identifications on list consist of artist, artist's dates, title of work, and date if known. Slides labeled. Orientation marked.

Purchasing: Slides sold singly, 75 pence each. No minimum order. Postage added. Prepayment requested in pounds sterling or by international money order. Slides kept in stock and shipped within one to four weeks. Rush orders filled as quickly as possible; no surcharge. Slides not sent on approval, and no returns accepted. Special photography undertaken on request.

238   Galleries
London

Profile: Exhibitions documented by University Colour Slide Scheme **(227)**, Miniature Gallery **(225)**, and World Microfilms Publications **(230)**.

239   Hunterian Art Gallery
University of Glasgow
82 Hillhead Street
Glasgow G12 8QQ Scotland,
United Kingdom
Telephone: 44 (0) 141 330 5431
FAX: 44 (0) 141 330 3618
Attn: June Barrie
E-mail: j.e.barrie@museum.gla.ac.uk
URL: http://www.gla.ac.uk/Museum/ArtGall/

Profile: Forty duplicate color slides offered of selected works from the permanent collection, including 10 from the Whistler collection and 20 from the Mackintosh Collection. In addition, set of six slides available of Mackintosh interiors. No additions planned to commercial slide holdings. Archive of approximately 1,000 slides exists, from which special-order duplicates might be obtainable.

Photography: Originals (slides and large-format transparencies) shot by university photographer, using tripod. No information available on film type.

Production: Sample slide set of Mackintosh House interiors produced in West Germany for Pitkin Pictorial Color Slides, Northway, Andover, Hants. SPIO 5BE. Producer of single slides, printed from internegatives, presumably the same. Color-corrected and contrast-controlled. Slides mounted and sleeved.

Documentation: Free single-page list. Artist, title, and date given on list. Slides also labeled.

Purchasing: Slides sold singly with exception of the one set mentioned. No minimum order. Singles priced 50 pence each, the set £2.50. Postage added. Prepayment from pro forma invoice required in pounds sterling. If paid in other currency, please add £10.00 to cover bank charges. Stock of slides kept, and orders shipped within two days of receipt of payment. Rush orders not accepted. Slides not sent on approval, and returns not accepted.

Other Products: Black-and-white photographic prints available.

Evaluation: Set of six samples sent: quality, 3; documentation, 1. Original photography of interiors excellent, but duplicates slightly soft. Documentation generally 2 to 3. Service rated 2 to 3 in 5th ed.

240   Iveagh Bequest
Kenwood, Hampstead Ln.
London NW3 7JR United Kingdom
Telephone: 44 (0) 181 348 1286
Attn: Publications Officer

Profile: Entry repeated from 5th ed. Sixty-three color slide titles offered of seventeenth- to eighteenth-century paintings in the permanent collection, as well as views of the architecture of Kenwood and the gardens.

Photography: Color negatives shot by an independent professional photographer.

Production: Produced by Woodmansterne (Woodmansterne is no longer selling slides as of 1997). Mounted in cardboard.

Documentation: List available. Slides labeled. Orientation marked.

Purchasing: Slides sold singly for 35 pence each or in sets of three for £1.00. No minimum order. Orders by educational institutions sent postpaid (in lieu of discount). Postage added to other orders. Payment in pounds sterling preferred. Slides kept in stock and shipped within one to two days. Rush orders filled same day. Slides not sent on approval. Returns accepted for exchange only. No special photography undertaken.

Evaluation: Reprinted from 6th ed. Four samples sent in 1984, two of architecture and two of painting: quality, 3; documentation, 3. Soft definition noted on architecture slides.

241 Laing Art Gallery

New Bridge St.
Newcastle-upon-Tyne NEI 8AG
United Kingdom
Telephone: 44 (0) 191 232 7734
FAX: 44 (0) 191 222 0952
URL: http://ris.sunderland.ac.uk/museums/laing.htm

Profile: No longer keeps "off the shelf" stocks but can provide images to order. Prices depend on the photography necessary and ease of access to the original work. Any photographs supplied will be subject to copyright; usage/reproduction must be approved in advance. No digital images available. The Laing Art Gallery is now administered by the Tyne & Wear Museums group; the above policy also is in effect for the Discovery Museum, Newcastle; Hancock Museum, Newcastle; Shipley Art Gallery, Gateshead; Art Gallery & Museum, South Shields; Arbela Roman Fort, South Shields; Museum & Art Gallery, Sunderland; and Monkwearmouth Railway Museum, Sunderland.

Evaluation: Quality, 4; documentation, 1; service, 1. (Evaluation by a single committee member; 6th edition rated quality, 3; documentation, 3; service, 3.)

242 Leeds City Art Gallery

The Headrow
Leeds LS1 3AA United Kingdom
Telephone: 44 (0) 113 247 8248
E-mail: Brenda.Copley@leeds.gov.uk
URL: http://www.leeds.gov.uk/tourinfo/attract/museums/artgall.html

Price Range: £18.00 per set (+ £1.50 postage and packing to United Kingdom; £4.95 postage and packing to United States).

Profile: Three sets of 15 slides each are available: "French Landscape Painting" (Corot, Rousseau, Courbet, Daubigny, Diaz de la Pena, Sisley, Pissaro, Picabia, Derain, etc.), "Images of Women" (Canova, Tissot, Bonnard, Gilman, Henry Moore, Kowalsky, etc.), and "The Camden Town Group" (Gilman, Gore, Sickert, Lucien, Pissaro, Bevan, Ginner, etc.).

Purchasing: Any orders from outside the United Kingdom must be paid for by a pounds sterling charge or money order drawn on a British Bank. Checks are to be paid to the Leeds City Council.

243 Manchester City Art Galleries

City Art Gallery, Mosley St.
Manchester M2 3JL United Kingdom
Telephone: 44 (0) 161 236 5244
FAX: 44 (0) 161 236 2880
Attn: Publication Dept.
URL: http://www.u-net.com/set/mcag/cag.html

Profile: Duplicate color slides offered of objects in the City Art Gallery, the Gallery of Modem Art, the Athenaeum, the Gallery of English Costume, Wythenshawe Hall, and Heaton Hall. British painting of the seventeenth through twentieth centuries featured. European painting of the eighteenth century also represented. The Gallery has a wide range of photographic material available for hire, especially eighteenth- and nineteenth-century works. The Gallery is looking to digitize its collection.

Photography: In-house photographer.

Purchasing: Slides are priced at £6.95 + postage and packing. Invoices to institutions not available under £30.00. All orders outside Great Britain must be paid in advance. Credit cards: VISA or MasterCard accepted. Postage and packing quoted on request.

Evaluation: Quality, 2 to 4; documentation, 1 to 4; service, 3.

244 Museum of London Picture Gallery

150 London Wall
London EC2Y 5HN United Kingdom
Telephone: 44 (0) 171 600 3699
FAX: 44 (0) 171 600 1058
Attn: Anna Payne
E-mail: alpayne@museum-london.org.uk

Price Range: £5 (+VAT for British customers) each. There is normally a reproduction fee on top of this depending on how the image is used.

Profile: The collection of more than 20,000 images covers objects within the museum galleries and stores, which include photos, prints, paintings, drawings, artifacts and costumes of London buildings, views, streets, and river scenes from the seventeenth century onward. Major events as well as social and political themes are represented. There also is a large suffragette collection (photographs and ephemera).

Other Products: Photographic prints (£10) and 4" x 5" transparencies (£30 rental).

245   National Galleries of Scotland

Picture Library
c/o Scottish National Gallery
Belford Rd.
Edinburgh EH4 3DR Scotland,
United Kingdom
Telephone: 44 (0) 131 624 6319
FAX: 44 (0) 131 315 2963
Attn: Deborah Hunter
E-mail: deborah.hunter@natgalscot.ac.uk

Profile: Initially part of the Publications Department, the Picture Library is now a separate section within the Commercial Department of the NGS. The Commercial Department supplies photographic material and permissions/licenses for works in all three galleries as well as material to scholars, publishers, TV companies, advertising agencies, and commercial companies. 50% of the business is overseas. Within three to five years this provider intends to have a digitized image service and to make use of the World Wide Web as a marketing and delivery tool.

Photography: Originals are photographed by professional fine art photographers, who supply black-and-white negatives and color transparencies from which 35mm slides can be made on appropriate film in carefully controlled conditions.

Documentation: No visual catalog of slides available. Refer to galleries' illustrated concise catalogs. Lists updated every two years.

Purchasing: A standard list of 35mm slides is available for retail sale. This provider also supplies specially made 35mm slides for individual customers from 4" x 5" color transparencies. Discounts are available for educational establishments purchasing 20 or more slides. Prepayment required by check/postal order/credit card. May accept purchase order forms from established clients. Costs of shipping based on volume/current postal costs. Dispatches within one week of receipt. Special orders can take two to three weeks.

Other Products: Hire of color transparencies, sale of black-and-white photographs, and permissions to reproduce. Retail Dept. can also supply postcards and gallery catalogs, etc.

Expansion Plans: Digitized catalog/ISDN delivery.

Evaluation: Quality, 3 to 4; documentation, 1 to 3; service, 2 to 3.

246   National Gallery Picture Library

Trafalgar Square
London WC2N 5DN United Kingdom
Telephone: 44 (0) 171 747 2814/2515
FAX: 44 (0) 171 753 8178
Attn: Belinda Ross
E-mail: picture.library @ng-london.org.uk
URL: http://www.nationalgallery.org.uk

This image provider also offers digital products and is listed in the digital section of the directory.

Profile: Entry reprinted from the 6th edition with some new information. Approximately 1,130 color slides offered of works in the permanent collection and a few items on loan: European paintings of the thirteenth to twentieth centuries. Most slides are duplicates, but a few originals remain, mostly of less-popular subjects. A few new titles added occasionally.

Photography: Currently, originals are 8" x 10" transparencies shot by staff photographers with a Sinar system on Ektachrome ASA 100 professional film #6122. Daylight flash used. Original slides were mostly shot on Agfachrome 5OL; a few may be on Ektachrome EPD ASA 200 daylight film.

Production: Printed from internegatives by Walter Scott Laboratories, Ltd., Bradford, on Fuji #8816. Color-corrected and contrast-controlled. Most mounted in plastic, some (originals) in cardboard.

Documentation: Free catalog. Artist surname and title of work given. Supplements issued approximately twice yearly. Most slides are labeled. Additional information available in published catalogs of the collection. Orientation marked on most slides.

Purchasing: Slides sold singly, 50 pence each. No minimum order. Postage added. Order form provided. Prepayment in pounds sterling required from pro forma invoice. International postal money orders accepted, as well as credit cards. Slides kept in stock and shipped within two to three weeks after receipt of payment. Rush orders sent within four days at no extra charge. Slides not sent on approval, and returns not accepted.

Digital Products: CD-ROM, *The Complete Illustrated Catalogue*, covers the entire collection and is offered for sale or loan.

Evaluation: Quality, 3 to 4; documentation, 2 to 4; service, 3 to 4.

247 National Museum of Wales

Cathays Pk.
Cardiff CF I 3NP Wales, United Kingdom
Telephone: 44 (0) 1 222 397951
FAX: 44 (0) 1 222 373219
Attn: Bookshop Manager

Profile: Entry reprinted from 6th ed. Sixty duplicate color slide titles offered of the permanent collection of archaeological artifacts and British and European paintings.

Photography: Original slides shot by staff photographer on Kodak film.

Production: Commercial duplicates made from originals. Mounted in plastic.

Documentation: Free list. Full identifications given in most cases for archaeological slides. Artist and title provided for art. Orientation marked.

Purchasing: Slides sold singly, 45 pence each. Postage added. Prepayment in pounds sterling from pro forma invoice required on overseas orders. Slides kept in stock and shipped within four days. Slides not sent on approval, and returns usually not accepted. Special photography undertaken on request.

Evaluation: Reprinted from 6th ed. One sample sent in 1984: quality, 3; documentation, 3. Color appeared too brown.

248 National Museums & Galleries on Merseyside (NMGM)

(Walker Art Gallery)
127 Dale St.
Liverpool 69 3LA United Kingdom
Telephone: 44 (0) 151 478 4685
FAX: 44 (0) 151 478 4790
URL: http://www.nmgm.org.uk/

Price Range: All slides are £1.00 each (85p + VAT) plus postage.

Profile: The NMGM offers 158 duplicate color slide titles of major works in the Walker Art Gallery, the Lady Lever Art Gallery at Port Sunlight, the Sudley Art Gallery, and Liverpool Museum. British and European paintings featured.

Photography: Originals are color transparencies.

Production: Duplicated on Ektachrome EPD film by Gilchrist Studios, Ltd. Color-corrected.

Documentation: Free list. Artist, artist's dates, title, and date given. Slides labeled. Orientation not marked.

Purchasing: Postage added to cost of slides. Non-U.K. customers £1.00 extra. Prepayment required; Eurocheque draft or a draft drawn on a British Bank or VISA, MasterCard, and American Express acceptable payment.

Evaluation: Reprinted from 6th ed. Quality, 3; documentation, 2 to 3; service, 2.

249 National Portrait Gallery

St. Martin's Pl.
London WC2H OHE United Kingdom
Telephone: 44 (0) 171 306 0055, x259, 260, 261
FAX: 44 (0) 171 306 0092
Attn: Publications Department/Picture Library
E-mail: bhorrocks@npg.org.uk or jcozens@npg.org.uk or jkilvington@npg.org.uk
URL: http://www.npg.org.uk/

Profile: Entry updated from website. Founded in 1856 to collect the likenesses of famous British men and women. The Gallery houses a primary collection of nearly 10,000 works, as well as an immense archive. There is no restriction on medium. There are approximately 10,000 titles in the Primary Collection and a further million items in the Archive. Not all of these are available for reproduction purposes due to copyright, ownership, and accessibility reasons. There are approximately 350 titles readily available. At present, digital images are not available. However, the entire Primary Collection has been digitized so this is a possibility at some future date.

Purchasing: 350 slides at 80 pence each. Special order one-off slides available through Picture Library, depending on copyright and accessibility, at £10 each.

Evaluation: Quality, 2; documentation, 1; service, 3. (Evaluation by a single committee member. 6th ed. rating: quality, 3 to 4; documentation, 2 to 3; service, 2 to 3.)

250 National Trust

36 Queen Anne's Gate
London SW1H 9AS United Kingdom
Telephone: 44 (0) 171 447 6790
FAX: 44 (0) 171 222 5097
Attn: Patricia Hix, Lecture Slide Librarian
URL: http://www.nationaltrust.org.uk/

Profile: Sell two slide sets: "Garden History" £41.00 and £3.00 postage; "Stowe Landscape Gardens" £4.35 (postage included). Slides are in color except for a couple of images taken from printed books. A few manuscript illustrations of gardens are also included. The Lecture Slide Librarian will provide single slides by arrangement.

Documentation: Paper printouts describing each slide.

Purchasing: Checks must be in British pounds sterling, and orders are filled upon receipt of payment.

Evaluation: Quality 4; documentation, 4; service, 4. (Evaluation by one member of committee.)

251 Percival David Foundation of Chinese Art

53 Gordon Square
London WC I H OPD United Kingdom
Telephone: 44 (0) 181 387 3909

Profile: Approximately 100 color slide titles offered of Chinese ceramics, tenth to eighteenth centuries. Slides available of the 1989–1990 exhibition "Imperial Taste" (Los Angeles County Museum of Art, Virginia Museum of Art, Kimbell Art Museum, and Museum of Fine Arts, Boston). New titles continually added.

Photography: Original slides shot by staff photographer on Ektachrome ASA 100 plus, using tripod and electronic flash.

Documentation: Mailing list kept. Free list, frequently updated. Slides labeled. Orientation marked.

Purchasing: Slides sold singly, £4.00 each, postpaid. No minimum order. Prepayment required in pounds sterling. Originals kept in stock and shipped immediately on receipt of payment. Original photography carried out at £12.00 additional charge per slide. Slides not sent on approval, and no returns accepted.

252 Royal Collection Enterprises Ltd.

Photographic Services
Windsor Castle
Windsor, Berkshire SL4 1NJ United Kingdom
Telephone: 44 (0) 1 753 868286
FAX: 44 (0) 1 753 620046
Attn: Gwyneth Campling, Head of Photographic Services

Profile: In 1993, Photographic Services was established to respond to photographic requests pertaining to the entire Royal Collection. The Royal Collection comprises 7,000 oil paintings, 30,000 drawings and watercolors, and other works including furniture, ceramics, Fabergé, and arms and armor. Interior views of Royal Residences are also available. The department handles everything from a single slide request or request for a color reference print, to requests for reproduction permission from television companies and publishers. Photographic Services also deals with in-house photographic orders. Enquirers must send a written order. The Royal Collection includes English, Italian, and German drawings as well as military, Roman, and Victorian drawings. Italian, English, Dutch, and Flemish paintings are included in the Royal Collection as well as Victorian and miniature paintings.

Documentation: A list of catalogs from various publishing houses of Drawings and Pictures in the Royal Collection will be sent on request. The lists include full bibliographic citations for the catalogs. Price list for the various formats and services will be sent on request.

Photography and Production: Slide requests are duplicated from existing transparencies, and special-order photography is carried out where location permits.

Purchasing: Individual slides from existing transparencies are priced at £3.50 each. Where new photography is requested, the following charges apply: Drawings/Watercolors/Prints—£35.00 plus individual slide price (£3.50); Oil Paintings—£45.00 plus individual slide price (£3.50); Three-Dimensional Objects—£60.00 plus individual slide price (£3.50). Where location photography is necessary, a 25% surcharge will be made. An administration charge of 10% minimum (£2.00) is added to all orders. VAT will be added where applicable. To order material, a written request must be sent either by post or fax to Photographic Services. An invoice will be sent upon receipt of the written order. Prepayment is required, but VISA, Access, and MasterCard credit cards are accepted where deadlines are short. All color material is sent out by registered first class post, but despatch of material by courier, where an account number is provided, can be arranged. After receipt of payment, a slide made from an existing transparency takes about five working days. A slide for which new photography is required may take four to six weeks depending on ease of access to the object in question.

Other Products: Black-and-white prints, color prints, microfilm prints for study. Reproduction permissions are also handled by Photographic Services. Contact Photographic Services for specific charges and details for permissions.

253   Sir John Soane Museum

13 Lincoln's Inn Fields
London WC2A 3BP United Kingdom
Attn: Photo Services Department
URL: http://www.demon.co.uk/heritage/
soanes/index.html

Profile: Sir John Soane designed this house to live in but also to show off his antiquities and works of art. In time, the architect established the house as a museum. Four sets of slides are available: "Views of the Museum," £5.00; "Hogarth's Election Series," £2.50; "Hogarth's Rake's Progress," £5.00; and "Drawings of the Interior of the House in Soane's Day," £3.75. The Photo Services Department handles single requests by arrangement.

Other Products: The museum supplies photographs in black-and-white and color. Color transparencies are available for rental. The store also sells publications related to Soane, his collections, and his times as well as catalogs of exhibitions.

Evaluation: Quality, 3; documentation, 3; service, 3. (Evaluation by one member of committee.)

254   Tate Gallery Publishing Ltd.

Millbank
London SW 1P 4RG United Kingdom
Telephone: 44 (0) 171 887 8869
FAX: 0171 887 8878 (from the U.K.) or
+ 44 171 877 8878 (from other countries)
Attn: David Watmouth
E-mail: carlotta.gemetti@tate.org.uk
URL: http://www.tate.org.uk

Profile: Publishing department of Tate Gallery established to publish key works from the permanent collections as 35mm slides (637 slides available).

Purchasing: Individual slides are priced at 80 pence each. Prepayment required.

Documentation: A catalog is available.

Other Products: Books, exhibition catalogs, slides, postcards, prints.

Evaluation: Quality, 2 to 4; documentation, 1 to 4; service, 3 (variable, but most of the ratings on the higher end of the scale for quality and documentation).

255   Victoria and Albert Museum

South Kensington
London SW7 2RL United Kingdom
Telephone: 44 (0) 171 938 8354 / 8452 /
9645 / 8352
FAX: 44 (0) 171 938 8353
Attn: James Stevenson
E-mail: picture.library@vam.ac.uk
URL: http://www.vam.ac.uk

Profile: Entry reprinted from 6th ed. No response to 1984 or 1989 questionnaires. Slides offered of selected masterpieces from the permanent collection.

Documentation: At least four lists available: "Paintings: Oil"; "Prints, Drawings, Photographs"; "Department of Sculpture"; and "Constable." Identifications consist of artist, artist's dates, title and date of work, and medium.

Purchasing: Slides sold singly, 30 pence each. Postage added. Prepayment by check or postal money order required.

Other Sources: Two 36-slide sets available from Scala (286): one on William Morris, the other on English furniture.

Evaluation: Reprinted from 6th ed. Quality, 3 to 4; documentation, 2 to 3; service, 3.

256   Wallace Collection

Hertford House, Manchester Square
London WIM 6BN United Kingdom
Telephone: 44 (0) 171 935 0687
FAX: 44 (0) 171 224 2155
E-mail: admin@wallcoll.demon.co.uk
Also trade@wallcoll.demon.co.uk
URL: http://www.the-wallace-
collection.org.uk

Profile: Entry updated from website. "The Wallace Collection was bequeathed to the British Nation in February 1897 by Lady Wallace. She was the widow of Sir Richard Wallace, a notable collector of works of art and, as the illegitimate son the Marquess of Hertford, the inheritor of one of the greatest of all private collections. Because nothing can be loaned or added, it enshrines a particular, Anglo-French nineteenth century taste. Among its main treasures are one of the finest collections of French eighteenth-century pictures, porcelain and furniture outside Paris, a remarkable display of seventeenth-century paintings and a superb armory."

There are 780 paintings, plus furniture, porcelain, medieval and Renaissance works of art, gold boxes, ceramics, and arms and armor. There is a total of 5,746 works of art in the museum.

Documentation: Slide list.

Purchasing: Individual slides are priced at 85 pence per slide from slide list; £8.00 for slides specially made from transparencies.

Other Products: Transparencies are rented for £50 for three months.

Expansion Plans: Researching the possibilities of selling digital images in the future.

Evaluation: Quality, 3 to 4; documentation, 2 to 3; service, 3.

ECUADOR

257 **Group for the Promotion of Art & Design**
See under Digital Section

FINLAND

Museums

258 **Suomen Rakennustaiteen Museo**

(Museum of Finnish Architecture)
Kasarmikatu 24
00130 Helsinki 13 Finland
Telephone: (90) 661918

Profile: Entry reprinted from 6th ed. Approximately 20,000 duplicate color slides offered of buildings by Finnish architects, especially Alvar Aalto and Eliel Saarinen. Two sets of 24 slides each available: one of Finnish architecture in the 1980s, the other of Aalto's works. Black-and-white slides can also be obtained from a photo archive of about 70,000 items.

Photography: Originals (slides and large-format transparencies) shot by independent professional photographers on various films.

Production: Duplicates made from originals without color-correction or contrast-control. Mounted in glass binders.

Documentation: No list. Slides labeled with architect, building name, location, and dates of construction. Orientation marked.

Purchasing: Slides sold singly. Sets also available. Price list sent on request. Prices vary according to intended use: research, publication, advertising. Duplicated to order and shipped within one week.

FRANCE

259 **Bibliotheque Nationale**

58, rue de Richelieu
75084 Paris, France
Telephone: (01) 47 03 81 26
Attn: Service Photographique

Profile: Entry repeated from 5th ed. Duplicate color slides offered of the library's holdings, including illuminated manuscripts, coins and medals, jewelry, etc. Not all objects in the collection can be photographed; some are too fragile.

Documentation: No catalog available. Slide sets listed on publications list: two sets of nine slides each offered of medical manuscripts, and 33 sets of six or nine slides each offered of objects in the Cabinet des Médailles. Identifications of made-to-order slides provided on pro forma invoice.

Purchasing: Ready-made slides sold in sets of six for 30 francs or nine for 43 francs, postpaid. Single slides (black-and-white) duplicated to order for 12 francs each (minimum 30 francs), and single slides (color) duplicated to order for 17 francs each (minimum 52 francs). Prepayment required from pro forma invoice.

Other Sources: United States orders can be placed through Mini-Aids **(076)**.

Evaluation: Reprinted from 6th ed. Quality of single made-to-order slides, 3; documentation, 2; service, 2. If prompt service is desired, the extra expense of using Mini-Aids would be a worthwhile investment.

260 Diapofilm

1, rue Villaret-de-Joyeuse
75854 Paris Cedex 17 France
Telephone: (01) 46 22 17 83
FAX: (01) 42 67 76 36

Profile: Slides and filmstrips offered for school use, documenting many subjects in addition to the history of art and architecture. Many French buildings represented. Also sells history and geography sets especially of French subjects.

Photography: Shot by staff photographers or obtained from agencies.

Production: Earlier slides printed on Eastman-color film; change to low-fade film announced in 1982.

Documentation: Free catalog, in French, issued annually. Sets described briefly in catalog, but individual slides not listed. Further information about contents of sets available on request. Each set accompanied by a booklet of commentaries on the slides.

Purchasing: Slides sold in sets of 12 to 36 with a price range of 109.45 francs to 326.70 francs. Quantity discounts given. Prepayment required. Airmail postage included in prices. Slides kept in stock and shipped within three days.

Other Products: Filmstrips available.

Evaluation: Reprinted from 6th ed. No current information available. Rated by one member of the Evaluation Committee: quality, 2; documentation, 2.

Museums

261 Musée des Beaux-Arts

20, quai Emile Zola
35100 Rennes, France
Telephone: (99) 30 83 87

Profile: Entry repeated from 5th ed. Color slides (originals and duplicates) offered of the permanent collection. Twenty-four paintings listed, Renaissance to twentieth century. New titles occasionally added.

Photography: Transparencies (slides and large-format) shot by staff photographer on Ektachrome using electronic flash. Cameras employed include a Mamiya 6" x 7", Linhof 4" x 5", and Contax 35mm.

Production: Duplicated on Ektachrome #5071 by L. C. B., Rennes. Color-corrected and contrast-controlled. Mounted in plastic.

Documentation: Free list, in French, revised biannually. Four sets of six slides listed. Artist, artist's dates, and title given. Slides labeled in French. Orientation marked.

Purchasing: Originals and duplicates sold singly or in sets. Limited edition sets available. No minimum order. Postage added. Slides shot or duplicated to order. No rush orders accepted. Slides not sent on approval. Returns accepted for exchange only.

262 Musée National d'Art Moderne

Centre Georges Pompidou
Place Beaubourg, rue St.-Merri
75191 Paris Cedex 04 France
Telephone: (01) 42 77 12 33, P. 4635
Attn: Service de Documentation
Photographique des Collections

Profile: Entry reprinted from 6th ed. Several thousand color slides offered of major works in the permanent collection. New titles continually added; 3,000 available that are not listed in catalog, and 300 added during 1989.

Photography: Original transparencies shot by staff photographers on Ektachrome ASA 100. Tripod and electronic flash used.

Production: Duplicated on Ektachrome by the laboratory of the Service Audiovisuel du Centre Georges Pompidou. Color-corrected and contrast-controlled.

Documentation: Free catalog, in French, gives artist, title, date, museum accession number, transparency number, and general medium. Slides labeled in French. Identifications consist of artist, title, and date. Orientation marked only when necessary.

Purchasing: Both original and duplicate slides available. No minimum order. Single slides priced 17.25 francs each for up to 30, 12.00 francs each for

31 to 50 slides, and 9.75 francs each for 51 to 100 slides. Sets also offered. Postage added. Slides kept in stock; if necessary, made to order. Shipped within 10 days of receipt of signed documents accepting terms of sale. Invoice sent upon receipt of these documents. No returns accepted.

Other Products: Black-and-white photographic prints sold, and 4" x 5" color transparencies rented for reproduction.

Evaluation: Quality, 3; documentation, 3. (Evaluation by a single committee member.)

263   Musée Rolin

5, rue des Bancs
71400 Autun, France
Telephone: 03-85-52-09-76
FAX: 03-85-52-47-41
Attn: Brigette Maurice-Chabard

Profile: Forty-six color slides offered of the permanent collection: 10 from the Roman period, 13 Romanesque, 14 Gothic and Renaissance, and 9 paintings from the sixteenth to twentieth centuries. Details included of major works.

Photography: Originals shot by a professional photographer using Kodak professional films.

Documentation: Mailing list kept. Free list, in French. Artist and title given, plus date when known for paintings. List updated annually. Slides labeled in French.

Purchasing: Slides sold singly and in sets. Slides kept in stock and shipped upon receipt of payment. No rush orders accepted. No returns accepted. Prepayment required. University purchase orders accepted.

264   L'agence photographique de la Reunion des Musées Nationaux

(formerly Services Techniques et Commerciaux de la Reunion des Musees Nationaux)
10, rue de l'Abbaye
75006 Paris, France
Telephone: 33 1 40 13 46 00
FAX: 33 1 40 13 46 01
Attn: Monsieur le directeur
E-mail: photo@rmn.fr
URL: http://www.rmn.fr/

This library also offers digital products and is listed in the digital section of the directory.

Profile: Did not respond to questionnaire. Entry from 6th edition updated where possible from website. Slides and CD-ROM of works in the Louvre and 33 other French national museums offered. Works from the following collections are represented:

Paris:

Galerie Nationales du Grand Palais

Musée des Arts d'Afrique et d'Océanie

Musées des Arts Asiatiques - Guimet

Musée des Arts et Traditions Populaires

Musée Eugéne Delacroix

Musée d'Ennery

Musée Hebert

Musée Jean - Jacques Henner

Musée du Louvre

Musée Gustave Moreau

Musée du Moyen Age - Thermes de Cluny

Musée de l'Orangerie des Tuileries

Musée d'Orsay

Musée Picasso

Musée Auguste Rodin

Ille-de-France (provincia parisina):

Musée des Antiquités Nationales

Musée de Céramique

Musée Fontainebleau

Musée des Granges de Port - Royal

Musées de Malmaison et de Bois - Préau

Musée de la Renaissance

Musées de Versailles et de Trianon

Acquitaine:

Musée du Chateau de Pau

Musée de la Préhistorie

Bourgogne:

Musée Magnin

Corse:

Musée de la Maison Bonaparte

Limousin:

Musée Adrien Dubouché

Pays-de-la-Loire:

Musée des Deux Victoires

Picardie:

Musée de Compiégne

Musée de la Coopération Franco - Américaine

Poitou-Charentes:

Musée de L´ille d´Aix

PACA:

Musée Fernand Léger

Musée Message Biblique - Marc Chagall

Musée Picasso "La Guerre et la Paix"

Photography: Original transparencies shot on Ektachrome by photographers employed by the Réunion des Musées Nationaux (ceased production).

Production: Printed from internegatives on low-fade Eastmancolor film. Mounted in cardboard. Versailles and Fontainebleau sets produced elsewhere.

Documentation: Mailing list kept of customers interested in exhibition coverage. Free catalog and supplements. Artist and title listed. Slides labeled. Since January 1983, label information consists of artist, artist's dates "if necessary," title, date if known, location, dimensions, and materials. "Diafiche" sets of 10 slides accompanied by text in French, English, German, and Spanish.

Purchasing: Slides sold singly or in sets. Some slides available only in sets. Single slides offered only of objects in the Louvre, the Musée d'Orsay, and the Orangerie des Tuileries. Large sets (18, 30, and 42 slides) also offered. Minimum order 54 francs. Airmail postage added. Order form provided. Prepayment required by traveler's check, money order, or check.

Other Products: Videocassettes, Super 8 films, and microfiche also offered. Large-format transparencies rented for reproduction.

Evaluation: Quality, 3 to 4; documentation, 2 to 3; service, 2 to 3.

GERMANY

265   Bildarchiv Foto Marburg

Wolffstrasse
Postfach 1460
D-3550 Marburg, Germany
Telephone: +0049 (0) 6421 28-3600
FAX: +0049 (0) 6421 28-8931
E-mail: bildarchiv@fotomr.uni-marburg.de
URL: http://fotomr.uni-marburg.de/index.htm

This vendor also offers digital products and is listed in the digital section of the directory. See K. G. Saur (268).

Profile: History: Founded in 1913 by Richard Hamann to provide the Art History Department of University of Marburg with pictorial material; with about 1.2 million negatives it became one of the greatest photoarchives for art history in the world.

Bildarchiv produces the following materials: art historical prints from the archive; microfiche publications; illustrated museum catalogues on CD-ROM; text-only museum catalogues on CD-ROM; museum information systems; and DISKUS (Digital Information System for Art and Social History) computer-aided verbal and visual information system developed by participating museum offices for the preservation of historical monuments, university departments and institutes of art history.

Photography: The photographs are directly photographed from the original works of art or architecture by professional photographers, mostly with Ektachrome 64.

Digital Products: CD-ROM. Photostyler 2.0 and Photoshop 4.0 used for manipulation and color-correction of images.

Documentation: Slides labeled in German. Orientation marked by label placement.

Purchasing: Slides sold singly and in sets. Sets with six slides cost 10 deutsche marks. Payment after delivery.

Other Products: Prints; several microfiche editions; Marburger Index, inventory of art with 1.2 million reproductions; France-Index with 100,000 reproductions; Italy-Index with 60,000 reproductions; Spain- and Portugal-Index with 30,000 reproductions; Austria- and Switzerland-Index with about 35,000 reproductions; Egypt-Index with 11,000 reproductions. The databank gives access to ca. 130,000 works of art. The products of the Bildarchiv (microfiche-editions, museum catalogs on CD-ROM, the Marburger Index [Guide to Art in Germany, CD-ROM Database]) are edited and sold by the publishing house K. G. Saur **(268)**.

For further information please consult the essay "Fritz Lauplichler: Photographs, Microfiches, MIDAS and DISKUS: The Bildarchiv Foto Marburg as German Center for the Documentation of Art History," *Visual Resources* 12(2), 1997, 157-76.

Expansion Plans: The availability of the Bildarchiv's data and images over the Internet is projected over the next three years.

Evaluation: Reprinted from 6th ed. Quality, 3 to 4; documentation, 3 to 4; service, 2 to 3.

266   Jünger Audio-Visuell
D-6050 Offenbach/Main
Schumannstrasse 161
Postfach 100962 Germany
Telephone: (069) 840003-22
FAX: (069) 840003-33

Profile: Entry reprinted from 6th ed. No response to 1984 or 1989 questionnaires, but 1989 catalog sent. Entry based on the catalog and information from the 4th edition. Slides sold among other audiovisual products. Other subjects besides art history covered. Products oriented toward audiences of all ages. Slides available of ancient art, European architecture from the early Christian era to the Baroque, and European painting from the tenth to twentieth centuries.

Photography and Production: Slides printed from large-format negatives.

Documentation: Lavish general catalog, in German, with color illustrations, 160 pages (of which seven are devoted to art history slides). Sets briefly described in catalog. German text accompanies slide sets. Optional audiotapes (presumably in German) may be purchased with some sets at extra cost. Orientation marked.

Purchasing: Order form included in catalog. Most sets composed of 24 slides, priced 59.80 deutsche marks. Sets sent on 10-day approval.

Other Products: Videocassettes, Super 8 films, filmstrips, and transparencies for overhead projection.

267   Vista Point Verlag
D-5000 Cologne 1
Engelbertstrasse 38A
Postfach 270572 Germany
Telephone: (0221) 21 05 87

Profile: Reprinted from 6th ed. Approximately 70 slide sets offered of the history of art and architecture, many on themes such as "The Window as Motif in Painting," "Music in Painting," and "Art and Nature." Several contemporary topics included: "Pop Art," "New Realism," and "Photography Today." Art and architecture of the Third Reich featured in three sets. Some 5% of holdings are black-and-white. New sets continually added (10 in 1989).

Photography: Original slides shot by independent professional photographers and traveling scholars, mostly on Kodachrome ASA 64. Tripod used. Some originals are large-format transparencies.

Production: Produced from originals. Color-corrected and contrast-controlled. Packaged in plastic folders.

Documentation: Mailing list kept. Free catalog, in German, updated twice a year. Author of each set cited in catalog. Set descriptions include brief contents list. Slides labeled in German. Identifications are complete. Orientation marked.

Purchasing: Slides sold in sets only. Prices listed in catalog in German, French, and Austrian currencies. Set of 24 slides, for instance, priced 59 deutsche marks. Postage added. No discounts. Duplicates kept in stock and shipped same day order received. Prepayment not required.

Other Products: Videos.

Evaluation: Quality, 3 to 4; documentation, 2 to 3; service, 3.

268 K. G. Saur
See under Digital Section

Museums

269 Ägyptisches Museum

D-1000 Berlin 19 Germany
Telephone: (030) 341 1085
Attn: Verein zur Förderung

Profile: Reprinted from 6th ed. A large set of 100 slides offered of masterpieces in the permanent collection. Several sets of six also available. New slide titles added occasionally.

Photography: Original large-format transparencies shot by staff photographer on Ektachrome.

Production: Produced on Kodak film (Eastmancolor #5381, apparently) from original transparencies by Heinze-von Hippel, Berlin. Color-corrected and contrast-controlled. Mounted in plastic and sleeved.

Documentation: No list or catalog. Slides labeled with title, date, and inventory number, in German. Orientation not marked.

Purchasing: Slides sold in sets only. Slides kept in stock and shipped within one week. Payment accepted in U.S. dollars. Sets not sent on approval, and returns not accepted.

Evaluation: Reprinted from 6th ed. Quality, based on 113 samples submitted, 2 to 3. Original photography mostly good, but film stock of duplicates unstable. Twenty-six of the samples were already pink. A few slides were out of focus.

270 Kunstsammlung Nordrhein-Westfalen

D-4000 Düsseldorf I
Grabbeplatz 5 Germany
Telephone: (0211) 13 39 61

Profile: Entry repeated from 5th ed. Ninety-six color slide titles offered of the permanent collection of twentieth-century art. Of special interest is the Paul Klee Collection.

Photography: Slides shot by an independent professional photographer.

Production: Produced by a commercial laboratory. Color-corrected. Mounted in glass.

Documentation: Free list, in German. Artist, title, and date provided. Slides labeled in German. Orientation marked.

Purchasing: Slides sold singly, 2.50 deutsche marks each. No minimum order. Postage added. Prepayment required on large orders from abroad. Slides kept in stock and shipped within one week. Rush orders filled same day; no surcharge. Slides not sent on approval, and no returns accepted. No special photography undertaken.

271 Staatliche Antikensammlungen und Glyptothek

D-8000 Munich 2
Meiserstrasse 10 Germany
Telephone: (089) 5591 551

Profile: Entry reprinted from 6th ed. Duplicate color slides offered of masterpieces in both collections of ancient art. No additions to holdings planned.

Photography: Slides of works in the Glyptothek photographed by Saskia **(086)**. Antikensammlungen works shot by a German professional photographer, Heinz Juranck. In both cases, originals are 35mm slides. Antikensammlungen slides shot on Ektachrome ASA 100. Tripod used.

Production: Saskia slides sold as originals; some available as duplicates. Antikensammlungen slides produced on Agfa film of varying types by Agfacolor Munchen. Contrast-controlled, but no attempt made to correct color.

Documentation: No list available of Antikensammlungen slides. Saskia slides of Glyptothek objects listed in Saskia catalog, or list may be requested from the museum. Saskia slides fully identified. Antikensammlungen slides labeled with artist, dates of artist, title of work, city, and collection. Orientation marked only when necessary.

Purchasing: It is unclear from the response to the questionnaire whether the museum distributes Saskia slides or merely refers inquiries. From the United States, at least, it would be most convenient to order directly from Saskia **(086)**. Slides sold singly, 1.20 deutsche marks each. No minimum order. Slides kept in stock (usually) and shipped within four weeks.

No rush orders accepted. Slides not sent on approval, and no returns accepted.

272   Staatliche Kunsthalle Karlsruhe

D-7500 Karlsruhe
Hans-Thoma-Strasse 2-6 Postfach 6149
Germany
Telephone: (0721) 926-3355
FAX: (0721) 926-6788

Profile: Approximately 90 duplicate color slides offered of works in the permanent collection. Paintings by Old Masters and modern artists featured. New slide titles occasionally added.

Photography: Original slides shot by staff photographer.

Documentation: Free list in German, revised annually. Artist, artist's dates, title (in German), medium, and dimensions given on list. Orientation marked on slides.

Purchasing: Slides sold singly and in sets. Individual slides priced at 11 deutsche marks per slide. Slides kept in stock, or if necessary duplicated to order. If the latter, shipped within six to eight weeks. Payment in deutsche marks requested. Shipping cost added. Special photography undertaken of objects not included on list.

273   Staatliche Kunstsammlungen Kassel

D-3500 Kassel
Schloss Wilhelmshöhe, Germany
Telephone: (0561) 36011

Profile: Approximately 100 duplicate color slides offered of works in the permanent collection: single slides of European Baroque paintings and sets of six slides each of ancient vases and ancient portraits. New slide titles occasionally added.

Photography: Original large-format transparencies shot by staff photographer on Kodak film ASA 32.

Production: Stable slides produced from original transparencies by V-Dia, Heidelberg. Color-corrected and contrast-controlled.

Documentation: Free list, in German. Artist and title given. Slides labeled in German with artist, title, date of work, and city and collection.

Purchasing: Slides sold singly except for the two sets of ancient art. Single slides priced 1.50 deutsche marks, sets of six 6.00 deutsche marks. Slides kept in stock. No rush orders accepted. Slides not sent on approval, and no returns accepted.

274   Staatliche Museen Preussischer Kulturbesitz

D-1000 Berlin 30
Stauffenbergstrasse 41 Germany
Telephone: (030) 266 2605 or 266 2628
Attn: Verlag und Warbung

Profile: Entry reprinted from 6th ed. Although slides are sold on site in the museums, there is no overseas mail-order service.

Photography: Original slides shot by staff photographers and independent professionals on Agfa and Kodak films.

Production: Printed from negatives. Color-corrected.

Documentation: Lists in German available free from the museum. Artist, title, and date provided. Slides labeled with complete identifications, except nationality of artist. Orientation marked.

Purchasing: Slides sold singly for 1.50 deutsche marks each, or in sets of six slides for 8.00 deutsche marks. No further discounts given. Postage added. Prepayment required. Slides kept in stock and shipped within two weeks. Other sources: Mini-Aids **(076)** can supply slides of art and architecture in Berlin. Saskia **(086)** offers superb slides of selected prints from the Kupferstichkabinett in addition to many slides of paintings. The set titled "Along the Ancient Silk Routes: Central Asian Art from the West Berlin State Museums," produced by the Asian Art Photographic Distribution **(030)**, is out of stock in 1989.

275   Städelsches Kunstinstitut & Städtische Galerie

D-60596 Frankfurt-am-Main 70
Dürerstrasse 2 Germany
Telephone: (069) 6050980

FAX: (069) 610163
Attn: Elisabeth Heinemann, Department
of Fotographs

Profile: Approximately 125 color slide titles offered of the permanent collection of European painting from the Renaissance to the twentieth century.

Documentation: Free list. Artist and title given, in German. Slides labeled.

Purchasing: Slides sold singly, 4.00 deutsche marks each. Shipping cost and bank fees added.

276　Von der Heydt-Museum

D-5600 Wuppertal-Elberfeld I
Turmhof 8 Germany
Telephone: (0202) 563 21 91
Attn: Kunst- und Museumsverein
Wuppertal

Profile: Entry reprinted from 6th ed. Entry based on 1986 correspondence and list. Approximately 115 duplicate color slides offered of works in the permanent collection: nineteenth- and twentieth-century painting and sculpture.

Production: Slides produced by Stoedtner. Mounted in glass.

Documentation: Free list. Artist, title (in German), and date of work given.

Purchasing: Slides sold singly, 2.50 deutsche marks each.

Other Sources: Slides may be ordered directly from Mini-Aids **(076)**.

GREECE

277　Agora Excavations

American School of Classical Studies
Souidias 54
GR-106 76 Athens, Greece
Telephone: (01) 3210162
Attn: Photographic Department

Profile: Entry reprinted from 6th ed. Approximately 1,500 color slides offered of archaeological finds from the excavation of the Agora (Agora Museum accessions). Site views and drawings included, as well as pottery, sculpture, architectural fragments, inscriptions, and jewelry. Fourteen slide sets available, based on the Agora Picture Book series. New slide titles continually added.

Photography: Original slides (and some large-format transparencies) shot by staff photographers on Ektachrome EPY ASA 50 (indoors) and Ektachrome Professional EPT ASA 64 (outdoors). Tripod, perspective-correcting lens, polarizing filters, and lamps used.

Production: Originals duplicated on Ektachrome #5071. Color-corrected and contrast-controlled. Mounted in plastic, sleeved, protected with cardboard, and mailed in Jiffy bags.

Documentation: Mailing list kept. Free list of sets, revised annually. Sets assembled and annotated by archaeologists on the Agora staff. Objects represented in sets that have been published in the Agora Picture Book series or in *The Athenian Agora* or *Hesperia*. Identifications brief, but bibliographic references included in slide notes accompanying sets. Slides keyed to notes.

Purchasing: Order form provided in mailings. Slide sets composed of 20 slides, sometimes 30, priced $30.00 or $40.00, respectively. Payment in U.S. dollars requested. No minimum order, but single slides not available from sets. Sets kept in stock. Shipped from Athens; postage added ($3.00 per slide set). Rush orders filled within three days; 100% surcharge. Orders usually filled within two weeks of receipt. Slides sent on approval, and returns accepted for exchange or refund, if slides are in "pristine condition" and are sent back within 10 days of delivery. Special photography offered of objects not available in sets; price list sent on request. Other products: *Agora Picture Books*, which serve as documentation for the slide sets, may be ordered from the American School of Classical Studies at Athens, c/o Institute for Advanced Study, Princeton, NJ 08540. Black-and-white photographic prints and 4" x 5" color transparencies available from Photographic Department.

Evaluation: Reprinted from 6th ed. Quality, based on samples, 3 to 4; documentation, 3 to 4; service, 4.

278　Archaeological Receipts Fund (TAP Service)

Ministry of Culture and Science
57, Panepistimiou St.
GR-105 64 Athens, Greece
Telephone: (021) 3253901-6

Profile: Entry reprinted from 6th ed. Approximately 2,500 duplicate color slide titles offered of Greek archaeological sites and of objects in Greek museum collections. Museums represented include the following:

Archaeological Museum, Thessaloniki

Byzantine Museum, Athens

Heraklion Museum, Crete

National Archaeological Museum, Athens

Photography: Original large-format transparencies shot by independent professional photographers. Tripod used.

Production: No information on film type. Slides ordered in 1985 were on unstable film. Color-corrected and contrast-controlled. Mounted in cardboard.

Documentation: Free list, in Greek or English, of sites documented. Slides labeled in four languages: Greek, English, French, and German. Title, date of work, materials, and city/collection given. Orientation marked.

Purchasing: Slides sold in sets of six, priced 300 drachmas per set. Postage added. Prepayment required in Greek or U.S. currency. Sets kept in stock and shipped immediately on receipt of payment (within eight days). No returns accepted.

Other Products: Videotapes available of sites and museums. Large-format transparencies also loaned for reproduction in publications.

Evaluation: Reprinted from 6th ed. Four sample slides sent of sculpture: quality variable, from average to 4; documentation, 3. Stability of film uncertain.

279   Hannibal

11 Arkadias St.
Halandri 152-34, Athens, Greece
Telephone: (021) 681 70 28
Attn: Constantine Tryfides

Profile: More than 1,300 duplicate color slides offered of art and architecture in Greece, ancient and medieval. Works in Greek museums represented, including the National Archaeological Museum in Athens (15 sets) and the Heraklion Museum, Crete (two sets). New slide titles continually added.

Photography: Originals in various formats shot on Kodak film by Mr. "Hannibal" personally (Hannibal Stamatopoulos, owner of the company).

Production: Copies made in-house on Kodak film, Eastmancolor #5384 according to the 5th ed. Color-corrected and contrast-controlled. No stock of Eastmancolor #5381 remains. Mounted in cardboard and shrink-wrapped as small sets.

Documentation: Free list in Greek and English. Set name and very brief description given on list. Slides also labeled. Identification list accompanying slides printed in Greek, English, French, and German. Orientation marked only when necessary.

Purchasing: Slides sold in sets of 10. Minimum order five sets. Prepayment required. Airmail postage added. Sets kept in stock and shipped within one week. Listing alternates is recommended. Sets sent on approval, and returns accepted for exchange. No refunds given.

Other Products: Large-format transparencies rented for reproduction in publications. Also, guidebooks sold for all archaeological sites in Greece.

Expansion Plans: Company plans to offer all slides in CD-ROM format by end of 1998.

Evaluation: Quality, 1 to 3; documentation, 1 to 4. (Evaluation of samples.)

HUNGARY

Museums

280   Magyar Nermzeti Galéria

(Hungarian National Gallery)
H-1250 Budapest PF.31 Hungary
Attn: Artfoto VGMK

Profile: Information repeated from 5th ed. Slides offered of works in the permanent collection, representing Hungarian art from the eleventh century to the present.

Photography: Large-format color transparencies shot by staff photographer on Kodak and Agfa films. Mamiya camera used.

Production: Color-corrected and contrast-controlled.

Documentation: No list available. Slides labeled in Hungarian or English. Orientation marked.

Purchasing: Slides sold singly. Minimum order five slides. Orders filled within one week. Special photography undertaken for $15 per slide.

Other Products: Black-and-white photographic prints also offered.

IRELAND

281　Trinity College Library

College St.
Dublin 2 Ireland
Telephone: 353-1 772941, x1757
Attn: Library Shop

Profile: Entry based on 4th edition and 1984 ordering experience. Three sets of six slides offered, two of the Book of Kells and one of the Book of Durrow.

Photography: Originals shot by a commercial photographer.

Production: Produced on Kodak film by a commercial laboratory.

Documentation: Free brochure, listing slides among other publications.

Purchasing: Price list and order form included in brochure. Postage included in prices. Prepayment required in Irish pounds, pounds sterling, or U.S. dollars, by credit card, personal check, or bank draft. Orders sent by surface mail and delivered within five to nine weeks to the United States and Canada, within 10 days to Europe.

Evaluation: Quality, 2; documentation, 3; service, 2.

Museums

282　National Gallery of Ireland

Merrion Square W.
Dublin 2 Ireland
Telephone: 353-1 6615133 or 6785450
FAX: 353-1 6615372 or 6619898
Attn: Vivienne Lynch (retail), Marie McFeely (Rights & Reproduction)

Profile: Gallery shop with extensive selection of books, videos, cards, posters, canvas reproductions, and National Gallery of Art publications. Rights and Reproductions Office deals with all academic/commercial requests for photo material and permission to use it. This section also photographs and duplicates master copies if required. More than 300 slides are readily

available. Special order slides for educational/research purposes on request. More than 5,000 medium format transparencies and 15,000 black-and-white negatives of everything in the collection. The National Gallery provides worldwide service and hopes to have E-mail and Internet facilities in the near future to provide easier access and speedier service to our customers. Due to lack of legislation, the area of electronic rights has been regarded with caution.

Photography: Our current photographers are fine art specialists using Sinar, Nikon and Canon cameras on Agfa RSX/Kodak 64T for color. Most photography is conducted in a new conservationally approved studio.

Documentation: Artist/artist's dates/title or work/date of work if known; copyright owner credited where different from museum.

Purchasing: Individual slides are offered with a 10% discount on orders over 50 slides. Prepayment is necessary. We can organize "swiftpost" mail/courier services (DHL/TNT/Federal Express). No handling charges. Orders put aside and then sent out on receipt of payment.

Rental: Only larger transparencies for use by publishers/TV/Film, etc. are hired out.

Evaluation: Quality, 2 to 4; documentation, 2 to 3; service, 4.

283　National Museum of Ireland

Kildare St.
Dublin 2 Ireland
Telephone: 353-1 76 55 21
Attn: Sales Office

Profile: Fifth edition entry repeated. One hundred seventy color slide titles offered of works in the permanent collection: archaeological artifacts, early Christian metalwork, traditional crafts, fine art, and natural history. No additions to slide holdings planned. 3% of slides are black-and-white.

Photography: Original slides shot on low-speed Ektachrome by staff photographers. Tungsten lighting used.

Production: Duplicated on Kodak Ektachrome duplicating film by GBS, Ltd., Bray, Co. Wicklow, Ireland. Contrast-controlled. Mounted in cardboard and packaged in plastic sleeves.

Documentation: Free list, in English, revised 1984. Title, date, and provenance given, as well as artist, if known. Slides labeled in English.

Purchasing: Slides sold in small sets or singly. Current prices sent on request. No discounts. Postage added. Slides kept in stock. Rush orders filled immediately. No special photography undertaken. Slides not sent on approval. Returns accepted for exchange only.

Evaluation: Reprinted from 6th ed. Quality, 2; documentation, 2 to 3; service, 2.

ITALY

284   Böhm, Osvaldo

San Moise 1349-50
30124 Venice, Italy

Profile: Entry reprinted from 6th ed. No response to 1984 or 1989 questionnaire. Entry based on a letter of March 1984. Archive of 30,000 black-and-white negatives accumulated since the 1860s of Venetian art and architecture from the Byzantine era through the nineteenth century. New titles (300 to 400) added annually. Permanent collections and exhibitions in Venetian museums documented.

Photography: Negatives shot mostly with large-format cameras.

Production: Black-and-white slides produced from negatives.

Documentation: Series of catalogs in publication, approximately one volume per year, starting 1983. Postage added to cost.

Purchasing: Slides sold singly, priced 8.000 lire each (1984).

Other Products: Photographic prints also offered, and a few large-format color transparencies loaned for publication.

Evaluation: No information on slides. Photographic prints are of good quality.

285   Colorvald S.A.S.

Zona Industriale 23
36078 Valdagno, Italy
Telephone: (0445) 40 11 55
Attn: Alberto Fomasa

Profile: Fifth edition entry repeated. Approximately 3,000 color slide titles offered of art and architecture: prehistoric, ancient, early Christian and Byzantine, medieval, European from the fifteenth to twentieth centuries, Islamic, and Oriental. A large portion of this vendor's business is production of slides in bulk for other companies.

Photography: Large-format transparencies shot by staff photographer (30%) or independent professional photographers (70%). 10% of originals are 35mm slides. Ektachrome film used, ASA 64 to 200.

Production: Produced in-house. Film type unspecified but apparently Eastmancolor. Color-corrected and contrast-controlled. Mounted in cardboard, plastic of various thicknesses, or plastic with glass.

Documentation: No list available. Sets accompanied by texts.

Purchasing: Slides sold in sets only. Copies made to order and shipped within three to four weeks. Payment accepted in German or U.S. currencies. Sets sent on approval for a fee of $3.00 each. Otherwise, no returns accepted.

Evaluation: Based on an order prior to 5th ed.: quality, 1 to 2. Film unstable; some slides already pink on receipt.

286   Nuova Italia Editrice (La)

Casella Postale 183
50100 Florence, Italy

Profile: Entry reprinted from 6th ed. Entry based on 1988/1989 catalog. Slides sets offered of the history of art and architecture among other subjects.

Documentation: Catalog available, in Italian. Sets briefly described.

Purchasing: Slides sold in sets only, most consisting of 50 to 80 slides. Eighty-slide sets priced 78.480 lire. More than 100 thirty-slide sets offered on individual artists, priced 29.430 lire each. Order form printed on back cover of catalog.

Other Products: Videocassettes, films, transparencies, and maps also available.

Evaluation: Reprinted from 6th ed. A visual resources curator in Great Britain, who purchased two sets in 1988, complained of poor color and focus and of scratches on several of the slides. No further information available.

*287   Scala Fine Arts Slides

SCALA Istituto Fotografico Editoriale S.p.A.
Via Chiantigiana 62-I
50011 Antella, Florence, Italy

Telephone: (055) 641-541
FAX: (055) 644-478
URL: http://scala.firenze.it

This vendor also offers digital products and is listed in the digital section of the directory.

Profile: Entry reprinted from 6th edition with updated address and distributor information. Some information from website. Nearly 10,000 duplicate color slide titles offered of art and architecture history of all periods, with emphasis on works in Italian collections. New sets occasionally produced from an archive of more than 80,000 transparencies. European churches documented in 55 eight-slide sets (TAC series). Italian painting surveyed in 122 twelve-slide sets (SAD series). Scala is the official photographer for most Italian museums and for several other European museums. Major exhibitions documented. Museum collections represented in Scala sets include the following:

Castello Sforzesco, Milan

Galleria Borghese, Rome

Galleria degli Uffizi, Florence

Galleria dell'Accademia, Venice

Monumenti, Musei e Gallerie Pontificie, Vatican City Museo Archaeologico, Florence

Museo Archaeologico Nazionale, Paestum

Museo di San Marco, Florence

Museo Internazionale delle Ceramiche, Faenza

Museo Nazionale di Villa Giulia, Rome

Museo Poldi Pezzoli, Milan

Palazzo Pitti, Florence

Pinacoteca di Brera, Milan

Victoria and Albert Museum, London

Photography: Original large-format transparencies shot by professional staff photographers on Kodak film using Sinar view cameras.

Production: Printed from internegatives on Eastmancolor #5384 at Scala Istituto Fotografico Editoriale, Florence. Color-corrected and contrast-controlled. Mounted in cardboard. Packaged in plastic sleeves.

Documentation: Free list, in English, of set titles available from Davis Art Slides (Scala distributor in United States and Canada) **(047)**. Slides labeled in Italian and keyed to accompanying identification list or booklet. Texts often multilingual (English, Italian, French, and German) or sometimes available in one of various languages by request. Images thoroughly identified in most cases; dates of works sometimes lacking. Orientation marked.

Purchasing: United States and Canadian orders must be addressed to Davis Art Slides **(047)**. Slides sold in sets only, with price list available. The Scala website (English or Italian) includes an online catalog of 30,000 low-resolution, watermarked images. The website also offers the Scala Archives on CD-ROM and image licensing. Customers can receive, on request, a CD-ROM catalog with images.

Other Sources: Scala sets occasionally sold by Miniature Gallery **(225)** at discount prices; when Scala slides are in stock, an issue of *Art-Slide News* will announce their availability.

Evaluation: Quality, 3 to 4; documentation, 2 to 4; service, 2 to 3.

Museums

288   Commune di Ferrara
Direzione Musei Civice d'Arte Antica
Palazzo Schifanoia,
Via Scandiana, 25
44 100 Ferrara, Italy
Telephone: (0532) 62038
Attn: Civica Fototeca

Profile: Duplicate slide titles offered of works in Ferrara's museums, including paintings, sculpture, prints, manuscripts, and archaeological artifacts. Slides of architecture in Ferrara also available. Archive of 15,000 images exists that is not covered by catalogs. 2% of holdings are black-and-white. New slide titles continually added.

Photography: 90% of original slides shot by staff photographers on Kodak and Ilford films. Tripod used.

Production: Copies made by photographic laboratory of the Museo Civico d'Arte Antica. No information about film type, but respondent affirmed that it is stable. Color-corrected and contrast-controlled.

Documentation: Free lists, in Italian. Annual supplements issued. For paintings, identifications consist of artist, title, medium, dimensions, and collection. Slides keyed to lists. Orientation marked by number placement (at center top).

Purchasing: Slides sold singly, priced 2.000 lire each. No minimum order. Slide copies made to order and shipped within one month.

Rental: Slides rented only for local use in Ferrara province.

NETHERLANDS

Museums

289 Frans Halsmuseum

Groot Heiligland 62
2011 ES Haarlem, Netherlands
Telephone: (023) 31 91 80

Profile: Entry repeated from 5th ed. Twenty-three duplicate color slide titles offered of works in the permanent collection. New titles occasionally added.

Photography: Original slides shot by an independent professional photographer.

Production: Produced by A.N.C. Productions. No attempt made to correct color or control contrast.

Documentation: Free list, in Dutch, English, German, and French. Artist, artist's dates and places of birth and death, title of work, and date of work provided. Slides labeled in English.

Purchasing: Slides sold singly, priced 1.50 guilders each. No minimum order. No discounts. Postage added. Slides kept in stock and shipped within two weeks. Rush orders filled within three days if slides are in stock. Slides not sent on approval, and no returns accepted.

Evaluation: Quality, 3; documentation, 2; service, 2. (Evaluation by a single committee member. Reprinted from 6th ed. Quality, 2 to 3; documentation, 3; service, 3.)

290 Haags Gemeentemuseum

P.O. Box 72
2501 CB The Hague, Netherlands
Telephone: (070) 51 41 81

Profile: Entry repeated from 5th ed. Approximately 250 color slide titles offered of items in the Gemeentemuseum, the Museum Bredius (12 slides), and the Kostuummuseum (11 slides). Subjects covered include modern art (of special interest, the work of Mondrian and M. C. Escher), nineteenth-century art, history of The Hague, costumes, and musical instruments. New titles occasionally added.

Photography: Large-format transparencies shot by a staff photographer.

Production: Produced by Fotoburo Niestadt, Panningen, on stable film. Color-corrected and contrast-controlled.

Documentation: Free list, in Dutch, revised annually. Artist, title, and date provided. Slides labeled in Dutch.

Purchasing: Slides sold singly, 1.75 guilders each. No minimum order. Discount of 10% given on 10 slides or more. Set of 35 slides of M. C. Escher's work priced 29.50 guilders. Orders filled within three weeks. No rush orders accepted. Slides not sent on approval, and no returns accepted. Special photography undertaken within four weeks at 7.50 guilders per slide.

Evaluation: Reprinted from 6th ed. Quality, 3 to 4; documentation, 2 to 3; service, 2 to 3.

291 Rijksmuseum Kröller-Müller

P.O. Box 1
6730 AA Otterlo, Netherlands
Telephone: (08382) 12 41

Profile: Entry reprinted from 6th ed. Forty-one duplicate color slide tides offered of works in the permanent collection: nineteenth- and twentieth-century painting and twentieth-century sculpture. No additions to slide holdings planned.

Photography: Original slides shot by staff photographer.

Production: Produced by Scala Fine Arts Slides **(287)**. Color-corrected and contrast-controlled.

Documentation: Free list. Identifications consist of artist, title (in Dutch and English), and date. Slides labeled in Dutch and English.

Purchasing: Slides sold singly, 1.75 guilders each. No minimum order. Postage added. Prepayment required in guilders or U.S. dollars. Orders shipped within 10 days of receipt of payment. No rush orders accepted. No returns accepted. No special photography undertaken.

Other Sources: Slides also available from Davis Art Slides (formerly Rosenthal Art Slides) **(047)**.

Evaluation: Quality, 3 to 4; documentation, 3 to 4; service, 3.

292 Stedelijk Museum

P.O. Box 5082
1007 AB Amsterdam, Netherlands
Telephone: (020) 5732 911
Attn: Reproduction Department

Profile: Entry repeated from 5th ed. Four hundred fifty color slide titles offered of selected works in the collections of the Stedelijk Museum (250 slides), the Rijksmuseum Vincent van Gogh (130 slides), and the Amsterdams Historisch Museum (70 slides). New titles occasionally added.

Photography: Large-format transparencies shot by staff photographer on Agfa film 100S.

Production: Printed from internegatives on Fujicolor film by Herrmann & Kraemer, Garmisch, Germany. Color-corrected and contrast-controlled. Mounted in plastic.

Documentation: Free list for each museum, in Dutch and English. Artist and title provided on list. Slides labeled in English. Orientation marked with an arrow only if necessary.

Purchasing: Slides sold singly except for one set of 12 slides from the Vincent van Gogh Museum. No minimum order. Single slides priced 1.75 guilders each. Quantity discount: 10 slides for 15.00 guilders. Prepayment from pro forma invoice required on overseas orders. Slides shipped within one week of receipt of payment. Rush orders filled within two days; no surcharge. Slides not sent on approval, and no returns accepted. Special photography undertaken within four weeks at 15.00 guilders per item.

Evaluation: Reprinted from 6th ed. Quality, 3 to 4; documentation, 3; service, 3.

293 Stedelijk Museum "de Lakenhal"

P.O. Box 2044
2301 CA Leiden, Netherlands
Telephone: (07) 25 46 20

Profile: Entry repeated from 5th ed. Approximately 60 duplicate color slide titles offered of works by artists who were born or lived in Leiden. Slides of painting of the fifteenth through nineteenth centuries, decorative arts of the seventeenth through nineteenth centuries, and some seventeenth- and eighteenth-century architectural interiors included.

Photography and Production: A few slides shot by a staff photographer on Ektachrome ASA 50

and produced by the University of Leiden. Majority of slides photographed by a commercial photographer and produced by Polyvisie. Copies sometimes produced from duplicates rather than originals. Color-corrected. No attempt made to control contrast.

Documentation: No list available. Slides labeled in English. Orientation not marked.

Purchasing: Slides sold in sets, 25 guilders for six slides. Slides kept in stock and shipped within two weeks. Slides not sent on approval, and no returns accepted.

Evaluation: Reprinted from 6th ed. Quality, 2; documentation, 2. No information available about stability of current production of Polyvisie slides; formerly unstable.

NORWAY

294 Norsk Filminstitut

Dronningensgate 16
Postboks 482 Sentrum
N-0105 Oslo, Norway
Telephone: (+47) 22 47 45 00
FAX: (+47) 22 47 45 99
E-mail: kunder@nfi.no
URL: http://www.nfi.no/nfi.html

Price Range: 235 Norwegian kroner per set (approximately $35).

Profile: Slide sets on Munch, Dahl, graphics of Kathe Kollwitz, Norwegian painting, Gustav Vigeland, Picasso, and Krohg.

Evaluation: Quality, 4; documentation, 3; service, 4. (Evaluation by a single committee member.)

295 Statens Filmsentral

P.O. Box 2655, St. Hanshaugen
0131 Oslo 1 Norway
Telephone: (02) 60 20 90
Attn: Anne Lise Rabben, c/o Nasjonalgalleriet

Profile: Entry repeated from 5th ed. Norwegian art systematically documented in 26 sets totaling 780 color slide titles. Project carried out since 1985. Variety of media and historical periods represented. Painting, sculpture, graphic arts, and tapestries included. Contributions received from most Norwegian museums.

Photography: Large-format transparencies shot by museum photographers and a staff photographer on Agfachrome or Ektachrome.

Production: Produced by an in-house laboratory and Laboratorie-Service, Oslo. Printed on Kodak Vericolor #5072 from 35mm internegatives on Kodak Vericolor #6011. Color-corrected and contrast-controlled. Mounted in plastic and glass.

Documentation: Free brochure, in Norwegian. Each set accompanied by booklet containing identifications and commentary by an art historian, in Norwegian. Slides labeled with artist and title.

Purchasing: Slides sold in sets of 30. Entire series offered by subscription, 150 Norwegian kroner per set. Minimum order one set, priced 180 Norwegian kroner.

Evaluation: Quality, 3 to 4; service, 3 (based on single committee member).

Museums

296 Oslo Kommunes Kunstsamlinger/ Munch-Museet

Toyengaten 53
P.O. Box 2812, Kampen 5
N-0608 Oslo 6 Norway
Telephone: (02) 67 37 74
FAX: (02) 67 33 41

Profile: Entry reprinted from 6th ed. Fifty-seven duplicate color slides offered of the works of Edvard Munch in the Munch-Museet and the Nasjonalgalleriet, Oslo. No additions to holdings planned.

Photography: Originals (slides and large-format transparencies) shot by Mittet Foto, Oslo, on Ektachrome ASA 64. Professional equipment used.

Production: Produced on Kodak duplicating film by Colorvald **(285)**. Respondent to questionnaire (an employee of Mittet Foto) stated that the film is stable. Mounted in plastic.

Documentation: Free list, in Norwegian and English. Slides labeled. Orientation marked.

Purchasing: Slides sold singly, 5.00 Norwegian kroner each. No minimum order. Postage added. Slides kept in stock and shipped within one to two weeks.

Evaluation: Reprinted from 6th ed. Two samples sent: quality, 4; documentation, 2. Slides labeled with artist and title only—title in Norwegian.

PEOPLE'S REPUBLIC OF CHINA

297 Beijing Slides Studio

51, Xizhimennei St.
P.B. 100035
Beijing, People's Republic of China
Telephone: 65-5356

Profile: More than 100 slide set titles offered of fine arts, architecture, cultural relics, parks, scenic locations, and folk customs. Works in the Palace Museum, Hubei Museum, and Shaanxi Museum represented. New slide titles periodically added. Slides intended for sale at tourist sites in China.

Photography: Negatives shot on Kodak film ASA 100 by various photographers, including staff. Tripod and perspective-correcting lens used.

Production: Copies printed in-house on Kodak film. The respondent to the questionnaire affirmed that the film is stable. Color-corrected. Mounted in cardboard.

Documentation: Free catalog, in Chinese, updated every other year. Slides also labeled with set name and slide number, keyed to booklet providing complete identifications in English and Chinese. Orientation marked.

Purchasing: Slides sold in sets only. Postage added. Discounts given to educational institutions. Prepayment of one-third total amount required. U.S. dollars accepted. Returns subject to negotiation. Slides kept in stock, or made to order if necessary. Orders usually filled within two months. Rush orders filled within one month.

Evaluation: Reprinted from 6th ed. Sample set of 12 slides of architecture sent: quality, 2 to 3; documentation, 3.

POLAND

298 Ars Polona

Krakowskie Przedmiescie 7
00-068 Warsaw, Poland

Profile: Entry repeated from 5th ed. Approximately 100 slide titles offered of works in the National Museum, Warsaw. Ancient art, medieval art, Polish art, European art, and contemporary paintings and drawings represented. No additions to slide holdings planned.

Photography and Production: Shot by an independent professional photographer and produced by KAW, Warsaw.

Documentation: Free list, in French. Artist, title, and date provided. Slides labeled in Polish. Back of slide mount white; otherwise, orientation not marked.

Purchasing: Slides sold singly or in sets. Orders shipped within one month. Special photography undertaken by KAW, Wilcra Str. 46,00-679 Warsaw. Payment accepted in U.S. dollars. Returns accepted for exchange only.

SPAIN

299 Ampliaciones y Reproducciones MAS

("Arxiu MAS")
Frenéria, 5, 3° D.
08002 Barcelona, Spain
Telephone: (93) 315 27 06
Attn: Dr. Montserrat Blanch

Profile: Founded 1900 by Adolfo Mas Ginesta. Black-and-white slides offered of art and architecture in Spain, made to order from an extensive archive of negatives (350,000). Systematic photographic campaign to document Spanish art carried out in the 1920s under sponsorship of the Frick Reference Library, the Hispanic Society of America, the Institute of Fine Arts at New York University, and the Fogg Museum Library of Harvard University. Present holdings include 250,000 negatives of art in Spain (Spanish and other), 20,000 negatives of art outside Spain (Spanish and other), and 80,000 negatives of Spanish personalities, folklore, and geography. Affiliated with the Amatller Institute of Hispanic Art, founded 1941.

Documentation: No comprehensive published catalog. Extensive indexes available on site. Lists, in Spanish, available on request of particular subjects. Telephone consultations possible. Slides keyed to lists. All correspondence written in Spanish.

Purchasing: Slides sold singly. Quantity discount possible. Postage and bank charges added. Prepayment required from pro forma invoice.

Other Products: Black-and-white photographic prints may also be ordered.

Evaluation: Reprinted from 6th ed. Quality, based on prints rather than slides, 2 to 3; documentation, 2; service, 3 to 4. Identifications are minimal and in Spanish. Service is reasonably prompt and extremely courteous. This is a valuable source for images unobtainable elsewhere.

300 Sanz Vega Fotografia de Arte e Historia

Concha Espina, 11
28016 Madrid, Spain
Telephone: (91) 259 58 34
Attn: Prof. B. Sanz Vega

Profile: Entry based on 5th ed. Approximately 7,500 duplicate color slide titles offered of art and architecture in Spain. Many details of paintings and sculptures included. Several exhibitions documented from the early 1960s, when this company was actively producing new material. Holdings not augmented since 1972. Works in the permanent collections of the following museums are represented:

Casa y Museo del Greco, Toledo

Colecciones del Real Monasterio El Escorial

Museo Arqueológico Artistico Episcopal, Vich

Museo Arqueológico de Barcelona

Museo Cerralbo, Madrid

Museo de Arte de Cataluña, Barcelona

Museo de Arte Modemo, Madrid

Museo de Bellas Artes, Bilbao

Museo de Bellas Artes de Granada

Museo de Bellas Artes de Seville

Museo de la Real Academia de Bellas Artes de San Femando, Madrid Museo de Santa Cruz Cervantes, Toledo

Museo del Prado, Madrid

Museo Español de Arte Contemporaneo, Madrid Museo "Lazaro Galdiano," Madrid

Museo Nacional de Esculturas, Valladolid

Museo Provincial de Bellas Anes, Malaga

Museo Provincial de Bellas Artes, Valencia

Museo Provincial de Cadiz

Panteón de Goya, Madrid

Production: Slides printed from internegatives. Current production is on low-fade Eastmancolor film. Old stock, which will continue to be sold until exhausted, is unstable Eastmancolor #5381. (The proprietors of Mini-Aids **[076]**, a distributor of Sanz Vega slides, believe that very little old stock remains as of mid-1989.)

Documentation: General catalog issued 1965, bound together with two supplements (1969 and 1972). Each slide briefly identified in Spanish. Slides labeled with artist and title, in Spanish, and keyed to catalog.

Purchasing: All business correspondence carried out in Spanish; communications in English may be misunderstood or go unheeded. For this reason, it may be advisable to deal with this company through Mini-Aids, although it is less expensive to order directly. Slides sold singly. Several sets offered as well, at a 20% discount from the price for singles: Spanish architecture (180 slides), Spanish sculpture (150 slides), and Spanish painting (234 slides). Orders invoiced; payment in U.S. dollars requested from U.S. customers. Postage added.

Other Sources: Sanz Vega slides are obtainable through Mini-Aids **(076)**.

Evaluation: Quality, 1 to 2; documentation, 1; service, 2.

301 Silex, Ediciones

Alcala, 202, 1° C.
28028 Madrid, Spain
Telephone: (91) 246 81 03

Profile: Entry reprinted from 6th ed. Three hundred fifty-six duplicate slide titles offered in 42 sets of art and archaeological artifacts in Spanish museums. About 2% of holdings are black-and-white. New titles occasionally added. Museum collections documented include:

Casa y Museo del Greco, Toledo

Museo Arqueológico Nacional, Madrid

Museo Arqueológico Provincial, Cordoba

Museo del Prado, Madrid

Museo Español de Arte Contemporaneo, Madrid

Photography: Original slides shot on Kodak Vericolor III by staff photographers, using tripod and studio lighting.

Production: Produced by Dinasa Laboratory on Eastmancolor #5384 or Geva #982. (The catalog erroneously states that all slides are on Ektachrome.) Color-corrected and contrast-controlled. Mounted in cardboard.

Documentation: Free catalog available, in English or Spanish, revised annually. Brief identifications provided for each slide (for painting, artist, title, and city/collection only). One large Prado set (120 slides) and four small sets accompanied by commentaries in English, Spanish, French, or German. Slides labeled in Spanish. Orientation marked by asterisk only when necessary.

Purchasing: Slides sold singly or in sets of six, ten, or twelve slides. Minimum order $50. Postage (by surface mail) added. Pro forma invoice issued to institutions. Prepayment required from individuals. Slides kept in stock and shipped within one week of receipt of payment. If necessary, slides duplicated to order. Rush orders accepted at no surcharge. Returns accepted on a case-by-case basis.

Other Sources: Slides may be obtained through Mini-Aids **(076)**.

Evaluation: Reprinted from 6th ed. Quality variable, 1 to 3; documentation, 2; service, variable, 1 to 3. One sample sent in 1984 of a cave painting: good quality. Two samples sent in 1989: one excellent detail of "Guernica," one slide of a Murillo painting that was both cropped and scratched.

SWEDEN

Museums

302 Nationalmuseum

P.O. Box 16176
S-103 24 Stockholm, Sweden
Telephone: (08) 24 42 00
Attn: Museum Shop

Profile: Entry reprinted from 6th ed. No response to 1984 or 1989 questionnaires. Entry based on 1984 list. Approximately 250 color slide titles offered, mostly of European paintings. A few sculptures, icons, portraits, and works of decorative art included.

Documentation: Free list, in Swedish and English. Artist and title provided.

Purchasing: Slides sold singly, 4.00 Swedish kronor each. Postage added: minimum 10.00 Swedish kronor per order.

Other Sources: Slides of seventeenth- and eighteenth-century European painting and Swedish paintings offered by Saskia **(086)**.

Evaluation: Quality, 4; documentation, 2; service, 3. (Evaluation by a single committee member.)

303   Statens Historiska Museum

(Museum of National Antiquities)
Storgatan 41
P.O. Box 5405
S-114 84 Stockholm, Sweden
Telephone: (08) 7839495
Attn: Museum Shop

Profile: Entry reprinted from 6th ed. Approximately 150 duplicate color slides offered of prehistoric art, Viking art, medieval art, and coins. Slides of Swedish textiles from the Middle Ages available.

Photography: Original slides shot by staff photographer.

Production: According to the 5th edition, duplicated on Kodachrome.

Documentation: Free list, in Swedish and English. Slides labeled. Orientation not marked.

Purchasing: Slides sold singly and in sets. No minimum order. No discounts. Payment requested in Swedish kronor. Sets of 20 slides priced 130.00 Swedish kronor. Single slides priced 6.00 Swedish kronor each. Surcharge of 50.00 Swedish kronor on foreign orders to cover shipping. Slides kept in stock and shipped immediately. Slides not sent on approval, and no returns accepted.

Other Products: A few audiocassettes available.

Evaluation: Reprinted from 6th ed. One advisor to the 5th edition rated these slides 4 on quality, 3 on documentation, and 3 on service. No further information available.

SWITZERLAND

Museums

304   Öffentliche Kunstsammlun-Kunstmuseum Basel

St. Alban-Graben 16
4010 Basel, Switzerland
Telephone: (061) 22 08 28

Profile: Entry reprinted from 6th ed. No response to 1984 or 1989 questionnaires. Entry based on list dated March 1983. One hundred twenty slide titles offered of European painting.

Documentation: Free list. Identifications consist of artist, title (in the original language), and date when known.

Purchasing: Slides sold singly, priced 2.00 Swiss francs each. Postage added.

Evaluation: Quality, 4; documentation, 2 to 3; service, 3.

305   Sammlung Oskar Reinhart

"Am Römerholz"
Haldenstrasse 95
8400 Winterthur, Switzerland
Telephone: (052) 23 41 21

Profile: Entry reprinted from 6th ed. List sent in response to 1989 questionnaire. Fifty-one slide titles offered of paintings, mostly nineteenth century. Other information in entry repeated from 4th ed.

Photography: Large-format originals shot by commercial photographer in the galleries.

Production: Copies made by a commercial laboratory.

Documentation: Free list. Artist, title, and date of work given.

Purchasing: Slides sold singly, priced 1.50 Swiss francs each. Prepayment required.

Evaluation: Three-star rating in 4th ed.

306   Schweizerisches Landesmuseum

(Swiss National Museum)
Museumstr. 2
8006 Zurich, Switzerland
Telephone: (01) 218 65 39
FAX: (01) 211 29 49
Attn: Mrs. Jeanette Frey
E-mail: jeanette.frey@slmnet.ch
URL: http://www.slmnet.ch

This museum also offers digital products and is listed in the digital section of the directory.

Price Range: 20 Swiss francs to 400 Swiss francs.

Profile: The photo archive of the Swiss National Museum contains pictures of the objects in the museum since its foundation in 1898. The collections cover archaeological objects through to the twentieth century and arts and crafts, including nineteenth- and twentieth-century photography. Existing collection of pictures includes 350,000 black-and-white prints, 30,000 slides, and 10,000 color transparencies. In two to three years, part of the photoarchive will be shown on the Internet for researchers. Some 20,000 slides already are digitized; digital photography is planned before year 2000. Download through the Internet or satellite network planned after 2005.

Photography: Original photography is carried out by Staff Professional Photographers, Otto Knel and Donat Stuppan. Equipment used includes: Camera: Sinar (4" x 5" up to 20 x 25cm), for reportage: smaller formats (6 x 6cm, 24 x 36mm). Two photo studios in-house. Different kinds of film are used, but normally Kodak Ektachrome and Ilford for black-and-white.

Production: Slides are duplicated.

Documentation: Catalog is sent to mailing list and updated when museum prices change, usually every three to four years. List with short text in German is included with slide orders.

Purchasing: 20 Swiss francs for 24 x 36mm; 100 Swiss francs for 4" x 5" or larger. Orders by fax or letter. Prepayment or invoice sent with material. Slides not sent on approval. Rush orders filled immediately and sent by Federal Express or DHL where required, at cost of the client. Normal delay: two weeks.

Rental: Rental of 4" x 5" Ektachromes or 24 x 36mm slides is available. Contact museum for details.

Digital Products: Kodak PhotoCD; Scan with Agfa DuoScan from 24 x 36mm original. Manipulated with Photoshop and color-corrected. .PCT and .JPG formats are available; others may be supplied if required. Digital products available for one-time, nonnetworked use. .JPG format requires Photoshop to view. Digital product delivered on floppy disk or CD within three weeks; protected by watermark. Federal Express/DHL, etc. when required at cost to client.

Other Products: Listings from object database and picture database (almost all kinds of objects concerning Swiss history).

Expansion Plans: Choice of posters and slides, digital products for the Museum Shop and Internet.

Evaluation: Quality, 4; documentation, 2 to 4. (Evaluation of samples.)

TAIWAN

Museums

307   **National Palace Museum**
Wai-shuang-hsi, Shih-lin
Taipei, Taiwan
Telephone: 881-2021
FAX: 886-2-8821440
Attn: Publications Division & Mail Order Division

Profile: Entry reprinted from 6th ed. Three hundred color slide titles offered of objects in the museum's permanent collection: Chinese painting, calligraphy, jade, porcelain, and bronzes. No additions to commercial slide holdings planned.

Photography: Most original photography carried out by museum staff. Slides and large-format transparencies shot on Ektachrome: EPY ASA 50 and films #6118 and #6117. Tripod and various lenses used.

Production: Copies produced on Kodak film #6117 by Jazz Laboratory, Taipei. Color-corrected and contrast-controlled. Mounted in cardboard.

Documentation: Free catalog, available in English. Slides also labeled with artist, dates or dynasty of artist, and title of work. Orientation marked only when necessary.

Purchasing: Commercial slides are duplicates, sold in sets of 10, but originals may be obtained singly through special photography. Prepayment required. U.S. dollars accepted. Per-slide price $5.00 (so states price list, but catalog indicates this is the price per set). 10% educational discount given. Postage added. Commercial slides kept in stock and shipped within one week of receipt of payment. No rush orders accepted. Returns accepted for exchange.

Other Products: Videotapes available. Black-and-white photographic prints offered for sale, and color transparencies loaned for reproduction in publications.

Evaluation: Quality, 4. (Evaluation by a single committee member.)

SLOVENIA (FORMERLY YUGOSLAVIA)

Museums

308   Narodna Galerija

(National Gallery)
Puharejeva 9
1000 Ljubljana, Slovenia
Telephone: 386 61/12 63 109
FAX: 386 61/12 63 138
E-mail: info@grohar.ng-slo.si
URL: http://www.ng-slo.si

Profile: Two sets of color slides offered of works in the permanent collection: one of Slovene art of the eighteenth and nineteenth centuries and one of Slovene Impressionist painting.

Photography: Shot by an independent professional photographer on Agfa or Kodak film.

Production: Copies made in a laboratory in Zagreb. No attempt made to correct color.

Documentation: No list available. Slides labeled in English. Orientation marked.

Purchasing: Slides sold in sets of six. Museum intends to resume slide sales in 1999.

PART IV
APPENDIXES

APPENDIX 1: Image Providers No Longer Selling Images

Editors' Note: The following providers did not respond to the original mailing or to follow-up attempts to contact them. To the best of our knowledge, the providers listed here no longer sell images.

UNITED STATES AND CANADA

309   A Space
183 Bathurst St.
Toronto, Ontario M5T 2R7
Canada

310   Alphabets Co.
59 Rusholme Rd.
Toronto, Ontario M6J 3H3
Canada

311   American Association for State and Local History (AASLH)
172 Second Ave. N.
Nashville, TN 37201

312   American Craft Council (ACC)
40 W. 53rd St.
New York, NY 10019

Images distributed by Crystal Productions (045).

313   American Institute of Architects (AIA)
1735 New York Ave.
Washington, DC 20006-5259

314   Art Color Slides
235 E. 50th St.
New York, NY 10022

315   Art Now Inc.
320 Bonnie Burn Rd.
P.O. Box 219
Scotch Plains, NJ 07076

316   Artpark

P.O. Box 371
Lewiston, NY 14092

317   Atlatl

402 W. Roosevelt
Phoenix, AZ 85003

318   Bolchazy-Carducci Publishers

44 Lake St.
Oak Park, IL 60302

319   Bonanza Group Inc.

220 E. 54th St.
New York, NY 10022

320   Center for Humanities Inc.

Communications Park
P.O. Box 1000
Mount Kisco, NY 10549-1000

321   Ceramic Arts Library

141 S. Martel Ave.
Los Angeles, CA 90036

322   Cinema Expeditions Inc.

17 Leisure Dr.
Kirksville, MO 63501

323   Dunlap Society

Lake Champlain Rd.
Essex, NY 12936

324   Educational Audio-Visual Inc. (EAV)

17 Marble Ave.
Pleasantville, NY 10570

325   ESM Documentations

201 Second Ave.
Suite 4A
New York, NY 10003

326   Esto Photographics

222 Valley Pl.
Mamaroneck, NY 10543

327   Fusaro, Florindo

3600 Spring Garden St.
Philadelphia, PA 19104

328   Gould Media, Inc.

44 Parkway W.
Mount Vernon, NY 10552-1194

329   Haeseler Art Publishers

P.O. Drawer 1518
Lafayette, CA 94549

330   Honolulu Academy of Arts

900 S. Beretania St.
Honolulu, HI 96814

331   Interior Design Magazine

270 Lafayette St.
#606
New York, NY 10012

332   International Structural Slides

P.O. Box 466
Berkeley, CA 94701-0466

333   Jefferson National Expansion Memorial

11 N. Fourth St.
St. Louis, MO 63102

334   John Michael Kohler Arts Center

608 New York Ave.
P.O. Box 489
Sheboygan, WI 53082-0489

335   KaiDib Films International

P.O. Box 261
Glendale, CA 91209-9643

336   Les editions l'Image de l'Art

C.P.292, Succ. "E"
Montreal PQ H2T 3A7
Canada

337   Light Impressions

439 Monroe Ave.
P.O. Box 940
Rochester, NY 14603-3717

338   McIntyre Media, Inc.

30 Kelfield St.
Rexdale, Ontario M9W 5A2
Canada

339   McIntyre Visual Publications Inc.

251 Portage Rd.
Lewiston, NY 14092

340   National Film Board of Canada

Phototheque, Tanney's Pasture
Ottawa, Ontario K1A 0M9 Canada

341   Palm Press, Inc.

14 Lomar Dr.
Pepperell, MA 01463

342   Religion and Ethics Institute
P.O. Box 664
Evanston, IL 60204

343   Ruhle, James L. and Associates
P.O. Box 4301
Fullerton, CA 92834

344   Sandak, Inc.
70 Lincoln St.
Boston, MA 02111

345   Sanders Art Media
1237 Masselin Ave.
Los Angeles, CA 90019

346   Snite Museum of Art
University of Notre Dame
South Bend, IN 46556

347   Steeplechase Slides
1115 Sherman St.
Denver, CO 80203

348   Streetscape Slides
A Division of Image Management Corp.
P.O. Box 10862
Denver, CO 80210

Note: The collection has been donated to the University of Colorado at Denver, College of Architecture and Planning. The images may be made available to a wider audience in the future. If so, readers will be informed about availability and terms in the "Slide Market News" column in the Visual Resources Association Bulletin and at the Image Providers Directory website.

349   Visual Education
6945 28th St. S.
St. Petersburg, FL 33712

350   VRI Slide Library
P.O. Box 1208
Imperial Beach, CA 91933

Note: Sold to Universal Color Slide Co. (095)

351   Woman's Building Slide Library
1727 N. Spring St.
Los Angeles, CA 90012

OTHER COUNTRIES

352   Ashmolean Museum
Oxford University
Beaumont St.
Oxford OX1 2PH United Kingdom

353   Blauel Kunst-Dias

D-8033 Planegg bei München
Egenhofenstrasse 8
Postfach 1105 Germany

354   Chester Brummel, Photography

Korlavagen 47A
11449 Stockholm, Sweden

Note: Moving to Boston, MA; temporarily out of business.

355   Craft Council of Australia

100 George St.
The Rocks
Sidney, New South Wales 2000
Australia

356   Documentation Photographique de la Reunion

des Musées Nationaux
89, Ave Victor-Hugo
75116 Paris, France

See L'agence photographique de la Reunion des Musées Nationaux (264).

357   Museum fur Ostasiatische Kunst

D-5000 Cologne I
Universitätstrasse 100
Cologne, Germany

358   Nasjonalgalleriet

Universitetsgaten 13
Postboks 8157 Dep
N-0033 Oslo 1 Norway

361   Rijksmuseum

Stadhouderskade 42
P.O. Box 50673
1007 DD Amsterdam, Netherlands

362   Stoedtner, Dr. Franz

D-4000 Dusseldorf 1
Feuerbachstrasse 12-14
Postfach 25 0162 Germany

Dr. Stoedtner's slides are distributed by Mini-Aids (076). He did not reply to our inquiries, and it appears he does not want to expand his cross-Atlantic business. For the adventurous who are prepared to communicate in German and pay with the deutsche mark, Dr. Stoedtner may be contacted directly at this address.

363   Trinity College Library

Cambridge CB2 ITQ
United Kingdom

364   University of Edinburgh

Department of Fine Art
19 George Square
Edinburgh, EH8 9JZ
Scotland, United Kingdom

365 **VEB DEFA Kopierwerke
Berlin**

1058 Berlin
Milastrasse 2, Germany

366 **Woodmansterne, Ltd.**

2 Greenhill Crescent
Watford Business Park
Watford, Herts WD1 8RD
United Kingdom

APPENDIX 2: Sources of Slides Coordinated with Texts

The image providers with slide sets coordinated with textbooks are listed below each text citation. The number in parentheses is the vendor's entry number in this guide.

Some vendors offer several sets per text, varying in size. Most sets provide selective rather than comprehensive coverage.

Note that many image providers liberally substitute images in these sets. Often a view different from that reproduced in the textbook is supplied, or a similar work of art is chosen to illustrate a point being made in the text. Most lists provided by the sellers indicate where substitutions have been made.

Adams, Laurie Schneider. *A History of Western Art.* 2d ed. Madison, WI: Brown and Benchmark, 1997.
Davis Art Slides (047)
Universal Color Slide Co. (095)

Arnason, H. Harvard. *History of Modern Art: Painting, Sculpture, Architecture.* 2d ed. New York: Abrams, 1977.
Heaton-Sessions (060)

———. *History of Modern Art: Painting, Sculpture, Architecture.* 3d ed. Revised and updated by Daniel Wheeler. Englewood Cliffs, NJ: Prentice Hall, 1986.
American Library Color Slide Co. (022)
Heaton-Sessions (060)
Universal Color Slide Co. (095)

———. *History of Modern Art: Painting, Sculpture, Architecture.* 4th ed. New York: Harry N. Abrams, 1997.
Heaton-Sessions (060)

Benton, Janetta Rebold, and Robert Diyanni. *Arts and Culture: An Introduction to the Humanities.* Vols. 1 and 2. Englewood Cliffs, NJ: Prentice Hall, 1997-1998.
Davis Art Slides (047)

Bishop, Philip E. *Adventures in the Human Spirit.* Englewood Cliffs, NJ: Prentice Hall, 1994.
Davis Art Slides (047)

Brommer, Gerald F. *Discovering Art History.* 3d ed. Worcester, MA: Davis Publications, 1996.
Universal Color Slide Co. (095)

Brommer, Gerald F., and George F. Horn. *Art In Your World.* 2d ed. Worcester, MA: Davis Publications, 1995.
American Library Color Slide Co. (022)

Brown, Milton Wolf, et al. *American Art: Painting, Sculpture, Architecture, Decorative Arts, Photography.* New York: Abrams, [1979].
Heaton-Sessions (060)

Canaday, John Edwin. *Mainstreams of Modern Art.* 2d ed. New York: Rinehart and Winston, 1981.
American Library Color Slide Co. (022)
Heaton-Sessions (060)

———. *What Is Art? An Introduction to Painting, Sculpture, and Architecture.* New York: Alfred A. Knopf, 1980.
American Library Color Slide Co. (022)
Heaton-Sessions (060)

Clark, Kenneth. *Civilisation: A Personal View.* New York: Harper & Row, 1970.
American Library Color Slide Co. (022)

———. *The Nude: A Study in Ideal Form.* New York: Pantheon Books, 1956.
American Library Color Slide Co. (022)

Cleaver, Dale G. *Art: An Introduction.* 3d ed. New York: Harcourt Brace Jovanovich, 1977.
Heaton-Sessions (060)

Craven, Wayne. *American Art: History and Culture.* New York: Brown and Benchmark, 1994.
American Library Color Slide Co. (022)
Davis Art Slides (047)

Cunningham, Lawrence, and John Reich. *Culture and Values: A Survey of the Western Humanities.* 4th ed. Fort Worth, TX: Harcourt Brace College, 1998.
Saskia Ltd. (086)

De la Croix, Horst, Richard Tansey, and Diane Kirkpatrick. *Gardner's Art Through the Ages*. 9th ed. San Diego, CA: Harcourt Brace Jovanovich, 1991.
    Davis Art Slides (047)

Dudley, Louise, and Austin Faricy. *The Humanities: Applied Aesthetics*. 6th ed. New York: McGraw-Hill, 1978.
    American Library Color Slide Co. (022)

Elsen, Albert Edward. *Purposes of Art: An Introduction to the History and Appreciation of Art*. 4th ed. New York: Rinehart and Winston, 1981.
    American Library Color Slide Co. (022)

Feldman, Edmund Burke. *Varieties of Visual Experience*. 4th ed.New York: Harry N. Abrams, 1992.
    Universal Color Slide Co. (095)

Fichner-Rathus, Lois. *Understanding Art*. Englewood Cliffs, NJ: Prentice Hall, 1986.
    Heaton-Sessions (060)

————. *Understanding Art*. 4th ed. Englewood Cliffs, NJ: Prentice Hall, 1995.
    Davis Art Slides (047)

Fiero, Gloria K. *Humanistic Tradition*. 3d ed. New York: McGraw-Hill.
    Davis Art Slides (047)

Fleming, William. *Arts and Ideas*. 9th ed. Orlando, FL: Harcourt Brace, 1995.
    American Library Color Slide Co. (022)

Groenewegen-Frankfort, H. A., and Bernard Ashmole. *Art of the Ancient World*. Englewood Cliffs, NJ: Prentice Hall and New York: Harry N. Abrams, 1972.
    American Library Color Slide Co. (022)

Gilbert, Rita. *Living with Art*. 4th ed. New York: McGraw-Hill, 1995.
    American Library Color Slide Co. (022)

————. *Living with Art*. 5th ed. Boston: McGraw-Hill, 1998.
    Saskia Ltd. (086)

Gombrich, Ernst Hans. *The Story of Art*. 15th ed. Englewood Cliffs, NJ: Prentice-Hall, 1990.
    Heaton-Sessions (060)

————. *The Story of Art*. 16th ed. San Francisco, CA: Chronicle Books, 1995.
    American Library Color Slide Co. (022)
    Heaton-Sessions (060)
    Saskia Ltd. (086)
    Universal Color Slide Co. (095)

Grieder, Terrence. *Artist and Audience*. 2d ed. Madison, WI: Brown and Benchmark, 1996.
    Davis Art Slides (047)

Hamilton, George Heard. *Nineteenth and Twentieth Century Art: Painting, Sculpture, and Architecture*. New York: Harry N. Abrams, 1970 and Englewood Cliffs, NJ: Prentice Hall, 1972.
    Heaton-Sessions (060)

Hartt, Frederick. *Art: A History of Painting, Sculpture, and Architecture*. New York: Harry N. Abrams, 1976.
    Heaton-Sessions (060)

————. *Art: A History of Painting, Sculpture, and Architecture*. 2d ed. New York: Harry N. Abrams, 1985.
    Heaton-Sessions (060)

————. *Art: A History of Painting, Sculpture, and Architecture*. 3d ed. Englewood Cliffs, NJ: Prentice Hall, 1987.
    Heaton-Sessions (060)
    Saskia Ltd. (086)

————. *Art: A History of Painting, Sculpture and Architecture*. 4th ed. New York: Harry N. Abrams, 1993.
    American Library Color Slide Co. (022)
    Heaton-Sessions (060)
    Universal Color Slide Co. (095)

————. *History of Italian Renaissance Art*. 3d ed. New York: Harry N. Abrams, 1987.
    Heaton-Sessions (060)

———. *History of Italian Renaissance Art.* 4th ed. Revised by David G. Wilkins. Englewood Cliffs, NJ: Prentice Hall and New York: Harry N. Abrams, 1994.
> American Library Color Slide Co. (022)
> Heaton-Sessions (060)
> Saskia Ltd. (086)
> Taurgo Slides (091)

Heller, Nancy G. *Women Artists: An Illustrated History.* 3d ed. New York: Abbeville Press, 1997.
> Universal Color Slide Co. (095)

Hobbs, Jack A., and Richard Salome. *The Visual Experience.* 2d ed. Worcester, MA: Davis Publications, 1995.
> Universal Color Slide Co. (095)

Honour, Hugh, and John Fleming. *The Visual Arts: A History.* 4th ed. Englewood Cliffs, NJ: Prentice Hall, 1995.
> American Library Color Slide Co. (022)

Hunter, Sam, and John Jacobus. *American Art of the Twentieth Century: Painting, Sculpture, Architecture.* New York: Harry N. Abrams, 1973.
> Heaton-Sessions (060)
> Universal Color Slide Co. (095)

———. *Modern Art: Painting, Sculpture, Architecture.* 2d ed. New York: Harry N. Abrams, 1985.
> Universal Color Slide Co. (095)

Janson, H. W. *History of Art.* 5th ed. Revised and expanded by Anthony F. Janson. Englewood Cliffs, NJ: Prentice Hall and New York: Harry N. Abrams, 1995.
> American Library Color Slide Co. (022)
> Davis Art Slides (047)
> Dick Blick Co. (050)
> Saskia Ltd. (086)
> Universal Color Slide Co. (095)

Janson, H. W., and Anthony F. Janson. *History of Art for Young People.* 5th ed. New York: Harry N. Abrams, 1997.
> Taurgo Slides (091)
> Universal Color Slide Co. (095)

———. *A Basic History of Art.* 5th ed. New York: Harry N. Abrams, 1997.
> American Library Color Slide Co. (022)
> Universal Color Slide Co. (095)

Janson, H. W., and Samuel Cauman. *A Basic History of Art.* 2d ed. Englewood Cliffs, NJ: Prentice Hall and New York: Harry N. Abrams, Prentice Hall, 1981.
> Heaton-Sessions (060)

Janson, H. W., with Dora Jane and Joseph Kerman. *A History of Art and Music.* Englewood Cliffs, NJ: Prentice Hall and New York: Harry N. Abrams, 1997.
> American Library Color Slide Co. (022)

Kissick, John. *Art: Context and Criticism.* 2d ed. Madison, WI: Brown and Benchmark, 1996.
> Davis Art Slides (047)

Knobler, Nathan. *The Visual Dialogue.* 3d ed. New York: Holt, Rinehart and Winston, 1980.
> American Library Color Slide Co. (022)

Lamm, Robert Carson. *Humanities in Western Culture: A Search for Human Values.* 4th ed. Brief version. Madison, WI: Brown and Benchmark, 1996.
> Davis Art Slides (047)

———. *Humanities in Western Culture: A Search for Human Values.* Vol. 1. 10th ed. Madison, WI: Brown and Benchmark, 1996.
> Davis Art Slides (047)

———. *Humanities in Western Culture: A Search for Human Values.* Vol. 2. 10th ed. Madison, WI: Brown and Benchmark, 1996.
> Davis Art Slides (047)

Lucie-Smith, Edward. *Art and Civilization.* New York: Harry N. Abrams, 1993.
> Universal Color Slide Co. (095)

Matthews, Roy T., and F. DeWitt Platt. *The Western Humanities.* 3d ed. Mountain View, CA: Mayfield, 1997.
> Davis Art Slides (047)

Mittler, Gene A. *Art in Focus*. 3d ed. Westerville, OH: Glencoe/Macmillan/McGraw-Hill, 1994.
American Library Color Slide Co. (022)

Myers, Bernard Samuel. *Art and Civilization*. 2d ed. New York: McGraw-Hill, [1967].
American Library Color Slide Co. (022)

Ocvirk, Otto G., et al. *Art Fundamentals: Theory and Practice*. New York: McGraw-Hill, 1998.
Davis Art Slides (047)

Preble, Duane, and Sarah Preble. *Artforms: An Introduction to the Visual Arts*. 5th ed. New York: HarperCollins, 1993.
American Library Color Slide Co. (022)
Universal Color Slide Co. (095)

———. *Artforms: An Introduction to the Visual Arts*. 6th ed. New York: Addison Wesley Longman, 1998.
Davis Art Slides (047)

Richardson, John Adkins. *Art: The Way It Is*. 4th ed. New York: Harry N. Abrams, 1992.
Universal Color Slide Co. (095)

Sayre, Henry M. *World of Art*. 2d ed. Upper Saddle River, NJ: Prentice Hall, 1997.
Davis Art Slides (047)

Snyder, James. *Northern Renaissance Art: Painting, Sculpture, the Graphic Arts from 1350 to 1575*. New York: Harry N. Abrams, 1985.
American Library Color Slide Co. (022)

Sporre, Dennis J. *Reality Through the Arts*. 3d ed. Englewood Cliffs, NJ: Prentice Hall, 1996.
Davis Art Slides (047)

———. *The Creative Impulse: An Introduction to the Arts*. 4th ed. Englewood Cliffs, NJ: Prentice Hall, 1995.
Davis Art Slides (047)

Stokstad, Marilyn, with Marion Spears Grayson and Stephen Addiss. *Art History*. New York: Harry N. Abrams, 1995.
American Library Color Slide Co. (022)
Davis Art Slides (047)
Saskia Ltd. (086)
Universal Color Slide Co. (095)

Tansey, Richard G., and Fred S. Kleiner. *Gardner's Art Through the Ages*. 10th ed. New York: Harcourt Brace Jovanovich, 1996.
American Library Color Slide Co. (022)
Saskia Ltd. (086)
Taurgo Slides (091)
Universal Color Slide Co. (095)

Wilkins, David G., Bernard Schultz, and Katheryn M. Linduff. *Art Past/Art Present*. New York: Harry N. Abrams, 1990.
Universal Color Slide Co. (095)

———. *Art Past/Art Present*. 2d ed. Englewood Cliffs, NJ: Prentice Hall and New York: H. N. Abrams, 1994.
Davis Art Slides (047)

Zelanski, Paul, and Mary Pat Fisher. *The Art of Seeing*. 3d ed. Englewood Cliffs, NJ: Prentice Hall, 1994.
American Library Color Slide Co. (022)

PART V

INDEXES

NAME INDEX

References are given as entry numbers, not page numbers. References in bold type indicate that the entry is devoted entirely to a vendor. Other numbers may refer to an entry in which the image provider is mentioned. In other cases, numbers indicate that materials of an institution are sold by the image provider described in the éentry even though the institution may not be listed in the image provider's entry. Numbers greater than 308 refer to vendors listed in Appendix 1. Vendor names printed in bold type represent additions to the guide since the 6th edition.

SUBJECT INDEX

References are to entry numbers, not page numbers. When an image provider specializes in a subject, the entry number is referenced in bold type.

Using catalogs supplied by the image providers and material provided at websites, this list has been compiled to reflect the wide-ranging variety of subject coverage offered by the vendors in this guide. Omissions are inevitable though regrettable.

In this edition, names of selected artists, architects, and cities are introduced into the index. Usually this indicates that an image provider sells at least 50 images of the works of that architect or views of that city. The works of painters need fewer images, so the appearance of a painter indicates the image provider's holdings have strong coverage of that artist.